METALLICA
ALL THAT MATTERS

T0151112

METALLICA
ALL THAT MATTERS

PAUL STENNING

Plexus, London

All rights reserved including the right of
reproduction in whole or in part in any form
Copyright © 2010 by Paul Stenning
Published by Plexus Publishing Limited
The Studio, Hillgate Place
18–20 Balham Hill
London SW12 9ER
www.plexusbooks.com

British Library Cataloguing in Publication Data
A catalogue record for this book is available
from the British Library

ISBN-13: 978-0-85965-538-5

Cover photograph by Mick Hutson/Redferns/Getty Images
Book and cover design by Coco Balderrama
Printed in Great Britain by Bell & Bain Ltd, Glasgow

CONTENTS

INTRODUCTION

*'I hope that Metallica will be remembered or
looked upon as a band that cut through all the political
and business bullshit. So then people will realise that it's possible to
control yourself and gain a certain level of popularity without having to
cater to anyone else's ideas or thoughts other than your own. If that's all
that Metallica will ever stand for, then that's news enough.'*
Lars Ulrich

Metallica are the biggest metal band in the world, a position they have held for over twenty years, selling some 58 million albums worldwide, almost 30 million more than their nearest metal rival, Ozzy Osbourne. There are many reasons for this enduring popularity – an immense desire and focus, carefully considered business decisions, a supreme likeability and, most importantly, a wealth of memorable material. Like other metal greats, Metallica produce entire cohesive albums rather than singular songs, though many of their tracks can be enjoyed separately.

Since 1983 Metallica have been releasing innovative and unique material and here, all eras are covered. This book is the first to finally do justice to the group's entire career – after all, the band did not split up in 1991! It covers every aspect of their genesis, from the troubled childhood of James Hetfield to the liberal upbringing afforded Lars Ulrich. Their first musical experiences are explored in depth with contributions from those who really knew (and in many cases, still associate) with the band. There are many interviews drawn from entirely new sources; hitherto undiscovered colleagues, close friends, and in some cases ex-girlfriends.

Naturally, all aspects of each Metallica album are covered in depth – from the story behind the recording and writing of the material, to lyrical meaning and legacy.

All That Matters is a work that owes much to the number three. Principally, the band has always revolved around three members: Hetfield, Ulrich and guitarist Kirk Hammett. Metallica would have been a vastly different band without any of these members, with the latter being particularly underrated by fans and journalists alike. Finally, Hammett's significance is acknowledged here.

The history of the band is split into three eras, all featuring different bass players. There is the fun-loving, carefree youthfulness of their first few records which featured one of metal's best loved and most missed four-stringers, Cliff Burton. This era produced three of the greatest heavy-metal albums of all time in *Kill 'Em All, Ride The*

Lightning and *Master Of Puppets*. These recordings are thoroughly examined with a wealth of intriguing and illuminating quotes from those who were there at the time.

We discover the duality of a frontman who lived with an alcohol addiction, which took him many years to consciously recognise. There was the juvenile don't-give-a-fuck Hetfield, and the more mature man who penned eloquent lyrics and elegant music.

As we segue into era two, which begins with the heartbreaking death of Cliff Burton, a new Metallica emerges, still underpinned by a youthful naivety that fails to diminish when all the while the trio are maturing in musical ability and appreciation of life.

Metallica are a band full of contradictions, all of which are fully explored within these pages. They were a group who demonised the thrash-metal tag, yet conversely created some of the most sublime thrash of all time. They grew up quickly after the death of their close friend, yet childishly vented their frustration upon their new bass player Jason Newsted, treating him with disdain. They are a band with more money than most people will ever see, yet they famously spoke out against their music being made available for free. They are a band unafraid to change their style who virtually disassociated themselves from metal, but just a few years later returned heavier and faster than they'd been for many years. They are intensely private, preferring to keep their business in house, yet amazingly they allowed themselves to be filmed for one of the most revealing musical documentaries ever produced; and bravely displayed their most vulnerable characteristics while struggling to keep the band together. Most irksome for some is the dichotomy that while Metallica are the ultimate perfectionists, they have released some of the worst, most simplistic album covers in heavy-metal history.

Their current incarnation sees the band rediscovering their form as metal titans, yet managing to combine an uncompromising sound with massive global popularity. After almost 30 years, Metallica are still vital to the metal scene. They are unafraid of risks, always refusing to play it safe. Their 2003 opus, *St. Anger*, was widely considered to be a disaster, with poor sound, and largely bereft of decent ideas – it revealed a band in crisis. It was this period that was filmed for the revealing documentary *Some Kind Of Monster*.

Despite *St. Anger*'s traumatic conception and subsequent critical panning, Metallica held strong – to return five years on with the much-improved *Death Magnetic*. However, even with this return to form, the album drew criticism for an over-distorted production that many felt detracted from the clarity of the material.

While Metallica enjoy mainstream popularity, they are far from being a regular band. Their strength is in their refusal to conform, something both James Hetfield and Lars Ulrich revelled in as adolescents. Few other bands can boast such diverse personalities among their ranks, or a history so colourful and turbulent. For this reason – not to mention their stunning contribution to metal as a whole – Metallica are worthy of closer inspection, and this book aims to explore the group's rich tapestry with greater precision and depth than those that have come before.

Despite their imperfections, contradictions and inconsistencies, all that really matters is Metallica.

Paul Stenning

CHAPTER 1
IN THE SHADOW OF GOD

'My dad was always one of these "Cut your hair!"
kind of guys. My mom was more open to things. She painted a lot.
She kinda reminded me of a Berkeley mom. She wasn't alive for any of my
success with Metallica. It really pisses me off. But you know,
I think she knows what's going on still.'
James Hetfield

Nineteen sixty-three was one of the most memorable years in history, as the world stood upon the cusp of a chaotic new era. As the Soviet Union and America continued to face off across the Iron Curtain, America saw the Civil Rights Movement gather momentum as Martin Luther King Jr. delivered his 'I Have A Dream' speech in August. Less than three months later, President John F. Kennedy was assassinated. Despite these epoch-defining events, 1963 would also be remembered for producing two of the greatest songwriters in the history of music – Lars Ulrich and James Hetfield.

Thirteen miles southeast of downtown Los Angeles sits the small city of Downey, California. It's an oppressive, almost bleak sprawl of urban living, most famous for being home to the oldest surviving McDonald's restaurant – only the third to be built. Indeed, Downey is something of a fast-food Mecca; the world's very first Taco Bell was also built here. Though the sun seems to perpetually shine, ever-present smog engulfs Los Angeles County like a toxic veil.

Doomed pop darlings the Carpenters moved to Downey from Connecticut in 1963 and subsequently became synonymous with the city. It was in this year that James Alan Hetfield arrived into the world, on 3 August. Interestingly, although Downey's municipal website proudly tells visitors that the city once housed the Carpenters, there is no mention of Hetfield.

The Hetfields are a family of Irish, Scottish, English and German descent.

James was born to Virgil and Cynthia Hetfield. His mother was a light opera singer and homemaker, while his father owned a Los Angeles trucking company and also taught at a local Sunday school. This was no fleeting interest for Virgil. Both he and Cynthia were staunch Christians and belonged to a branch of the religion known as Christian Science.

The Hetfields' faith is often dismissed as a mere footnote in James's early life. Yet how many people truly know what Christian Science is? It requires explanation, as this doctrine informed much of the frontman's childhood experiences. Formative exposure to this belief system would play a significant part in shaping James's character and provide inspiration for some of Metallica's most heartbreaking – and at times ferocious – material.

The foundations of Christian Science are rooted in a textbook written by Mary Baker Eddy in 1867: *Science And Health, With Key To The Scriptures*. Baker Eddy was a sickly, fragile child and suffered interminably from a variety of infirmities, for which she could never find an explanation or cure.

In February 1866, the middle-aged Baker Eddy suffered a debilitating spinal injury after a fall, and it was during her convalescence that she turned to the Bible for solace. According to her testimony, she recovered from all her physical ailments the moment that she devoted herself to God.

Seized with religious zeal, she spent the subsequent three years studying the Bible intently and creating the defining principles of Christian Science. After claiming that God, spirit and man combined and created a platform for healing, Baker Eddy became convinced that illness could be cured by a heightened sense of God's power and potential. To facilitate this, all temporal remedies were forbidden, particularly the use of any form of drugs or prescribed medication. This dogma was based on the premise that Jesus Christ could heal without the aid of any manmade substances.

Having recovered from her injury, Baker Eddy felt she could now help heal others through Christianity. Essentially, Christian Science teaches that God's power overrules all external illness or misfortune. The reality of God overrides the reality of sickness, death, sin or the material world. According to Christian Scientists, God is ever-present and cares spiritually for each and every individual.

Christian Scientists 'believe in the saving, healing power of God's love, that no one is beyond redemption, that no problem is too entrenched or overwhelming to be addressed and healed. Christian Scientists don't believe that salvation occurs at some point in the future, but that the presence of God's goodness can be experienced here and now, and by everyone.'

As James Hetfield would reveal some time later, 'The main rule is, God will fix everything. Your body is just a shell, you don't need doctors. No medicine is necessary and anything you have is God-given and basically comes down to huge faith and a lot of belief in yourself, that's something you don't really quite get when you're a kid.'

Accounts of so-called miracles among Christian Scientists are commonplace – whereby even the most irreversible conditions have been cured by sheer belief and trust in God. Christian Science's headquarters are in Massachusetts, Mary Baker Eddy's home state. She died in 1910 aged 89.

Virgil and Cynthia Hetfield were staunch advocates of the doctrine, which though understood by Christian extremists is still relatively unfamiliar to many, and in 1963 this awareness was even less widespread. The religious influence suffused every aspect of the young James Hetfield's life. For a small child who didn't understand the implications or ramifications of the religion, his confusion led to isolation and uncertainty.

Cynthia had two boys from a previous marriage and this, along with the perplexing beliefs of Christian Science, made James a particularly unsettled youngster. 'I'd say that in every child's life there is some form of abuse, there's some form of traumatic experiences that happen that scar and help form your survival techniques later on in life,' observed James. 'It was very isolating as a kid having two half-brothers that weren't really brothers *per se*, because they had a different dad and they were a generation away, but not quite father figures. So they were just kind of my brothers who were sometimes home and sometimes not. And my dad threw one of them out of the house. And I can just imagine my dad, he's married someone and he's got an eleven- and twelve-year-old, two boys – man, that's gotta be tough.'

The typical difficulties that result from divorce and remarriage were hard enough for kids to adjust to, never mind the parents. But for James, the ever-present glare of Christian Science was the hardest part of his difficult childhood. He subsequently went so far as to claim it was 'cult-like'.

Though it is an officially recognised form of Christianity, there is perhaps some truth to James's assertion, in much the same way as Scientology is often referred to as a 'cult'. However, Scientology (which, incidentally, many people wrongly believe to be the same as Christian Science) can lay claim to some eight million members – which is stretching the boundaries of what can be considered as a 'cult'. By comparison, today sources estimate that Christian Science boasts between 300,000 and 400,000 devotees.

Due to his parents' beliefs, James was not permitted to study health education, biology or physical education. 'I was very isolated at school, feeling that I'm just different because of this religion,' recalled James. 'I'm really different. Like, why does Jamie leave the room every time we get our health books out? I have to go and stand out in the hallway. Pissing down rain and I'm standing outside the classroom while people are learning about the body, learning about health, learning about what shell we have for our souls. I couldn't even learn about it. It was either stand in the hall, and other teachers would walk by and give you the dirty eye, because you're in trouble, because you're standing "outside the classroom". Or you go and sit in the principal's office and wait in there. Any kid who goes into the principal's office, something's the matter. So you get this shameful look. Like you're shamed. And I took that all in.'

Though he was bright and inquisitive, if a little shy, James's parents chose not to nurture his nascent intellect. Where a simple explanation could have worked wonders he was left to subsist within a fantasy world, unsure of his place in life or the reason for his seclusion. 'There was no explanation of why that doesn't work,' he observed. 'It was just, "No this is the way." And kind of going through life trying to believe it and feeling that I'm faulty, I'm defective because I can't believe this, and my parents completely do.' Clearly, this would rankle deeply and generate a lifetime of unresolved angst and pain.

Evangelists and overzealous clerics have long been figures of (often justifiable) vilification. Unfortunately for James, his father was one such preacher, albeit with a far more sedate manner. Yet regularly, when his father taught Sunday school, which James was obliged to attend, the young boy would see things that beggared belief. Whereas the child sees clearly and concisely, the adult explanation proved sorely lacking. As Hetfield remembered of one particular incident, 'There was a girl that had her arm broken. She stood up and said, "I broke my arm but now look, it's all better." But it was just like, mangled. Now that I think about it, it was pretty disturbing. So as a kid it didn't make any sense to me, and I battled it quite a bit through my teens and twenties.'

James's most traumatic years came during early high school. Though he began to mature into a man physically, emotionally Hetfield was still short of full development. He also possessed a vulnerable streak, which many were apt to take advantage of. 'It was alienating and hard not fully understanding the religion,' Hetfield told *Playboy*. 'I just knew that there were rules around it, which were pretty frustrating. I couldn't get physical to play football. It was weird having to leave health class during school, and all the kids saying, "Why do you have to leave? Are you some kind of freak?" As a kid you want to be part of the team. They're always whispering about you and thinking you are weird. That was very upsetting.'

For the young James, such isolation was both all encompassing and hard to cope with. At school he would be teased, ignored or berated and then would have to go home and be strictly admonished for even the slightest indiscretion. Life was harsh and alienating, a state of affairs which would only ease when he discovered music. Still, this torrid upbringing proved essential in forming Hetfield's personality and would provide him with plenty of firepower for the future.

'You can't even joke around with the guys because you weren't a part of it,' explained Hetfield. 'Just looked at as outsider. And you know, there's good qualities to that. I've taken on the power of the rebel somehow but still, it's always been a lone wolf kind of mentality.'

Eventually, the strain of raising kids who were not his own seemed to overwhelm Virgil and after one too many arguments with Cynthia, he walked out on his family. At the time, James and his siblings were blissfully unaware of any marital strife simply because arguments were always staged away from the kids and any conflict between the parents was kept private.

In the vain hope that Virgil would return, Cynthia told the children that her husband was merely away on a 'business trip', but as the weeks passed and Virgil remained out of touch it eventually became clear that he had left for good.

In addition to enduring the tough first few years of junior high school, James suddenly had to come to terms with the absence of his father who, while strict and difficult to understand, represented the male role model James so dearly needed. There was no note from Virgil and no explanation as to why he had left – one day he was there, the next, he had disappeared, seemingly permanently.

Yet, Virgil was still in the area, as James soon began to realise. While the young

Hetfield was at school, his father would return to the house to pick up extra belongings or some of his prized trophies. By the time James would return home from school he realised his father's things had been moved. This left James with a supremely negative sense of worthlessness – his dad had left but still came back to the house when he wasn't there – therefore, it must be something he had done.

Cynthia Hetfield stayed home with the kids. James's younger sister DeDe often fought with her brother, and unsurprisingly, James released his pent-up anger upon his sibling. 'There were some bad times,' he recalled, 'my mom needed to be home when we kids were home, or I'd have killed my sister. We beat the living hell out of each other. I remember burning her with hot oil and I realised, "Wow, it went too far."'

For financial reasons, Cynthia simply had to find a job to support her children. This would be the start of a spiral of sickness that would engulf her. 'It was all tough on my mom, having to get a job and support the kids was too much for her, she couldn't deal with it,' recalled James. 'Mom was not the strongest woman there was. Very passive and sweet. I learned love, the caressing and stuff like that – that's what mom does. She doesn't offer really hard advice or good life lessons, she was there and comforting, but not the strong woman who could go out and work.'

This pressure began to show, and before long Cynthia was diagnosed with cancer. She remained brave, especially as at the time the children were virtually unaware of the pain she was in and just how close to death she was. 'My mom worried a lot, and that made her sick,' James recalled. 'She hid it from us. All of a sudden, she's in the hospital.' Ultimately, Cynthia's beliefs denied her the medical treatment she desperately needed. The religion that she had subscribed to all her life was now called upon to cure her illness and give her the strength to take care of her kids and herself. However, as James's lyrics would later observe, her God failed.

'She got sick and denied her illness and the denial of pain was a major thing, for Christian Science, to be able to get better,' said James. 'As soon as you acknowledge the pain you are giving into the negative aspect of the error, or the evil or whatever. So she's withering away in front of us and we can't say anything.'

Cynthia Hetfield passed away when James was just seventeen years old. It is one of the biggest criticisms of Christian Science; that the true believer of the faith shuns medical treatment for even the most virulent sickness.

In order to better understand this, the author spoke with a devout Christian Scientist, asking for an explanation as to how this belief so deeply penetrates the faith and why it is considered to be beneficial.

Heather Hayward lives in London and is a fervent Christian Scientist. 'Christian Science teaches that all problems, no matter how material they may appear, have a mental basis,' she explains. 'This means that the patient is actually not the body, but the thought of the person. Therefore, a quick solution through medicine would not address the real issue, since such a treatment doesn't deal with the mental aspect of the condition.

'There's no doubt that Christian Science would be the choice for me in trying times, simply because, for more than 30 years as a full-time Christian Science practitioner, I've seen how effective spiritual healing is for whoever chooses to rely on it. I've faced some severe physical situations of my own, as well, but my instinctive reaction, based on previous experiences of spiritual healing, has been to always trust God for the resolution.'

In common with many Christian Scientists, Heather experienced a moment of epiphany that cemented her belief. 'One time late at night, I was lying awake in excruciating pain. I turned my thought to God and didn't waver from my position to rely on spiritual healing, because I trusted that God would heal me as He'd done in the past. The result was that I experienced a healing in less time than it would have taken to try to find a medical solution.

'Throughout society there is currently a massive accent on medical solutions,' adds Heather, 'material ways of dealing with physical and mental anguish and pain. But the assumption that medical theory is exact and that reliance on spiritual healing means putting one's life at risk rests on a comparison that's unfair. For me there is no contest, because medical theory changes. Whilst many wonders occur in the field of medicine, I've found that permanent healing happens when spiritual truth, not material remedies, transforms the bodily condition. In this way Christian Science removes focus from the human body, not just attempting to fix matter. Spiritual healing renews thought and reforms character.'

Though her beliefs did not save Cynthia Hetfield, it is perhaps admirable that she still remained resolute in her convictions to the very end.

Although James was now even more isolated, he managed to make some friends through a shared interest in music. Ron McGovney was a relatively close confidant, yet even he remembers that there was barely a whisper from James regarding his mother's death. 'We had no idea,' he says. 'He was gone for like ten days and we had thought he went on vacation. When he told us that his mom had just died, we were stunned. And as he's cleaning out his locker he's telling us that he's got to move in with his brother in Brea.'

James subsequently made the thirteen-mile trip from Downey to Brea to live with his older half-brother David, an accountant. This hardly represented the kind of stability a teenager in James's situation needed. By the time of his mother's death, the young Hetfield had established a relationship with a girl of the same age, but soon after Cynthia passed away, his girlfriend left him. 'Lots of big stuff happened at that same time,' James told the Metallica fan club, 'as a sixteen- and seventeen-year-old: girls, insecurities – and there are tons of insecurities already. Me wigging out on marijuana and all this kind of paranoia just all of a sudden hit me. And abandonment issues were huge.'

Despite this less-than-ideal domestic situation, living with David did supply James with some pointers towards how to begin making music. 'David was kind of a hippie, kind of a hairy guy,' revealed James. 'He went to college and stuff. He played drums in a band, and I used to go bash on the shit.'

Now required to support himself, James went through a succession of menial jobs including working as a high-school janitor, in a sticker factory, and as a removals handyman. Though he was still young and perhaps not mature enough to deal with his mother's death on his own, the influence of Christian Science throughout the family forbade any formal grieving. The religion proscribes funerals.

Thus, James was left to deal privately with his sense of loss, with no means of expression regarding his feelings. 'There was no grieving process,' he recalled. 'And grieving, I've come to learn, is an extremely healthy way of cleansing feelings. You have to go through that process and we never did. We just kind of shoved it down – way down.'

It would be many years before James was able to confront his feelings for his parents via songwriting. Though he would write several lyrics that referenced his childhood and adolescence, the full grieving process was not addressed until he was into his thirties.

By the time of 1991's *Metallica* (often referred to as the 'Black Album'), James had made peace with his father, and become relatively close to his estranged dad, explaining, 'We talked a lot about religion, and I let him know there were no bad feelings. I felt, over the past few years, we had been closer. I had sorted out a lot of my anger in his departure, his never being around.' Yet just a short time later cancer would also take the life of his father, after he had battled against the disease for two years – again, using no standard medical forms of treatment.

Such absolute denial of conventionality was something James Hetfield would come to admire as he grew older. 'He stuck with it to the very end, and that, I think, helped him keep his strength – his knowledge that he did it his way. He studied the religion religiously. He got up every day before the milkman, before the cows, studying his lesson for the day. How that could give him such strength was amazing to me.'

As James reached his mid-teens he started to socialise with others who, like him, were surplus to requirements among the jocks and other 'beautiful people' at school. Ron McGovney remembers, 'When we first started high school, which was September of 1977, everybody had their little clique – there was the cheerleaders, the jocks, the marching band people, and you end up with the laggers hanging around without any real social group, and that included James and I. We actually got stuck at the same lockers, and we just started hanging out.'

Buoyed by a mutual love of all things hard and heavy, this friendship led James towards taking music more seriously, perhaps even as a profession. He now no longer needed to worry about his parents' wants or wishes. With his mother passed away and his father still absent, James could define his own path.

At the time, 'James's favourite band was Aerosmith – he was a total Steven Tyler freak,' recalls McGovney. 'And our friend Dave Marrs was a total Kiss freak. Dave Marrs, Jim Keshil, James and I started hanging out and they would make fun of the music I listened to – I was into bands like the Doobie Brothers, ZZ Top, the Eagles... things like that – so in return I would tell them "Kiss sucks" and "Aerosmith sucks", and it went back and forth; we did this in class all the time. I remember having James in my driver's ed class, James had drawn a big picture of Steven Tyler on his Pee-chee and I wrote "fag" across his face, just to piss James off, and he had a fit in class!'

James later revealed his passion for heavy metal and the reason it appealed, paving the way for a blackened future. 'There were three reasons the first Black Sabbath album appealed to me. First, it scared the shit out of me. Second, it crushed the fuck out of all the "peace and love" and "everything's groovy" bullshit that was still hanging around in the early seventies. And third, my friends' moms wouldn't let them own it!'

James Hetfield's early life had been hard to deal with and doubtless provided the inspiration he later required to become a success. Though he didn't yet know it, his discovery of hard rock music was to be a pivotal turning point in his young life. It was within this medium that he would find the motivation to turn his back on his past and concentrate on becoming a full-time musician. It would certainly not be easy, but nothing James would face in the future would be as difficult as his childhood. Yet, out of crippling adversity a phenomenal musician and songwriter would emerge, as James Hetfield became a man of whom his parents could be proud.

CHAPTER 2

ACES HIGH

'In 1973 I got dragged along to see Deep Purple.
That was the turning point. I didn't know what was going on,
but I saw Ritchie Blackmore throwing his guitar around and doing
all these silly poses, and I was pretty impressed.'
Lars Ulrich

Five thousand miles from California, on Boxing Day 1963, former tennis professional and musician Torben Ulrich and his wife Lone welcomed a newborn child into their affluent home in Gentofte, Denmark. They named their son Lars, and his birth would later come to influence the entire spectrum of heavy metal. Lars was actually brought up in the small town of Hellerup at Lundevangsvej, number twelve. Hellerup is part of the municipality of Gentofte, located in Eastern Denmark close to Copenhagen.

'Gentofte is the municipality; Hellerup is the city/area primarily located along the "Strandvejen,"' explains local resident, musician Henrik Jespersen. 'This is the most fashionable and expensive shopping area in Gentofte. But then again it's not like Prada and Bentley, more like Hugo Boss and Volkswagen. The most expensive shops are in the downtown tourist part of Copenhagen – Hellerup is where the locals go shopping, because it's more convenient.'

Interestingly, the year Ulrich was born saw Gentofte at its most populous. In the early 1960s the town's population almost reached 90,000, whereas today that figure has decreased by a third. There are 10,040 houses in Gentofte – 2,466 of which occupy more than 200 square metres, a remarkable statistic.

Gentofte divides into two distinct areas, one highly fashionable and wealthy, the other less so – but hardly a ghetto. Not surprisingly, given that his father made a decent living from tennis, Lars was born into a family who resided in the more affluent district.

Henrik Jespersen (whose photo of Lars's family home can be seen in the photo section), recalls, 'It is not typical of even the biggest houses in Gentofte, but then again Gentofte is one of the places you would live when you can afford a house this size. Gentofte is part of an area up the "Strandvejen" – a famous Danish upper-class road beside the Øresund Ocean – this particular part runs from Gentofte up to Rungsted for about 25 kilometres, called the Whisky Belt. The people there don't work much anymore, spending time drinking whisky.'

Jespersen surmises that the people of the area would not have been likely to mingle with the Ulrichs. 'Being in the upper "Whisky Class", the old school Hellerup mentality is one of snobbery, feeling above "the people" – I can imagine that Lars despised that kind of snobbery, living with a hippie intellectual tennis pro father. I could also imagine that one of the reasons Lars seems to be so down-to-earth is that he never would be part of "I'm better than the other fellow" Hellerup society.'

Not only was Lars able to have any material object he desired, his laidback father made sure the environment young Lars was subjected to was free and easy. Popular musicians of the time were regulars in the Ulrich household. One of Lars's best friends in his youth was vocalist Neneh Cherry, who was raised in part by her stepfather Don Cherry. Don lived just a few houses away from the Ulrichs.

'I grew up in as open an upbringing as you can imagine,' recalled Lars. 'Americans would call it spoiled. From that point of view, I was left alone a lot. But in terms of culture, there was always shit going on around the house. My dad was always around music. He was hanging out with Sonny Rollins, Don Cherry, Dexter Gordon. Dexter Gordon was my godfather.' Indeed, the jazz saxophonist was just one of many jazz musicians who regularly visited the Ulrichs, as Torben's jazz criticisms and reviews often appeared in Copenhagen newspapers.

As a highly accomplished professional tennis player, Torben amassed a staggering number of titles throughout his career and he retained his professional status until he was well into his fifties.

Unlike today, where a parent who travels the world would often leave their young child to be looked after by a spouse or nanny, in the 1960s kids were often privy to everything their parents experienced. Thus, little Lars accompanied Torben on his many travels.

Even before he started school, the future Metallica drummer had travelled the world several times over. And it wasn't all business – Torben's passion for music led him and young Lars to several landmark concerts of the period, not least the Rolling Stones' 1969 performance at Hyde Park.

Sometimes Torben and Lone were a little too chilled out. 'Every day I'd wake my parents up when I got home from school,' remembered Lars. 'I always had to wake myself up in the morning and bike myself to school. I'd wake up at 7:30, go downstairs, and the front door would be open – 600 beers in the kitchen and living room and nobody in the house. Candles would be burning. So I'd close the doors, make breakfast and go to school. I'd come home and have to wake my parents up.'

Although there were clearly difficulties in having to sometimes assume adult responsibilities, it served to introduce Lars to the realities of the world, and from a very tender age he was fiercely independent. Equally, the hedonistic lifestyle of his parents led them to assume a very non-judgemental stance in regard to Lars's future career (and personal) choices.

Lars subsequently revealed that he 'was very independent. I had nothing tying me down. At the same time, anything I wanted I had to get it myself. It's 1975, and I want to go see Black Sabbath. As far as my parents were concerned, I could go see Black Sabbath twelve times a day. But I had to find my own means, carrying the paper or whatever, to get the money to buy the tickets. And I had to find my own way to the concert and back.'

It was perhaps inevitable that Lars would follow in his father's footsteps by taking up either tennis or music. As it happened, he pursued both paths. Tennis came first, with Lars picking up a racket properly at around age five. During his early years, Lars was mentored by his father, but it wasn't until he became a teenager that an assessment of his true tennis potential could be made. Torben honestly believed his son had a lot of ability, but in truth was worried that he would not grow much more than he already had, and that this height disadvantage may halt his career before it began.

Today tennis is certainly more about height and strength than it once was, but even in the late 1970s height was an advantage, simply because a taller player had a greater chance of serving an ace (or one that was difficult to return). Even then, the average height for a professional player was around six feet tall. Lars meanwhile had reached five-foot-six and stopped growing. Nevertheless, when he was sixteen he was sent on a year's residential course at renowned tennis coach Nick Bollettieri's training academy in Florida. Bollettieri has mentored word champions Andre Agassi and Maria Sharapova.

'That was the entire idea,' Torben says today, 'to test whether he would really want to explore that whole tennis scene, because if that was the case, then that would be high time, the way things have to start so early these days. But I think it was absolutely right for him to have that situation really tested so that if he chose to go away from the ball playing, that he felt that he'd had the chance to explore it and not have to regret it later.'

'In 1979 for someone to join the academy they needed to show a willingness to work day in and day out,' Bollettieri says. 'They had to exhibit effort, self-discipline and sacrifice at all times. Today the admissions process at the academy is different. For legal reasons there is much more paperwork involved, but students must still have the same work ethics.'

The Ulrich family's tennis heritage provided a mitigating factor in favour of Lars's admission to the academy, as Nick explains. 'Torben Ulrich was a tremendous, very skilled professional tennis player. He did have a great deal of influence on Lars joining the academy because he believed in our philosophy. He felt his son would have discipline here and perhaps become a professional tennis player in his own right.'

After being used to getting his way and being free to do whatever he wanted, when he wanted, the academy's strict regime came as something of a shock to Lars. Bollettieri recalls, 'I remember them coming to the academy. Mr Ulrich was very tall and had a beard. Lars was small and not very keen on attending a tennis boot camp and he did not have the work ethics the other students had. He was more interested in the social scene, especially music.'

As Lars's passion for music grew, he began attending numerous concerts in the Florida area. This drew a reprimand from Bollettieri – it was simply unacceptable for a potential tennis professional to 'carry on' in such a manner. Tennis is about discipline and hard work and, though Ulrich had some natural ability and a keen interest in the sport, the combination of his upbringing and new musical interests gradually eroded the possibility of him playing it for a living.

Previous works on Metallica have stated that the academy decided they did not want to keep Lars on for another twelve months. However, Nick Bollettieri tells a different story. During the six months that he oversaw Lars's training, Bollettieri recalls that his charge's 'improvement was remarkable. We wish he would have stayed longer. It was his decision not to stay and we could not force him to do so. He was more like a small rebel, wanting to do his own thing. That was the primary reason he left. Lars was very flamboyant on the court. He could run, move extremely well and had a lot of ability. However, he was not willing to stay out on the courts for extra practice like the other students. His weakness was his size.

'When you review the majority of top players today, the physical make-up of both the men and ladies clearly show being tall and athletic are a major asset. We knew Lars was not going to be as tall as his father, nor did we expect for him to really bulk up. He was not dedicated to the rigorous work it would require.'

Despite this, Bollettieri believes that Lars's time at the academy prepared him for his subsequent career. He explains, 'I don't think Lars really had the passion to devote his life to tennis, but I am sure some of the work ethics he was exposed to when at our academy helped him achieve greatness in his field of music.'

After Lars had been in America for a year, his family came to join him, settling in Newport Beach, California. Irrespective of his relocation, Lars Ulrich will forever be associated with his home country. He can still speak fluent Danish, pays homage to Denmark by draping the national flag over his drum kit, and regularly returns 'home' to visit old friends. He is also officially the most famous musician to emerge from Hellerup, Gentofte, Copenhagen and indeed Denmark.

'Every kid in Denmark – and therefore also Gentofte – knows Lars is playing in Metallica,' says Henrik Jespersen, 'but because of the Metallica style, this is *not* played in the big houses in Hellerup, here it's Vivaldi and Mozart. If you had asked people in their sixties in the street: "Who is Lars Ulrich?" I guess their answer would be: "The son of the tennis player Torben Ulrich."'

Music had been a key element of Lars's childhood, and by the time he decided to quit tennis he had been a fan of bands such as Deep Purple for several years. When he was just nine years old, a friend of his father's, South African tennis pro Ray Moore, took Lars to see the British legends during their 1973 tour. The day after the concert Lars travelled to his nearest record store and purchased a copy of their latest album, *Fireball*. For Lars, who had – aside from occasional blasts of Hendrix or the Doors – been weaned on jazz, the supercharged metal sound of Deep Purple provided him with something of a musical epiphany.

This discovery compelled Lars to seek out harder and heavier sounds. In doing so, he demonstrated his precocious spirit of independence. 'In those days in Denmark, a child of eight or nine could take the bus to the concert hall and listen and then come back on their own,' explains Torben. 'And then sometimes he would fall asleep in the bus and the conductor would say, "Now it's time to get up and go home." I don't know that one could send one's child away to a concert nowadays in the city that easily and still be called a responsible parent.

'He heard a lot of different kinds of music at home. We were listening in those days to the Stones, the Beatles, Cream, Eric Clapton. All of those people were beginning to emerge, and we as Europeans were certainly listening with big ears to that. And also in our household we had always been extremely interested in the whole blues and gospel situation that related to jazz. Then of course after Deep Purple, Lars would hear a lot more Kiss and Thin Lizzy, and all of those bands. So on the one hand, he was hearing Indian music, all kinds of Asian music, Buddhist chants, classical music. His room was right next to the room where I played all this music all night long, and sometimes maybe he would have heard them even while he was sleeping, so he could have picked up a lot of this stuff even without being conscious of it.'

When he was thirteen, Lars asked his grandmother for a set of drums and was finally able to play a real kit – having had to improvise with pots and pans for the past few years. Given Lars's exposure to jazz from such an early age, it is perhaps unsurprising that it exerted a noticeable influence on his style. Equally it was not as out of place in hard rock and metal as many would have presumed.

In modern metal, many presume the jazz influence begins and ends with 'math metal' bands who favour technique and precision over actual songs. Meshuggah and the Dillinger Escape Plan are two of the foremost exponents of an approach that combines bludgeoning noise with occasional forays into 'jazzy' landscapes – which, some might argue, are there simply to portray an 'arty' influence.

Metal bands citing jazz as an influence seems to be a relatively modern phenomenon. The New York band Candiria, who formed in 1992, can claim to be perhaps the first modern jazz-metal band. Swedish noise mongers Meshuggah began as a technical thrash band, but by the mid-1990s were incorporating jazz elements into their sound. A more recent example would be the 'avant-garde' metal of Yakuza, who have released four albums of jazz-tinged crossover material to date.

Of course, the fathers of heavy metal were heavily influenced by jazz – be it Ginger Baker in Cream, or indeed Black Sabbath's Bill Ward – and these secondary influences may also have been assimilated into Lars's nascent style.

As Black Sabbath drummer Bill Ward explained to *Black Sabbath* author Steven Rosen, 'If you listen to the structure of Sabbath music, you'll hear Gene Krupa [big-band drummer]. On the song "War Pigs" I'm swinging at the beginning, playing in swing time. On "Black Sabbath" I'm playing in swing time too. And I used to get real big cymbals, about the biggest you could get.'

According to Torben, Lars had an intuitive feel for music, perhaps due to all the years of exposure to his father's record collection. 'I always thought that he had a very compositional approach to drumming in his very early years,' his father says, 'meaning actually before he started to be more involved in beating on the twos and fours and playing along with his records. And by compositional I mean that we could ask him to play a certain song that he had named and he could bring it out on the spot and repeat it. That kind of thing.'

However, by anyone's standards, Lars's early forays on the sticks were clumsy at best. This again made Bill Ward a perfect influence simply because his style of drumming was relatively easy to pick up. 'I tend to think my drumming was reachable by the common man,' Ward says, 'because my drumming is very, very simple. I'm notoriously out of time and I'm not ashamed of that at all.' This casual influence would subsequently be evident during many of Lars's Metallica performances.

James Hetfield's musical initiation was far less convoluted, traversing a fairly typical aural adolescence during the 1970s. Bands such as Kiss were the order of the day, though interestingly neither Hetfield nor Ulrich seemed particularly enraptured by the band. Metallica have never played any Kiss covers, and there is no recorded suggestion of Kiss having informed their musical direction.

In particular, James was far more interested in southern rock bastions Lynyrd Skynyrd. Through his half-brother David, James learned to appreciate the swamp-boogie tones of the band that brought the world the likes of 'Freebird' and, most recognisably, 'Sweet Home Alabama'. His enthusiastic immersion in Skynyrd's back catalogue also provided Hetfield with the basis for his later fascination with all things patriotic and confederate.

There were also the likes of Sabbath and AC/DC, of course, but James's exploration of heavy rock took a huge leap forward when he purchased the first Iron Maiden LP. 'I was with James when we picked up the first Iron Maiden album at Middle Earth Records in Downey, California,' recalls Ron McGovney. 'We bought it just because of the album cover. We had never heard of the band. After we listened to it, we became Iron Maiden fans.'

Hetfield was directed toward playing an instrument from an early age, learning the piano when he was nine years old. 'We originally started him on the piano when he was little, his sister and him, but he ended up on guitar,' explained his father, Virgil. 'A good friend of his taught him how to play guitar and I think he did a nice job.' Along the way James also taught himself how to play drums and began to improve on guitar by playing along to Scorpions and UFO albums, slowing the turntable down to hear every note of a Michael Schenker solo and then painstakingly working it out for himself.

James formed his first band while he was still in high school, a heavy-metal outfit named Obsession – after the 1978 UFO album of the same name. It featured brothers Rich and Ron Veloz on bass and drums respectively, with Jim Arnold on guitar. At that time, James was merely a bit-part singer doubling on guitar and sharing vocals with Arnold.

Ron McGovney and Dave Marrs provided the band's entourage, the duo tending to simply hang out and watch the band fumble around at practice, or occasionally help carry the gear. They were later cited as being 'roadies' in subsequent interviews, but this was a rather exaggerated description of their role.

'We would go to their practices on Friday and Saturday nights at the Velozes' house on Eastbrook in Downey,' McGovney explains. 'The Veloz brothers were like electrical geniuses, they wired up lights all over the place and they built this loft in their garage, Dave Marrs and I would sit up there and work the control panel doing the lights, strobes and stuff, it was like this whole show in a tiny garage.'

Obsession played cover songs, from Sabbath's 'Never Say Die' to the obligatory UFO tunes 'Lights Out' and 'Rock Bottom'. McGovney also recalls Deep Purple's 'Highway Star' being a particular favourite. 'Jim Arnold sang the Zeppelin songs. James sang "Doctor, Doctor" and I think the other UFO songs. Ron Veloz sang on "Purple Haze" – they would switch on vocals. I remember when Black Sabbath's *Heaven And Hell* had just come out; they started doing that too, as well as Scorpions. They played primarily backyard parties, this was 1979 or 1980; we were, like, sixteen.'

After a year and a half, Obsession split up when James, along with Jim Arnold and his brother Chris, formed a short-lived band known as Syrinx. The band specialised in Rush cover versions but this soon became tedious.

While James was in Brea he had formed a band – known as Phantom Lord – with Jim Mulligan, a drummer he befriended within the first few days of starting his new school. While Hetfield and Mulligan were jamming on lunch break one day, they saw a fellow student by the name of Hugh Tanner who, promisingly, was clutching a Flying V guitar. The three soon bonded over a mutual love of hard rock and before the end of the day, Tanner was part of Phantom Lord. The band was little more than a hobby for James, who could never quite find a steady bass player nor progress beyond playing covers.

After graduating, Hetfield left Brea to return to Downey, whereupon his reunion with Ron McGovney produced a group known as Leather Charm. The band played at a number of local parties and even managed a (now almost totally unavailable) demo before folding. 'Leather Charm was the band we started after high school,' McGovney remembers. 'We played covers such as "Slick Black Cadillac" by Quiet Riot, "Hollywood Tease" by Girl, "Rescue Me" by Y&T, and two covers by Iron Maiden: "Remember Tomorrow" and "Wrathchild". The band never really got out of the garage.'

Indeed, Leather Charm's greatest contribution to rock was introducing James Hetfield to Lars Ulrich. After Lars had placed an advert in a local magazine called *Recycler* asking for musicians to join his 'band' (which really was just Lars on drums), James and co decided they wanted the young Dane as a drummer for Leather Charm. What they did not realise was that Lars was not about to join anyone else's band. He had a vision that expanded far beyond garage rehearsals and almost instantaneously decided that only James Hetfield would be good enough for his group. 'Back then you'd look under the music section of the *Recycler* for heavy metal, and there's like two people,' James later explained. 'The same people every fucking week into "sex and Motörhead".'

After contributing to a procession of lightweight garage bands, James Hetfield was ready to step up a gear. Lars Ulrich, meanwhile, would only ever play in one band, and they would just happen to become the biggest metal group of all time.

Ulrich and Hetfield's childhoods could scarcely have been more different. On a personal level, they would arguably never quite gel in the way most close friends do. Yet there was something about their union that clicked right away and set aside the difficult youth James Hetfield had lived through. Suddenly, nothing else mattered except playing in a band full time. In his high-school yearbook under 'Plans', James wrote: 'Play music, get rich.'

CHAPTER 3

BANGING ON THE DOCK OF THE BAY

'The true story about Dave Mustaine will never be told, because there's something of a pact between Dave, Metallica and myself.'
Jonny Zazula

Without the New Wave Of British Heavy Metal, Metallica would not exist today. Lars's discovery of the harsh, reductive metal that was sweeping the United Kingdom and beyond irrevocably changed his life – from the moment he heard Diamond Head he wanted to be in a heavy-metal band. Ulrich's fascination with the NWOBHM led him far beyond the sub-genre's leading lights such as Diamond Head, Def Leppard and Iron Maiden. The likes of Holocaust, Jaguar, Budgie and Sweet Savage were also regularly occupying his turntable.

Once he hit his teens, record buying became Lars's principal obsession, and it was the discovery of the NWOBHM that sowed the seeds for a lifelong association with heavy metal. 'I'd been in America for some time during the autumn of 1979 playing tennis and had briefly returned to Denmark over Christmas of that year,' he remembered. 'Now, at the time my big idol was a guy called Ken Anthony who had a heavy-metal record store. It was he who introduced me to Samson's *Survivors*, alongside the Marseille LP *Red, White And Slightly Blue*, though I don't really regard Marseille as part of all this.' Samson were most famous for featuring the future Iron Maiden vocalist Bruce Dickinson, while Liverpool's Marseille are perhaps best known on account of guitarist Neil Buchanan's subsequent career in children's television.

However, along with Diamond Head, it was Iron Maiden who would exert an enduring influence upon Lars. 'It was March 1980 and I walked into a record store in America searching for the latest Triumph album or some such shit and I was over at the import bin poking around,' Ulrich explained. 'Now, this was still before I was truly aware of what was going on in England, so when I came across an album called *Iron Maiden* I had no idea who or what they were. The front cover illustration of "Eddie" could have been done by any one of 100 bands, but the exciting live shots on the back of the sleeve really stood out. There was something so fucking heavy about the whole vibe. What really hooked me was a small shot of the two guitarists, Dave Murray and

Dennis Stratton, in the bottom left-hand corner. I'd never seen any band look like *this* before. Such aggression. Funnily enough, I never even heard the record until I returned to Denmark because I didn't have a record player with me on the road.'

In contrast to the immediacy of Maiden, Diamond Head had a more gradual impact on the young Dane. 'The first time I heard Diamond Head was via the "Helpless/Shoot Out The Lights" single. Ken recorded it for me in the summer of 1980. It was good but not outstanding. Then in an issue of *Sounds* I recall seeing a letter from someone who said they'd gotten a copy of the band's mail-order-only *Lightning To The Nations* LP and wanted a track listing for it. That's how I became aware of the fact that Diamond Head did have a bit of a vibe. *Lightning To The Nations* was a white label album only sold through *Sounds* on mail order. Each copy was signed by one member of the quartet and it was pot luck whose autograph you ended up getting – I got Sean Harris's, the vocalist.

'So anyway, I sent away for this LP, never got it and sent away again. It took me six to eight months to get the record but in the meantime I'd struck up a writing relationship with Linda Harris, Sean's mum and co-manager of the band. She wrote really nice letters to me, sent me embroidered patches and singles – but still no album! Finally, in April 1981 the white label arrived and the riffing and freshness just amazed me.'

Ulrich also spoke with reverence of Diamond Head's 'It's Electric' – which Metallica would later cover. 'The compilation album *Brute Force* featured "It's Electric",' Lars recalled, 'and that was fucking unbelievable! And if you take a look at the sleeve of the record now and compare the photo of Diamond Head with all the other groups there, they had an attitude and a vibe about them that none of the others could match. There was something *special* about Diamond Head, no doubt about it!'

The Ulrich pad was besieged by a deluge of cassette tapes and pristine vinyl. An early friend of Lars's, writer and DJ Bob Nalbandian, describes Lars's growing obsession. 'I first met Lars Ulrich, this must have been 1981 just as he was forming Metallica. I lived in Huntington Beach, California and my friend Patrick Scott called me up one day and said, "I just met up with this guy who has the ultimate metal record collection! You got to meet this guy!" The guy he was speaking of was Lars Ulrich. Lars was really cool but he was very sarcastic too. He was incredibly determined and driven and he was one of those guys that would be able to weasel his way into anywhere, like, backstage to any metal show.'

When James Hetfield hooked up with Lars he was certainly impressed by the young Dane's stash of hard-to-find metal. 'I would spend days just going through Lars's record collection, taping over my REO Speedwagon cassettes with bands like Angel Witch and Diamond Head and Motörhead. I was in heaven at his house.'

Bob Nalbandian remembers, 'Patrick and I were huge metal fans and we were heavily into all the NWOBHM that was just coming out and we went to all these record stores in Orange County and Los Angeles to find the latest import albums and singles. Lars lived in Newport Beach with his mother. Newport was about fifteen minutes south of Huntington Beach, so Patrick and I went down to visit Lars a couple of times and he made us some killer metal compilation cassette tapes with bands like Diamond Head, Sledgehammer, EF Band, Angel Witch, Trust, Bow Wow, Black Axe, Raven, Tygers of Pan Tang, Holocaust etcetera.

'In fact, I only know of a few people in Orange County that were into NWOBHM and such. It was totally underground back then. Some people knew of the bigger bands like Motörhead, Maiden, Saxon and, of course, Def Leppard – but nobody apart from a handful of people knew of bands like Blitzkrieg, Diamond Head, Holocaust, Tygers of Pan Tang and other bands that we were into. Like I said, during this time even bands like Mötley Crüe were still playing the local clubs so to be an underground metal fan was like being a member of an exclusive club.'

John Kornarens was the very first person young Lars hooked up with when he arrived in California. As the area's only truly dedicated headbangers, Kornarens, Nalbandian and Ulrich formed something of an elite metal trio. 'I look down the road and there's this little guy with long hair and a wrinkled Saxon T-shirt on,' Kornarens recalled, 'and I thought I was the only one in all of LA so I went over the way. Lars was all excited 'cause he thought he was the only one in LA [that was into these new bands]. So we started talking about the NWOBHM and the next day or the day after I'm 'round at his house for like a NWOBHM marathon.'

Soon, the two were firm friends and regularly went on record-buying trips together. Their tastes were specialised to the extent that they often had to order via mail directly from record labels based in England. One particular time Kornarens remembers Lars's less than respectable behaviour concerning one particular order. 'We ordered two copies of Holocaust's "Heavy Metal Mania" twelve-inch with a few other things. And Lars had ordered it so the package was coming to his house, which back then would take a month! I get a call one day and he says, "The package is here." I go, "Great I can't wait to hear it," and he says, "Yeah but there's a problem – your copy of 'Heavy Metal Mania' got taken out of the wrapper and left on the stove." Note he said *your* copy! So my copy got warped. So I get in the car and drive 70 miles to his house just to hear it and it's awesome. I wasn't going to argue with him about my copy being all screwed up – I'm, like, "Where am I going to get another copy of 'Heavy Metal Mania'?" There were two copies: Lars had one and I had the other one. So I got my mum's ironing board out and tried to get it back into shape!'

'I suppose being removed from the centre of it all just increased my determination to stay in touch with the scene,' observed Lars. 'I was *truly* obsessed by the NWOBHM. You see, I landed in the States and there was Van Halen, Journey and Styx happening. None of these new bands had yet got a look in. America had just about heard of Judas Priest and UFO, who were old warhorses as far as the UK were concerned.

'I kept heavily in touch via *Sounds*,' Lars continued, 'which back then was my bible. Each week I'd eagerly pore over every printed word in the paper, spending hours going through the whole thing. I had a long list of every single band in the NWOBHM who got a name check – even if it was only in the gig guide. I ended up with over 200 names, not knowing that about 180 or so were just garage bands who had only written one song themselves!'

Although the NWOBHM would be best known for producing the likes of Def Leppard and Iron Maiden, the fast-paced reality of the scene was that many bands only lasted for the time it took to release one demo or a debut single.

Around the same time Bob Nalbandian clicked with Lars, he also met James Hetfield. 'I first met James outside a small rock nightclub in Anaheim called the Woodstock in 1981. He had just joined forces with Lars. At the time I didn't know he was forming a band with Lars, but I always used to see him checking out my jacket – I had a jacket with patches of Motörhead, Saxon, Maiden, Priest, Rainbow etcetera. When Pat told me that he was the singer in Lars's newly-formed band called "Metallica", I saw him in the parking lot at Woodstock and he again was commenting on my jacket and I said to him, "You're the lead singer for Metallica aren't you?" And James totally freaked out that he was recognised because they hadn't even played a show at that time, and they were still looking for a guitarist and bassist. He said, "Yeah! I sing for Metallica, how did you know?" Then I told him how I knew Lars and we chatted for a while about metal. James was a very nice guy, a really, really cool and genuine person. But he was always very reserved as well.'

It seems that James and Lars's little band were making waves almost from the moment of their formation. Yet it nearly didn't happen. The first jamming sessions between the two were less than impressive, partly due to the fact that Lars's cymbals fell over every time he hit them. James was also far more accomplished with his chosen instrument than his new partner.

'Lars really was not a good drummer,' asserted James. 'When we were done jamming it was, "What the fuck was that?" He had a fucked up, hella fucking cheap Gemco kit or whatever. We told him, "Yeah, we'll give you a call," and we never even called him back! There were so many different things about him. His mannerisms, his look, his accent, his attitude, his smell.'

According to Lars, he rarely washed, so his smell was particularly memorable. 'I can't really comment on his bathing habits,' Bob Nalbandian says today, 'all I can say is that his bedroom didn't have the most pleasant aroma, if you know what I mean!'

'I think that even back then Lars saw something in James that he wanted, so he kept on bothering him,' observed James's old school friend, Dave Marrs. James had little expectation of making much of an impact with Lars in the band, but Ulrich would not give up and was soon further motivated by his beloved NWOBHM.

In summer 1981 Lars travelled to England ostensibly to see Diamond Head at London's Woolwich Odeon, but he also blagged his way into sessions by bands such as NWOBHM underdogs Jaguar. He even managed to sneak into Motörhead's rehearsals for their *Iron Fist* album.

Diamond Head guitarist Brian Tatler remembers, 'The first time I met Lars was in the summer of 1981 on the last night of a Diamond Head tour. We were at the Woolwich Odeon in southeast London. Lars showed up backstage and introduced himself to us. He was just seventeen years old but he'd come all the way from California to see Diamond Head play live. We were really impressed! That night Lars ended up kipping in my brother's old sleeping bag on the floor of my bedroom at my mum and dad's house; the same room where Diamond Head used to practice. After that he stayed for a month with Sean Harris. Lars used to go everywhere with us, squashed into the back of Sean's Austin Allegro.'

'He goes, "I'm going to England, I'm gonna buy a bunch of records and just hang out for a couple of weeks,"' recalls John Kornarens. 'I get a phone call from Lars the week after he's gone and I'm asking him what records he got and he rattles a few off, then he says, "Guess who I'm with?" He says, "Diamond Head, I went to one of their shows and now I'm on tour with them!" I said, "No way." He says, "Yeah, do you want to talk to Sean Harris?" I'm thinking, this guy is unbelievable, you know, he's got a one-track mind and he always makes things happen in the most abstract manner. So I talk to Sean and he's real genial. Lars gets back on and says he's been throwing up 'cause he's been drinking too much with these guys!'

It was perhaps surprising that Lars's English sojourn did not become permanent. He was living the dream – town-hopping with his heroes and generally living the rock-star lifestyle while still a teenager. Yet, after five weeks, Lars returned home. The chief reason he felt inspired to leave the UK was the fact he now had the conviction that his future lay in rock music. He wanted to play to hundreds of people a night – hell, he wanted to play to thousands. So, despite his technical limitations, Lars set his sights on enlisting the apparently apathetic Hetfield. With James, Lars felt the band would have a chance to eclipse his heroes. By the time he'd convinced Hetfield to give the project another chance, not only had Ulrich progressed; he even had a record deal of sorts.

Lars had convinced his buddy Brian Slagel to allow his new band onto a compilation Slagel was putting together for his new record label. In the winter of 1981 Slagel agreed to include Lars's band despite the fact Ulrich had no songs and no band. Slagel had been a veritable local celebrity in the metal world, running a fanzine known as the *New Heavy Metal Revue*, and he often went on shopping splurges with Lars as he added to his already impressive stash of metal.

Bob Nalbandian remembers this period as an exclusive small group of friends who would share their esoteric knowledge – like some clandestine heavy-metal boys' club. 'Oh yeah, there were only a handful of us underground metal fans in the US, let alone California, so it seemed everybody knew everybody. I know Brian Slagel from when he sold metal imports at the Hollywood Record Swap Meet, then he started working at an independent record store called Oz in the valley. It was over an hour's drive from Huntington Beach but we would still take the drive out there every month or so to buy our favourite metal imports. I knew Ron Quintana from a letter he wrote in issue number four of *Kerrang!*. We instantly became pen pals and tape traders, this was just before he started his fanzine *Metal Mania*. I knew Ron and Brian about a month or two before I first met with Lars.'

Quintana would also become close friends with Lars, and subsequently became known as the man who gave Metallica their name. 'That's pretty true,' explains Ron today. 'We were always throwing band and 'zine names around when we would hang out or go to local record stores – I still didn't even know that Lars could actually play drums! – for when we might start a "super heavy metal magazine" or band. He showed me a list of the funniest band names like Black Lightning or Red Vette.'

With the prospect of appearing on Slagel's compilation proving too good to turn down, Lars snagged James for his new group. By now Lars, complete with new drum kit, had, according to Hetfield, 'improved a whole lot'.

Hetfield and Ulrich were always going to be the mainstays of the band, and initially Ron McGovney seemed like a reliable bass player. It was simply a case of who would fill the lead guitar slot. There were many who passed through the garage rehearsals – names that would forever be synonymous with Metallica, despite never recording anything still in existence. Brad Parker and Jeff Warner lent their mediocre talents to the nascent line-up. Parker went by the exotic stage name of 'Damien C. Phillips' and the brief time he was in the band remains the only time Metallica were a five-piece. By the time the band recorded their track for *Metal Massacre*, however, they had slimmed down to a trio.

In order to settle the line-up, the band even considered switching James to rhythm and lead guitar and hiring a full-time singer. 'I think his name was Sammy DeJohn,' Ron McGovney remembers. 'I think he was a singer for a metal band with Jim Durkin from Dark Angel at the time. At first, James wanted to be the lead singer without playing guitar. He didn't feel comfortable on stage without his guitar, so he decided he would just play guitar. We tried out Sammy and he was a good singer, just not Metallica style. He reminded me of the singer for Dante Fox. James decided to be the lead singer again, but this time he would also play guitar.'

Although he was capable of playing leads, at such an early stage in his musical development James felt unready to go public with his more experimental solos. The song 'Hit The Lights' was selected for the compilation – this required an extra-short lead guitar solo. It would actually be a mere ten seconds, but suited the song perfectly. The blistering lead was performed by Lloyd Grant, a tall, Jamaican-born guitarist whose contribution to 'Hit The Lights' would be the high-point of his career. Grant later tried his luck with his own band, thrash metallers Defcon, but after just two demos (one in 1985, the second in 1989), they folded.

Hours before 'Hit The Lights' was due for submission, Metallica decided a second lead was needed, and hastily drove around to Lloyd Grant's home. 'I remember we had this four-track recorder, it had tracks for drums, bass, guitar and vocals,' James explained. 'Because there were no vocals in certain parts of the song we could punch a lead in on the vocal track. I remember we wanted to get another solo on, so we stopped by Lloyd's house and hooked up some little fuckin' amp and just ripped through a solo. It was the first take. We went into the studio and that solo ended up on the record. It's a fuckin' great solo!'

Despite his talent for thrashing out devastating leads, Grant was not destined to become a permanent member of Metallica. 'Lloyd could play leads like a motherfucker, but his rhythm stuff was never very tight,' revealed James. Still, Lars subsequently spoke highly of Grant, telling *Metal Forces* a few years later that 'he's really talented; he's like a black Michael Schenker. There were problems with people because of the

Above: *Lars's fairytale childhood home in Gentofte, Denmark.*
Left: *The teenage Lars, soon to trade his tennis racket for a pair of drum sticks.*
Below left: *'I don't think success has changed us as people at all,' claimed Kirk. But one look at this flyaway, high-school hair says different.*
Below right: *A cherubic young James.*

Above: *Lars realises that he has been given milk and not vodka.*
Opposite: *Estranged bandmates James Hetfield and Dave Mustaine put their creative differences aside onstage.*

Above: *James and a very young Dimebag Darrell (then Diamond Darrell) goofing around at El Cerrito.*
Below: *James and Lars: sobriety reigns.*
Opposite: *Cliff, 'the most headbangingist bassist we had ever seen', in his element.*

Opposite: Clad in bell-bottom jeans, bass guitar welded to him, long mane flowing, Cliff imbued his performances with a unique energy.

Left: Cliff tries out Hetfield's six-string. The versatile musician was proficient in many instruments.

Below: The writing's on the wall: Cliff and James admire one of the band's posters.

Next page: Kirk Hammett prepares to rock his socks off.

fact that Lloyd was black, but to me he was just a great guitarist and it didn't matter if he were black, green, yellow or purple. I just hope something can happen with his band because he really deserves it.'

Even once 'Hit The Lights' was completed, the band faced further problems. 'When we went to mix the album February 1982; I remember it was at Bijou Studios, but Lars wasn't there,' John Kornarens remembers. 'At ten to three he comes running up, out of breath, and he pulls this cassette out of his back pocket and says, "Here it is." Brian goes, "Okay, I need 50 bucks," 'cause it costs 50 dollars to take the cassette and transfer it reel to reel. Lars looks at Brian and says, "I thought you were paying?" And Brian says, "No, I told you *you* had to pay," and it goes back and forth like this.

'Lars suddenly starts to panic and he gets all frantic and he looked over at me and goes, "Dude have you got 50 bucks?" And you know 50 dollars was a lot of money back then. I pull my wallet out and there was 52 dollars in there, which was a lot of money for me to be carrying around back in 1982, but I had it, so I gave it to Lars and he says, "You're going to be known as John '50 Bucks' Kornarens on every Metallica release in the future!" Anyway, he made it onto *Metal Massacre*.'

Kornarens still has the very first test pressing of *Metal Massacre* – now a valuable and highly sought-after item on account of being the very first official Metallica recording. The appearance on the *Metal Massacre* compilation was hardly exemplary – it seemed that the Metallica line-up was destined to change.

The sleeve notes incorrectly credited 'Ron McGouney' as bass player. McGovney, as he should be known, was in for a bigger shock when first meeting Metallica's new lead guitar player. Desperate for a full-time lead guitarist, Ulrich posted an ad in the local newspaper *Recycler*. McGovney remembers, 'I answered the phone one day and this guy Dave was on the other end, and he was just spieling this baloney like I could not believe.'

It is safe to say that the young Dave Mustaine, a flame-haired six-string wizard from Huntington Beach, California, was not short on confidence – even if it were mostly vacuous, substance-fuelled bravado. David Scott Mustaine was born on 13 September 1961 in La Mesa, California, to Emily and John Mustaine.

His parents divorced while he was still a young boy and Dave and his mother were forced to relocate frequently in order to avoid the continued attentions of his abusive alcoholic father. By time he met up with Hetfield and Ulrich, Mustaine was dealing drugs and living alone. Though they may not have discussed their childhoods, it is clear Hetfield and Mustaine had both experienced difficult upbringings and in some small way felt a bond because of this. Indeed, in 1983 Mustaine was quoted as saying, 'I think that James and I are very much the same man. I think that we grabbed an angel, split him in half, and both of us are possessing that power.'

However, Hetfield never really warmed to Mustaine, whom he found to be a little too bold and brash. As would soon become clear, he would also try to usurp Hetfield's lead vocal duties on stage.

Mustaine had been playing in an obscure band called Panic, of whom little is known, but he was clearly two steps ahead of his new bandmates. Despite his relative poverty, Mustaine had an impressive guitar set-up, and before he'd even played a note was invited to join Metallica. Luckily, when he actually played, both Hetfield and Ulrich were impressed. Mustaine later recalled the easy initiation, 'I was convinced that I should be in the band and went to rehearsal. I was tuning up when all the other guys in the band went into another room. They weren't talking to me, so I went in and said, "What the fuck? Am I in the band or not?" and they said, "You've got the gig." I couldn't believe how easy it had been and suggested that we get some beer to celebrate.'

Metallica's first demo combined 'Hit The Lights' with a rough rehearsal that was notable for being Mustaine's earliest recording with the band. It was produced on 1 March 1982, but few people outside the band's closest friends ever got to hear it. More memorable was their first gig, which took place two weeks later in Anaheim, Los Angeles. 'I remember their first show at a club called Radio City – next door to the Woodstock,' recalls Bob Nalbandian. 'Dave Mustaine broke a guitar string in the first or second song and he didn't have a back-up guitar, so the band had to take a ten-minute break while Dave put on a new string. And then they started back up again. They played mostly all covers songs from Diamond Head and other NWOBHM bands at the time and their only original then was "Hit The Lights".'

According to some reports, Metallica insinuated that the obscure cover songs were their own original material. 'Only certain people in the audience, like Pat and I, knew they were covers because we were familiar with the NWOBHM bands,' Nalbandian explains. 'The band didn't actually announce that the songs were "theirs", but they also didn't mention that it was a cover song so I'm sure most people in the audience assumed it was their original songs.'

Indeed, Lars would later confess to the band's creative obfuscation. 'It's quite weird to note that back in the early days of Metallica we had a live set that consisted of "Hit The Lights" plus "The Prince", "Am I Evil?", "Helpless" and "Sucking My Love" from Diamond Head; "Killing Time" from Sweet Savage, "Blitzkrieg" from Blitzkrieg and "Let It Loose" from Savage. We also did a four-track demo of "Hit The Lights", "Let It Loose" and "Killing Time", from which a bootleg seven-inch single now exists featuring the latter pair of cuts. Our trick back then was not to tell people that these songs were covers; we simply let them assume they were ours. We just didn't introduce them, so we never actually laid claim to them, but... well, you get the idea.'

'The first gig was at Radio City and I was just singing,' recalled James. 'There were a lot of people there, maybe 200, because we had all my school friends and all Lars's and Ron's and Dave's buddies. I was really nervous and a little uncomfortable without a guitar and then during the first song Dave broke a string. It seemed to take him an eternity to change it and I was standing there really embarrassed. There was no experience there. We didn't know what to do. Tell a joke? We learned a lot from that gig though. We were really disappointed afterwards. But there were never as many people at the following shows as there were at that first one. I don't think anyone from the band had gotten up onstage before and played. Maybe Dave in his previous band, but I know Lars hadn't. I had played a couple of parties but I know Ron hadn't played before either. Everyone was pretty fuckin' new, very green on that stage!'

Lars's diary entry for the band's first gig read: 'Crowd: 75. Pay: $15. Remarks: 1st gig ever. Very nervous. Only band. Dave broke a string on the first song. Played so-so! Went down pretty good.'

It's hardly an alien concept to most new bands; such trial by fire is almost the only way to learn and develop. Unlike most other groups, Metallica learned extremely quickly, and by the end of the month they were not only twice as good, but they had also secured a pair of gigs with NWOBHM legends Saxon.

On 27 March, the band supported Saxon at the Whisky A Go-Go on Sunset Strip – a show that saw Hetfield sporting a pair of incongruous leopard-print trousers. Although this could be retrospectively viewed as the frontman indulging in some post-modern irony, he was simply conforming to the mix'n'match styles of the day. 'At the time pretty much all the metal bands, whether glam or not, wore stuff like spandex pants,' explains Bob Nalbandian. 'Even Biff from Saxon wore spandex. So that was not that unusual back then. This was a year or two before the big glam wave hit and Metallica kinda combined the LA look of Van Halen – i.e. spandex – with the British metal look: studded wristbands and bullet belts.'

It would soon dawn on Metallica that as they had little else in common with the likes of Van Halen or Mötley Crüe, so their wardrobe should reflect their more pertinent influences. After just a few shows the band reverted to 'street clothes' and instantly felt far more comfortable, both conceptually and physically. For the gig with Saxon, Hetfield again chose to sing without playing guitar, but soon found he was uncomfortable when stripped of his axe.

It has been suggested that at this time Ron McGovney managed Metallica. However, despite the early exposure he brought the band through simple campaigning, he refutes this. 'I really wouldn't call it managing the band. I was the one who got us and the equipment to the gigs, but I only set up two shows myself, which was the Saxon gig; two shows on a Saturday night. I was standing outside of the Whisky when all of a sudden Nikki and Tommy from Mötley Crüe came by. They told me that they were offered the Saxon gig, but turned it down. They introduced me to the girl who booked the gigs. She liked what she heard and gave us the gig.'

In the well-respected pages of the *LA Times*, Terry Atkinson accorded Metallica their very first review. 'Saxon could also use a fast, hot guitar player of the Eddie Van Halen ilk,' he wrote. 'Opening quartet Metallica had one, but little else. The local group needs considerable development to overcome a pervasive awkwardness.' Lars enjoyed recording the fact that the band received a dollar more than their first gig and he also cheekily transcribed, 'Great sound this time. Dave and me played great. Ron and James so-so. Went down pretty good. Had a good time but never met Saxon.'

Just a month after their first demo, Metallica had recorded a new improved version of 'Hit The Lights' (which appeared on all subsequent pressings of *Metal Massacre*) and were clearly beginning to gel with Mustaine. The band opted not to give their second demo a title, but eventually a bootleg version called *Power Metal* would surface, taking its name from an old Metallica business card.

'I went to make Metallica business cards to send to the club promoters along with our demo,' explains Ron McGovney. 'The card was supposed to just have the "Metallica" logo and a contact number. But I thought it looked too plain and decided it should say something under the logo. I didn't want to put "hard rock" or "heavy metal", so I coined the term "power metal"; I thought it had a nice ring to it. No band had used that term before as far as I knew. I remember bringing the business cards to the band and Lars got so pissed off at me. He said, "What the hell is power metal? I can't believe you did such a stupid thing! We can't use these cards with the words 'power metal' on them!"'

Lars's gig diary from the time reveals that, in keeping with thousands of other aspirant bands, Metallica found that their earliest performances were more of a trauma than a triumph. Given the group's subsequent successes, Lars's notes clearly demonstrate that even the world's biggest metal band began by having days when no one showed up:

5 June 1982, Radio City, Anaheim, CA.
I played like shit! Fucked up a lot! The others were pretty good. Went down so-so!

3 July 1982, Concert Factory, Costa Mesa, CA.
Shitty gig. Played 2nd, were suppose to headline. Everything was very rushed, both before and during the gig and played like fucks. Shortened set, coz of the times. Great pay!

5 July 1982, Troubadour, Hollywood, CA.
Played okay, but went on late, so everybody had gone home. Nothing really went down, just a normal gig.

27 August 1982, Whisky, Hollywood, CA.
SHIT!! Ron broke a bass string on 'PL' ['Phantom Lord] and the rest of it was just awfull [sic]. Started at 9:15 with no one around.

'In the early days, when we were playing clubs around LA, people didn't understand what we were about,' explained James. '"Oh," they'd think, "a goddamned punk band," and they'd throw chairs at us.'

The band did manage an encore at an early performance at the Troubadour in Hollywood, but even this did not pass off without a hitch. 'I remember the first time we ever got an encore,' recalled James. 'It was a Monday night at 2:00 in the morning at the Troubadour and there were about ten people there but they were clapping and we came back for the encore. We were deciding on what song we were going to play and Lars starts up a different song! He just decided he wanted to play. And we hadn't practiced that song for like three months. I had forgot all the lyrics, but I went through the motions. And after the gig, I just turned right around and punched him out onstage. "You fucker!" I shouted. Got him in the gut. And people were going, "Huh?"'

Matters improved with the band's first show in San Francisco. They played the famous Stone nightclub in September 1982 and the reaction from fans, critics and the band themselves gave the first indication that Metallica were going places. There were 200 people in attendance and Lars's diary was brimming with enthusiasm. 'First real great gig,' he beamed. 'Real bangers, real fans, real encores. Had a great fuckin' weekend. Fucked up a lot onstage!'

Indeed, even at this early stage in the group's development, there were committed Metallica fans in attendance who knew their songs inside out, singing along to every word. 'It was our first encounter with real fans,' said James. 'It was like, these people are here for us, and they like us, and they hate the other bands – and we like that 'cause we hate them too. These people appreciated us for our music, and not because of how we looked, which was how LA was.'

Local writer Brian Lew heaped plaudits on the band from the pulpit of his *Whiplash* fanzine. He wrote, 'The heaviest band in the US of A, Metallica, rampaged into the city by the bay and spread more havoc than the 1906 earthquake!'

Leah Storkson (then known as Leah Schechter) was James Hetfield's girlfriend from 1983 to 1985. She describes the San Francisco scene of the time: 'We called ourselves the SF bangers,' she remembers, 'there were about 200 young kids who made up the SF metal scene, from ages twelve to 21, and the bands were more like nineteen, twenty years of age. I met up with a guy called Chris Harris on one of my trips to England with my family; he used to write for the Motörheadbangers [a Motörhead fan club]. He turned us on to Motörhead, Girlschool, Angel Witch, Satan, Holocaust, and all these killer English bands. My family had been going to England every summer because my dad worked over there a lot as an architect; and I wound up bringing back all this cool and rare stuff that no one ever knew about, and Ron just ate it up.'

Storkson recalls that as 1982 progressed, Metallica became 'just so hungry to get out of LA as the metal scene there were all mostly posers, and the fans actually hated real metal. The guys in the band seemed extremely happy to play in San Francisco and played a few shows, there they met all their new SF fans, and everyone and anyone who wanted to meet them got to meet them. They were a fun bunch of guys, Dave Mustaine being by far the craziest of all four of them. We partied with them, we watched as they wrecked hotel rooms; the drinking was out of control. We went to all their shows in the Bay Area – we were not groupies or anything, we were just friends.'

In July, Metallica released their most famous demo – one that would garner them worldwide attention. *No Life 'Til Leather* (a title based on Motörhead's *No Sleep 'Til Hammersmith*) was a sudden hit on the underground tape-trading circuit. 'We had been listening to Metallica for a really long time – six to eight months, because we did tape trading, so we had heard all the San Francisco metal bands, like Exodus, Slayer and Possessed and of course Metallica,' explains Storkson. 'My friend Ron Quintana had this radio show at, like, 2:00 in the morning called KUSF and every Saturday night we would go up there, listen to the music and party all night long. My parents were so cool; either they didn't know or they didn't care – I don't know which, but we always had to be home by 10:30 on the Sunday morning, wherever we had been we had to be home for breakfast at that time. My parents were very cool; they actually started taking us to metal shows when we were very young, like, before high school.'

This penchant for velocity was inspired by the likes of Motörhead (who just two years earlier had released the riotous 'Ace Of Spades') and punk heavyweights such as Misfits and Discharge. The latter, a British group who had formed as far back as 1977, would come to prominence with their 1982 debut album *Hear Nothing See Nothing Say Nothing*, although Metallica had long been spinning their early EPs such as 'Realities Of War', Fight Back' and 'Decontrol'. 'Back in the partying days,' James Hetfield later explained, 'we'd put on a Motörhead record, Angel Witch, then Discharge – and no one flinched. It all belonged together. It was aggressive, it had guitars. It felt good. Discharge's guitarist Bones was pulling off some serious metal riffs.'

At the time, *No Life 'Til Leather* seemed resolutely heavy and certainly much faster than most of the NWOBHM heroes of the day. In hindsight, however, it is difficult to believe this is Metallica. Compared to their subsequent studio output, *No Life 'Til Leather* is a sonic homage to Lars and James's British heroes. Metallica would eventually be deemed responsible for the speed-metal movement of the early 1980s, mostly due to the ferocity of their 1983 debut album, *Kill 'Em All*.

Yet *No Life 'Til Leather* gives little indication of the speed-metal behemoth that would become evident with the issue of *Kill 'Em All*. On one hand, the guitars were tinged with a chunky, heavy depth, overlaid with Dave Mustaine's audibly talented lead, and the chugging low riffing at the base of most songs was indeed quite fast. However, James's youthfully exuberant, echo-drenched vocals made the material sound as if it were played by a group of fourteen-year-olds, rather than young metal gods in waiting.

Hetfield's vocals were reminiscent of Holocaust's Gary Lettice, with a sprinkling of Diamond Head, and his tendency to raise the pitch at the end of certain lines in order to place emphasis on a particular word was an irritating affectation, and far removed from the vocal style Hetfield would soon adopt.

The one song that sounded most like the subsequent album version was the almost note-perfect 'Motorbreath' – perhaps because this was one of the band's most basic tracks. Similarly, the demo's other songs were far more straightforward than their later versions, the likes of 'Phantom Lord' and 'Metal Militia' being considerably shorter than those on *Kill 'Em All*.

Several other tracks, notably 'Seek And Destroy', were clearly slower on the demo, which detracted from their impact. One listen to Diamond Head's *Borrowed Time* and the track 'Dead Reckoning' will alert the listener to the remarkable similarities between this and 'Seek And Destroy'.

Ironically the high point of the demo is Lars's colossal drumming, which, though largely simplistic, often carried the song when Hetfield's vocals weakened or the guitar fell too low in the mix. Yet for all its imperfections and naivety, for a demo *No Life 'Til Leather* was remarkable – pulsing with an excitement that most metal bands of the time would fail to match.

Original Metallica fan-club chief K.J. Doughton remembers, 'In 1982 Patrick Scott sent me the first Metallica demo tape, asking for some local band's demo in return. Patrick was the light man for Metallica at the time. The demo tape he sent included "Hit The Lights", "The Mechanix", "Motorbreath", and "Jump In The Fire". After hearing the demo, I freaked out. Metallica had a distinctly European slant to their music, at a time when most US bands were light alloy at best. There were heavy Yank bands like Y&T, Riot, and the Rods, but Metallica took on the big, biblical, slash-and-burn, good-versus-evil issues. No party music. No girl-magnet ballads. Just brutal, attack-oriented audio death.'

'Metallica were definitely the first thrash or speed-metal band in the US at that time,' insists Bob Nalbandian. 'Most of the other bands in LA and even Orange County were more glam or they were still doing the Van Halen kind of thing. There were heavy bands around, but no metal band had adopted the speed riffs here in the US like Metallica did at the time. Punk rock was really big in Orange County and a lot of people thought Metallica was punk just because they played so fast. Not too many people here in the US had even heard of bands like Motörhead, Diamond Head or Iron Maiden at the time, so many people didn't know what to think about them. But once they went up to San Francisco their music was much more accepted then here in Los Angeles, or even Orange County.'

The new-look Metallica was so impressive that Lars proudly wrote to his newfound friend and Diamond Head guitarist Brian Tatler to wax lyrical about his improved group. 'After Lars went home to America he'd write to me,' Tatler remembers. 'It was in early 1982 that he told me he'd formed a band called Metallica. He said they were rehearsing six nights a week and that they were sounding really tight.'

Although the group was progressing to the satisfaction of both Lars and James, the streak of ruthlessness that would later signal the end for a number of band members and friends soon became evident for the first time. Despite their close friendship, James realised that Ron McGovney was never going to work for Metallica full time. He was too staid, too much of a 'yes' man, and musically bereft of his own ideas. As McGovney himself would admit, he played what he was told.

Fatefully, Hetfield and Ulrich soon spotted the ideal four-string titan for Metallica. Visiting the Whisky A Go-Go the duo caught a band named Trauma, featuring one Cliff Burton. They were taken aback, declaring Burton to be 'the most headbangingist bassist we had ever seen'.

Burton literally swung his mane throughout Trauma's set and, replete with bell-bottom jeans and tight vest top, he was evidently a man without any regard for what people thought of him. Then there was his actual bass playing. Using liberal amounts of wah-wah was largely unheard of for metal bassists, as was approaching the instrument as if it were a guitar. Burton used his instrument like a lead, leaving

Hetfield and Ulrich certain that this was the bass player for them. 'Cliff just blew the doors off of anyone we've ever played with. He's the new Steve Harris of metal,' observed Dave Mustaine.

Flemming Larsen (later Metallica's drum tech) recalled Metallica's reaction to Cliff, 'I could just see them go, "Oh my God! Look at that guy!" The thing that struck them most was that while you see lead guitar playing, here you had a guy playing lead bass! They thought that was great.'

Burton was approached after the show and offered a position in Metallica. Although he initially declined, the band kept hounding him, retaining McGovney's services in the interim. Cliff's mother Jan would later recall, 'He was a very loyal person, extremely loyal, and he didn't want to leave Trauma. But Trauma wanted him to go plunk, plunk, plunk, plunk. He wanted to play lead bass and they said, "No way." He really became so frustrated at wanting to express himself musically. Metallica kept calling every week. They'd call him from LA and he'd say, "No, no." When they finally got together he'd say, "I wanna play lead bass. I want some spot in here where I can go off. And they said, "You can play anything you want, just come with us."'

Eventually Burton gave in to the relentless pressure – on the proviso that the band would uproot from Los Angeles to San Francisco. Given the importance of Burton to the sound the rest of the band were working toward, this was a no-brainer, and the group quickly set forth in a decrepit old van for the trip to the Bay Area.

As the end of 1982 neared, James, Lars and Dave moved into their friend Mark Whitaker's house at 3132 Carlson Boulevard in El Cerrito. Whitaker later worked as producer for local metal heavyweights Exodus on their *Bonded By Blood* album and would also double as Metallica's sound engineer and general all-round helper as the band began to gain popularity.

The El Cerrito house would become part of the Metallica mythos, being the setting for long nights of crazy partying. Lars would later explain the house was the source of 'every heavy metal cliché that you could muster up. Me and James shared a bedroom. Dave Mustaine slept on the couch. Dogs were running around. We had the old garage converted into a rehearsal room with egg cartons. It was the refuge, the sanctuary for everybody in the neighbourhood. People would come over and live there, hang there. It was a lot of fun, when you're nineteen.'

'We'd throw parties and take all the furniture out of the place, so you could get wild without breaking stuff,' recalled James. 'If there was something there, it would get broken.'

Despite the mythologising, the El Cerrito house was scarcely wilder than any other location Metallica happened to frequent – if anything it was a little more controlled. Buffo Schnädelbach, whose exclusive photos can be seen in this book, was a guest at the house for a couple of weeks when the band were rehearsing material for the *Master Of Puppets* album. In his experience the band did not go mad at El Cerrito as 'they had an agreement with Mark to keep the house in order'.

To make way for Burton, Ron McGovney was officially relieved of his services; though he is adamant he left Metallica of his own volition. According to him the downslide began even before Dave Mustaine entered the picture, and then proceeded to get worse. 'I guess you could say that I was the most responsible band member when it came to drinking or getting out of control,' asserted McGovney. 'James and I were very good friends before Metallica. Once Lars was in the picture, he kind of hung out with him more than me. I guess I distanced myself from all of them. Lars is Lars now as he was then. Dave and I never really got along. I didn't trust him at all. That caused a lot of tension between me and the rest of the band. To get along with Dave, you had to let him think he was the rock star of the band. Dave thought he was God's gift to the guitar and to women. As long as he thought he was better than you, you could get along with him fine.'

The band's volatile mix of egos made for a fraught dynamic within the group. On one occasion, Dave Mustaine found himself sacked, then re-instated within 24 hours. 'Dave was kicked out for one day,' explains McGovney. 'I don't know how it got so blown out of proportion. Dave let his dogs jump all over my car and scratch it up. James came out of the house yelling at him and Dave punched him in the mouth. I saw what was happening so I jumped on Dave's back and he threw me across the room. James kicked him out of the band then and there. Dave came back the next day crying and apologising, so James let him back in the band.

'It just got to the point to where I couldn't take it anymore,' confesses McGovney. 'Dave was stealing from me or trying to destroy my equipment most of the time. That situation coupled with them hanging out with Cliff at gigs when I was playing for them really got to me. I had finally had it after we returned from our San Francisco trip in November of 1982. I told all of them to get the hell out of my house. I took James aside and told him that I was sorry, but he would have to move out. They moved to San Francisco shortly afterward, and the rest is metal history.'

'Ron was a great guy,' Bob Nalbandian insists. 'He was probably the nicest and most easygoing guy in Metallica at that time. And he will be the first to say that he didn't fit in with the guys in the band and was still just learning to play bass at the time. So he didn't quite have the experience of the others and I think the main reason they kept Ron in the band is that he had his own condo where the band rehearsed and where James was living rent-free. He also funded their initial shows in San Francisco and their ads for many of their shows.'

'I did sell my gear after I quit Metallica because the end was so heart-wrenching for me that I figured I would never be in a band again,' McGovney reveals. 'I sold my Washburn B20 bass to an old high-school friend. I started a band in 1986 called Phantasm and I had to buy all new gear. Phantasm had booked a gig in Oakland near San Francisco in 1987. Just as we were about to leave, the old friend with the Washburn bass showed up at my door and asked if I wanted to buy the bass back. I bought it back on the spot. It looked the same as when I sold it to him in 1983. It even had the same pickups. I loaded the bass up and headed for the gig in Oakland with my old Metallica bass.

'Apparently the bass still had the old Metallica curse on it because our band sucked really bad that night. I put it back in the case until 2004 when I decided to sell it on eBay. I put a reserve price of $5,000 because I knew nobody would pay that much. The bidding got to $4,950 and the bass didn't sell. Some people have written that it was sold, but it was not. I still have it to this day.'

Though many would sympathise with McGovney's situation, there was no doubt that Clifford Lee Burton was the best bass player they could have enlisted. He didn't know it at the time, but Burton was about to help take Metallica to the next level.

CHAPTER 4

HERO OF THE BAY

*'I had seen Cliff in this band called EZ Street when
I was, like, sixteen years old at a club called International Café in
San Francisco, it always stuck out in my mind. This guy with wild red
hair flying all over the place and a Rickenbacker and a real distinct
bass style and I thought to myself, "This guy is fucking wild!"'*
Kirk Hammett

Cliff Burton was born in Castro Valley, California on 10 February 1962, to Jan and Ray Burton. The author obtained exclusive permission from Metallica photographer Harald Oimoen to quote a rare and hitherto unpublished interview Oimoen conducted with Cliff's parents in 1986.

'Cliff was a great kid,' Jan Burton revealed to Oimoen, 'he was never a problem; he was really very quiet. He just led a really normal life except for one thing: he was always his own person, even when he was a little bitty kid. I used to say, "All the kids are playing outside, why aren't you out there playing with them?" And he said, "They're not playing, they're just sitting around talking. That's boring." Then he'd go in the house and read his books or put on his own music. Even when he was a tiny little kid, he would listen to his music or read. He was a big, big reader and he was very bright; in the third grade they tested him and he got eleventh grade comprehension. He just heard a different drummer; he never went with the crowd if he didn't want to. He was always popular and had a lot of friends. He was a very kind, very gentle kid but always his own person.'

'Cliff was 22 months old before he started walking on his own and we were quite concerned about it,' recalled Ray Burton, 'but the doctor said, "There's nothing wrong with him. He's just smart enough to know that mom and dad will carry him around." When we look back on it, it's quite humorous. He damn near broke Jan's back!'

Cliff had two older siblings, Connie and Scott. Scott passed away when Cliff was just a teenager. Like James Hetfield, Cliff had been taught the piano from a young age, a passion instilled by his father, who also opened Cliff's ears to the majesty of classical music.

'He didn't take music lessons until he was thirteen, after his brother died,' Jan Burton told Oimoen. 'He said to a couple of people, "I'm gonna be the best bassist for my brother." We didn't think he had too much talent at all [laughs]; we had no idea!

We just thought he'd plunk, plunk along, which he did at first; it was really not easy for him at first. Then, about six months into the lessons, it started to come together. I thought, "This kid's got real potential," and I was totally amazed 'cause none of the kids in our family had any musical talent! He took lessons on the boulevard for about a year, and then he totally outgrew the teacher and went to another place for a couple of years and outgrew him, too.

'Then he went to the school and took lessons from a very good jazz bassist, a very fine musician. He was the one who made Cliff take Bach and Beethoven and Baroque and made him learn to read music and stuff like that. He was with him for a long time, and then he really outgrew him, too. He really got so good that he didn't need that anymore. He really did sit down and study and play Bach. He loved Bach.'

Burton was taught by Steve Doherty, who resides in the ABC Music Studio. 'He was a good student, very focused. He knew what he wanted,' recalled Doherty. 'He was a kind of student who always came in with the lesson prepared, which is not all that common. I had many serious students, but Cliff had that rare inner drive to get out and do something about his music, I can't take credit for that; it was already there even when I taught him.'

Upon graduating from Castro Valley High School in 1980, Cliff travelled to Chabot Junior College during the week to study music.

Though classical music was Cliff's first aural love he also opened his ears to country, blues and jazz, all before he discovered heavy metal and punk. But even as his abilities progressed far beyond his peers, Cliff remained humble. 'He would practice between four and six hours a day, every single day, even after he got into Metallica,' explained Jan Burton. 'He was a very modest kid. He always said, "No, there's somebody in their garage that hasn't been discovered that's better than I am."

'Even in the last year with Metallica, when they had made it, it didn't make a difference to him. He still practiced every bit as much; he'd stay up all night and sleep late. But then when he got up, that's what he would do, is put on his bass first thing and play. One thing about him that probably was unusual was his consideration of us, 'cause he used to stay up all night. He didn't want to change his lifestyle; it was too hard on his body. His friends Dave Donato and Jim Martin would come over and they'd play *Dungeons And Dragons* or watch videos and he'd fix these huge meals, like omelettes, he loved to cook all this stuff, and he'd very seldom wake us up. He was exceptionally considerate and loving.'

Corinne Lynn, Cliff's last girlfriend, would transcribe the following interview, which was again undertaken by Harald Oimoen and is quoted ahead with kind permission.

'I started playing in 1976,' recounted Cliff. 'My influences would be... well, first off, with bass playing it would be Geddy Lee, Geezer Butler, Stanley Clarke, and Lemmy also had an influence in the way he uses distortion. That was different, new, and exciting. Also, certain guitar players had an influence. People like, well, everything Thin Lizzy did has had an influence. I used to jam around with some local friends, then I got together with these guys who called themselves EZ Street, named after a strip joint in San Mateo. It was all kinds of weird shit. It was pretty silly, actually. We did a lot of covers, just wimpy shit. But I was with them for a while, for a few years. And that slowly but surely disintegrated. Then I saw Trauma and I thought, "Well, I might as well do that." Didn't have anything better to do.'

'When he was about 21 or 22 he said, "I'm going to be a professional musician. I'm going to make my living as a musician,"' Ray Burton recalled. 'And that's what he did.'

'We said, "Okay,"' added Jan. ''cause Cliff never gave up on anything! I've never seen that boy give up on anything or anybody. So I knew that when he said that, he 110 per cent was going to go into it. Because we loved him very much and we respected him, we really tried to give him 110 per cent because we felt he was very deserving of it. He had been playing with other little local bands up until that time. We said, "Okay, we'll give you four years. We'll pay for your rent and your food. But after that four years is over, if we don't see some slow progress or moderate progress, if you're just not going anyplace and it's obvious you're not going to make a living out of it, then you're going to have to get a job and do something else. That's as far as we're going to support you. It should be known by then whether or not you're going to make it, so he said, "Fine." And, boy, did he make it! Two years later. Of course, *Kill 'Em All* was the first.'

Call it luck or the recognition of evident talent, but the Metallica boys noticed Cliff very early in his professional career. Once the band had arrived in Cliff's home city they were quickly seen as the leading lights of the burgeoning Bay Area movement. Bands such as Exodus were also synonymous with the genre that was soon to be tagged speed metal. Yet, where many speed metal bands were focused on vicious velocity and tended to lack catchy songs, Metallica shone above their peers from the outset. The songs they were beginning to construct had just as much grounding in the NWOBHM as anything Venom released, and there was always the punk influence, which James and Cliff brought to bear. As such, Metallica's wider range ensured that they transcended the sub-genre.

Cliff Burton's first show with Metallica was at the Stone nightclub, San Francisco, in March 1983. Writing in the *Bay Area Club Days Revisited* fanzine, Brian Lew gushed, 'Metallica, those supreme metal gods, those purveyors of raging sonic decapitation, those rabid vodka-powered maniacs, blew our faces off as they stormed onstage through a flurry of smoke and blinding lights and got things banging with "Hit The Lights". It was time to *die*! The moment many had been waiting for soon arrived – bassist Cliff Burton's solo spot! Cliff built his solo from a haunting classical guitar-sounding ballad up to a crescendo of some of the fastest, most apocalyptic bass raging ever performed!'

Soon after this show (which would be Dave Mustaine's last appearance with Metallica in San Francisco) the band would compose their next demo tape, the first to feature their new bassist.

By now Brian Slagel had formed a proper record label, which he named 'Metal Blade' – and it seemed inevitable that Metallica would sign with Slagel for their debut recording. Slagel was certainly interested, but his fledgling label had little to offer the band by way of financial backing. However, he was in touch with a friend on the East Coast by the name of Jonny Zazula. Zazula, the owner of a record store in East Brunswick, New Jersey, was well versed in the local metal scene of the time but had heard nothing like Metallica. In a bold move, and one of immense foresight, he made a commitment to borrow some extra money to start a record label in order to release Metallica's full-length debut LP. He named the label Megaforce.

Metallica's East Coast debut also featured an appearance from a band known as ANTI. The group featured future Savatage guitarist Chris Caffery. 'I was in high school when ANTI started to play,' he recalls. 'My brother was on drums. We had a pretty cool singer named Blais [pronounced "Blaze"]. We had a large local following. We were invited to open for Overkill at a show and did very well. Metallica was playing their first ever show on the East Coast. It was to be at the same venue. It was the State Theatre in Port Jervis, New York. Overkill was on the bill and we were again asked to play.

'Metallica did not have much money and needed a place to stay. Their record company contacted me about this. I offered to have them stay at my house but my mom refused to let them! I was only sixteen at the time! The night of the show my crazy singer Blais set up pyrotechnics on the stage without anyone knowing, including myself or Metallica. After a couple songs he set it off. I then see a huge guy, one of the Metallica crew, on the side of the stage holding a sign. It read, "This is your last song – sorry." We left the stage and the crowd was chanting "An-ti... an-ti..." It was funny, not because someone could have gotten hurt, but 'cause we could have finished a great show!'

It was around this time that Leah Storkson began her relationship with James Hetfield. 'At the time I was a brooding teenager, a total tomboy, who rarely had any girlfriends to speak of, only one or two,' she recalls. 'I felt like no one understood me, I had no boyfriend, I felt depressed and I decided to do something highly questionable and I landed myself in an institution for disturbed persons. At the time I was very good friends with a girl named Rebecca who was Kirk Hammett's girlfriend and she wound up marrying him later. She decided to come visit me and she brought James, Lars and Kirk to the hospital. I think Lars stayed in the car with his girlfriend or something.

'So that's where I re-met James,' she continues. 'I remember thinking, "Wow, he's just so intense and so shy – could this really be the same person that I've seen onstage all these times?" because he really was a maniac onstage. He seemed very shy, quiet, moody and not at all like I remembered him from previous meetings with him. I wasn't sure he even remembered me at all. With freckles, long brown hair, sort of a petite build, with plain clothes, not that memorable – is how I viewed myself. And I think we said "hi" and talked about music or something, realising we had the same exact musical taste. I wasn't even embarrassed at him seeing me in this place for some dumb reason. And then they left. I now *had* to get out of there, realising there was more life to live out there.

'Two weeks later I was told that there was a show at the Keystone Berkeley, Metallica playing with Exodus and Raven. My cool mom and I went AWOL a week later, and

I got out of the institution. My friend Ron Quintana, and my sister and I took this train called BART [Bay Area Rapid Transit] to the show and we were standing at the front for the show and James walked up to me and said, "You're out!" and I was laughing, and we just really hit it off. He invited us to come in and put us on the guest list. I remember a couple of people yelling, "Are you James?" And he's like, "No, I'm not, go away." He never wanted anybody to ask him questions. He never signed anybody's shirts or pieces of paper or nothing – he was just not into it.'

Storkson describes the development of her relationship with James: 'We started hanging out a lot more and started dating immediately after that, though it started out as more of a friendship. We went to all these gigs and parties together – shows at Ruthie's Inn and other tiny venues in San Francisco and around the Bay Area, and they held a lot of parties at the El Cerrito house. I recall that none of the guys had jobs, and had very little to live on. Once in a while I loaned James money for what I hoped would be for toothpaste, toilet paper, socks – the bare necessities. The next Friday night a big bottle of Popov Vodka would be on the coffee table again. Oh well, the fun was not to be stopped. I wasn't complaining!'

Metallica almost didn't make it to New York – at least, not with their frontman. Fred Cotton was James Hetfield's best friend throughout the 1980s. He would become well known for his Spastik Children project, which featured James along with Cliff Burton and Kirk Hammett. Cotton is a hulking presence, yet supremely easygoing and speaking with the same twang as James Hetfield. His words are punctuated with belly laughs and deferential respect to his old buddy.

'I met them at their first gig at the Stone,' Cotton remembers. 'I hit it off with James, not immediately but we started palling around. I used to go down and visit him after my work in a restaurant at the time. I always made sure our friendship was on a real level and had nothing to do with the band and I guess that's how we got close.

'We had this party at Tom Hunting's [Exodus drummer] house and James started throwing bottles at the street lights and he broke one,' continues Cotton. 'One of the neighbours saw it and called the cops, so the cops were coming and James ran inside. Everybody took a vote and told James to hide in the garage and they told Robbie [McKillop, Exodus bass player], 'cause he was the weakest one in the band, to tell the cops it was him, and he had to go to jail! James couldn't go to jail 'cause he had to go to New York the next day and Robbie was crying, "Waah, I didn't do it!"'

The drunk and belligerent youngster who would destroy everything and anything in his path is a side of James that few are aware of. Though he would become resolutely sensible in front of a camera, even early on in the band's career, behind the scenes with his closest friends, James would play out the role of resentful rebel. As Cotton rightly points out, many of the crowd around Hetfield at the time were all fighting their own demons from the past. These demons were not discussed directly, nor confronted in any formal manner; the seething wellsprings of resentment and bitterness being given some release through violence.

'He was volatile then,' Cotton says of James. 'He wasn't an asshole, we would just get drunk and belligerent, rowdy – like breaking glass and shit.' Alcohol was a mainstay of Hetfield's diet and freed him from his inhibitions in a very direct way. 'We were at this one party and were standing in a car port of a garage and we were thrashing shit and James started kicking the post from this car port and the whole fucking roof came down and the neighbour came out with a gun and chased everybody away,' recounts Cotton.

This kind of destructive behaviour wasn't confined to James, however. 'I remember when Slayer first came up here to play with Exodus they had a hotel room at the Berkeley Plaza Hotel,' Cotton recollects. 'We just destroyed that place. We were nailing pizza to the ceiling; we cut a hole in the wall to go into the next room, which was the manager's room. Anything we could get down the toilet we stuffed it down the toilet and clogged it, we were bowling down between the two beds with bottles. We fucked that place up, they got sued big time. The next time they came up to play we had a party at my buddy's house. He lived in this shack right next to Paul Baloff [Exodus singer]. The toilets weren't working, the whole bathtub was full of shit and piss and everything else – even the chicks were going to the bathroom in there, you name it man, it was foul.'

Liberated by alcohol and metal, Hetfield and Cotton felt invincible and fought back against the isolation of their respective childhoods. 'It was powerful,' says Cotton, 'it was like a movement; it was us against the world. We used to like to go into places for dinner, our money was as green as the other people in the place, you know, but just act the way we did – just to do it. We were proud of that. The attitude was to thrash, thrash ourselves and people's houses.'

James had his own explanation. 'Call it anarchy or whatever you want to, there's times when you wanna be able to do whatever the fuck you want and, y'know, life's always short, so why shouldn't you?'

Within Metallica, despite heroic levels of alcohol consumption, there was little in the way of violently destructive behaviour, aside from that displayed by James. As Cotton indicates, Lars was often taking care of business while Cliff would be too mellow for the destruction of property. 'They were serious when it came to the music, they really meant it,' insists Cotton. 'I knew the first time I saw them and heard them play, I knew there was something special there – I could feel it, it was intense.'

Yet, just when it seemed Metallica were going somewhere and had brokered a significant deal, the recurring problem of Dave's attitude reached crisis point. He was becoming a constant source of irritation, on and offstage, and eventually Hetfield and Ulrich took it upon themselves to fire the errant guitarist. The very same afternoon Mustaine was fired, the band invited Exodus guitarist Kirk Hammett into the band and he accepted.

That Kirk joined up with Metallica was somewhat bizarre given Exodus were a band Hammett had helped to form, along with drummer Tom Hunting. With admirable foresight, Hammett decided that he would achieve success far quicker with Metallica and left his bandmates without a second guitarist.

By many accounts, Dave Mustaine was an aggressive drunk who was unreliable and problematic, but also clearly had two sides to his character. Lars's father Torben remembers Dave as 'someone smiling and always friendly, very courteous and quite articulate, and when I say courteous I think particularly about the way he was always attending to Lars's mother and asking her if she'd had a good day and so on. So when he was around the house he was always very well liked and received. Obviously Lars's mother and I could not know how things were going once the guys left the West Coast and things began to unfold, or unravel, out East. Obviously it cannot be very nice to wake up in the morning and be told that it's over, and here's a ticket to take you back home, if your whole life is involved with this kind of music and that kind of travelling. But since we were not there, it seems impossible to be able to go further than that, except to give to Dave that kind of sympathetic thought, that I think also everybody would give, even given that he of course could not think that that was enough, ever.'

Bob Nalbandian also has a positive perspective on Mustaine. 'I always loved Dave and I thought he was one of the main focal points of the band. He seemed to have the most presence, so of course I was surprised when he was ousted from the band. But we all knew of Dave's alcohol problem, as it was very prevalent at the time. I mean, Dave was pretty out of control back then but that, I think, was what also gave the band that "I don't give a fuck" attitude. He had such a dominant role in the band's live performances back then and was a key songwriter, so I think every Metallica fan back then was pretty shocked about the news that Dave was out.'

However, Fred Cotton is more critical. 'I can totally see why they replaced him,' he says. 'Dave's a good guy but when he got drunk he would always get into the mic and say shit between songs. He was just too much of a presence I think, really rowdy. He needed to go off and do his own thing, it seemed like he was always trying to get up in the mix and that didn't sit too well with James. It stuck out; it was definitely something you could notice. Dave being obnoxious between songs made James look kind of silly.'

Leah Storkson also recalls Mustaine's intolerable attitude. 'He was crazy and so arrogant – he was such a rock star. I brought him to one of my friend's apartments who was a photographer for Mötley Crüe, who Metallica hated, of course. And she had all her black-and-white photos on the wall and Dave spat beer all over them. Of course, I had to drag them out of her house apologising and saying, "I'll pay for your pictures, I'm so sorry." The guy was such a freakin' jerk. I mean that stuff happened every time we went out, hotel rooms and people's houses were left in terrible shape, we got kicked out of everywhere we went – it's all true.'

Although Mustaine's alcohol and drug addictions are often cited as the cause of his sacking, the substances which fuelled his cantankerous behaviour were not the cause. His personality and intrusive japes were always likely to cause friction and this was something that even sobriety couldn't temper. Hetfield was no slouch when it came to drinking and rowdy antics, but when it was time to play he channelled all of his aggression into the music, not between-song rants or demonstrations of one-upmanship aimed at other band members. Mustaine crossed the line.

For many years after, Mustaine rarely passed up any opportunity to criticise his former band, reserving particular venom for the guitarist who took his place. He would insist that Hammett 'stole my job, but at least I got to bang his girlfriend before he took my job. How do I taste, Kirk?'

In a 1985 interview for *Metal Forces* magazine, Mustaine attacked Hammett, saying, 'It's real funny how Kirk Hammett ripped off every lead break I'd played on that *No Life 'Til Leather* tape.'

Kirk responded in the same publication several years later. 'The first thing I want to clear up is this thing about me playing Dave Mustaine's solos on *Kill 'Em All*, that's total bullshit. My style is totally different to Dave's; he likes to masturbate on the fretboard, play 10,000 notes in a small time measure. I don't come from that school of guitar playing. All my notes are thought out. As for him inventing this type of guitar technique, that's bullshit too! Let's face it, we all come from a basic school of heavy-metal guitar playing, he didn't invent jack shit.'

Twenty years later, the two would eventually bury the hatchet. 'It was really unusual because I was standing there and I'm always polite about it – "Hi Dave, how ya doin'?" And he goes, "Hey, how ya doin'?" And basically he just came up to me and apologised for all the bad-mouthing that he did to me and the band,' explained Kirk. 'I was really surprised. I think that was a result of him cleaning up and actually being able to think with a clear head. I thought it was very decent of him.'

Kirk Lee Hammett was born on 18 November 1962 in El Sobrante, San Francisco. His father was an Irish merchant marine and his mother a Filipino housewife. Kirk has described himself as an 'introverted kid. I read a lot. I had a fascination with comic books, monster magazines, and monster movies, which carries on through now. I'm still heavily into monster movies and monster toys.'

Kirk's older brother Rick was responsible for igniting a passion for music in his younger sibling. Rick was a guitarist and a serious music aficionado with a vast collection of LPs from UFO to Status Quo and the Rolling Stones to Black Sabbath. Crucially, he also owned a number of Jimi Hendrix albums, which would soon become musical manna for Kirk. 'My brother got me into music,' Hammett revealed. 'He started playing guitar around 1968. He was a hippie. He exposed me to the Haight-Ashbury scene, so I was exposed to Hendrix, Zeppelin, and Santana right when that stuff was released – 1967 through to 1969.'

Rick Hammett also owned several guitars as well as a couple of Rickenbacker basses, and by the time Kirk was fifteen he was copying his brother's six-string moves and teaching himself to play whenever he could. Kirk was not afforded the luxury of his brother's guitar collection, as he had been raised to work for his own money and his own possessions. And so Kirk's first guitar was straight out of a cheap catalogue – a Montgomery Ward special. His first amp came with the guitar and was a simple practice amp about the size of a shoebox with a tiny four-inch speaker.

In 1978, after just a year of playing, Kirk was able (thanks to a job in a local

Burger King) to afford a Fender Stratocaster and Marshall amp. Not long after that he bought a 1974 Gibson Flying V in honour of UFO's Michael Schenker – an item that he still prizes.

Before Kirk reached the age of twenty, he had formed Exodus along with Tom Hunting, a drummer in the Bay Area. Exodus were arguably more of a thrash band than Metallica, exploring the more vicious extremes of speed metal and, early on, demonstrating a distinct lack of subtlety.

Not long after forming the band, Hammett and Hunting enlisted Gary Holt as second guitarist. Holt, who is now the acknowledged leader of the band, and the longest-serving member, says of his Exodus initiation: 'When I joined the band I had only been playing guitar for about six months. I had first seen Kirk when Exodus played my high-school band room. We first hung out when we went to see Ted Nugent and the Scorpions together with some other dudes.

'Kirk taught me my first chords, a couple of scales and some Rolling Stones song – I can't remember which. We became partners in crime right off the bat. I took it from there until they asked me to play a song with them at rehearsal – it was Judas Priest's "Grinder", and then they asked me to join. I said, "Fuck, yes." Kirk was always super fun to be around, he was sort of geeky back then, but so was I! But he changed my life by being the first to play some old Scorpions for me. Uli Jon Roth has been God ever since.'

In 1982 Kirk made his first and only recorded appearance with Exodus for their untitled debut demo. 'At the time we all thought it was way cool, first real demo and all,' remembers Holt. 'I still think it's cool, although some of the lyrics are pretty funny, especially "Whipping Queen"!'

To many it somehow seems incongruous that the shy, retiring Hammett founded and played in a band so violently insane as Exodus. Indeed, the line-up, which featured Holt and six-string partner Rick Hunolt (the two became known as the H-Team) certainly seemed more closely matched. However, Holt says that in 1982 Kirk was completely suited to the group. 'At the time, of course it was right. Who knows what the band would have been like if he stayed, or if there would have been some kind of conflict over writing control and band direction? But when we found Rick it was when we found our groove, so to speak. Not musically, but our path.'

When Kirk left for Metallica he bequeathed his second guitarist with an unspoken role as the leader of Exodus. 'It was Kirk's baby when I joined, he wrote all the music,' explains Holt. 'I was still a beginner, although I picked up the knack of playing really quickly. But at the time he left, I was starting to write my share of stuff too. So when he left, I felt like, "Yeah, she's all mine now!" Seriously, we were all very happy for him, and I was put in the driver's seat writing-wise. That's when the band headed for a more violent direction, I guess you could say.'

Intriguingly, the bond between Exodus and Metallica was strong enough (after several shows together) that by the time of Dave Mustaine's departure it seemed probable rather than possible that Hammett would switch bands. 'I was surprised when Kirk left,' Holt reveals, 'but when Dave was out many people in the Bay Area thought someone from this band was going to join Metallica. But we had a big party for Kirk, and we cut his picture out of a bunch of our promo pics and taped them up all over this club, the Old Waldorf. Girls' bathroom and everything! He chased those things down all night.'

This close association ensured that there was no bad blood between the two bands when Hammett changed groups. Indeed, throughout the 1980s and 1990s the Bay Area would give rise to a tight scene of friends. The bands were not in competition with each other, but rather fed off each other's reputations. 'When we first played together was the first time I had heard them,' Holt says of Metallica. 'We were surprised to hear someone else playing music similar to what we were, and we all hit it off immediately. Us and Metallica, we were good friends, and they certainly stood out for sure. Later, with some of the other bands, we were all friends but at the same time there was a healthy competition. Things were newer and more underground in the beginning, but later it had become apparent that this type of metal was going somewhere. But early on we were creating something new.'

Ironically, though Metallica were essentially considered a Bay Area band and had many friends in and around San Francisco, Kirk Hammett found himself flying to New York to join a band that came from his home state. Though Hammett was not officially given the Metallica job until after the debut album, he felt confident enough to give up his college studies in English and Psychiatry, and pooled enough money together for a flight to the East Coast. Like Ulrich before him, Hammett clearly thought this band, who had secured a record deal (unlike Exodus), had the talent and potential to become at least marginally successful.

Metallica and Exodus had first shared a bill at the Old Waldorf in San Francisco in late 1982. Kirk later recalled his first impressions of his future band. He told *Kerrang!* magazine: 'Within the first few minutes of seeing them, I thought to myself, "These guys are so goddamn original, but that guitar player isn't so hot, they should get me." That was really strange because two or three months later I got that phone call to join.'

Hammett also remembered feeling slightly uncomfortable in front of two people who were certainly not your average guys. 'I was speaking to Lars in the dressing room, and he just got undressed in front of me and it just seemed so bizarre. I remember James as a man of few words until you added alcohol.

'I had talked to Lars and James briefly, in passing when Exodus had played with Metallica,' Kirk explained. 'They were planning to go to New York to hook up with Jonny Z and do their first album. They had been having problems with Dave, and they were looking for someone who was more a melodic, controlled player. Our soundman played them some tapes of Exodus live, and they liked what they heard. They gave me a call in April 1983 and asked me if I wanted to join Metallica. I thought it was an April Fools' joke, but I said "sure" anyway.'

The band's first show with Kirk Hammett was on 16 April 1983 at the Showplace nightclub in Dover, New Jersey. Just one month later, Hammett would be in the studio making his first contribution to Metallica's debut album. Though there was a palpable sense of 'something' about to happen, the reality was far less explosive before the recording of *Kill 'Em All*. 'You gotta remember Metallica back then were kids trying to survive and have fun,' Bob Nalbandian says. 'Lars worked at a gas station; James worked at a print shop to make money. Even though they talked about "making it huge", you have to remember "making it huge" in their eyes would be to be as big as a band like Diamond Head or Saxon. In those days I'm sure they never thought they would ever become bigger than a band like Motörhead! And I'm sure they looked to those bands when it came to drinking and being crazy just because they wanted so much to be like the NWOBHM bands at that time.'

Most bands want to 'make it big', but unlike the vast majority, Lars Ulrich really did have the vision to see this ambition through. 'He used to say things like, "My band is gonna make it huge," and that kind of thing, but back then all local musicians used to say that kind of thing, so you would just take it with a grain of salt,' Bob Nalbandian recalls. 'I do remember one day in his room Pat and I were talking with him and he kept commenting about how his band is gonna rule in Europe and then in America and I commented back to him saying something like, "This kind of metal can never be big in America." And, fuck! Did he prove me wrong!'

CHAPTER 5

LOSING MUST

'Kill 'Em All *just melted your face off.*'
Fred Cotton

Making the flight to New York was the least of Metallica's problems. Given that money was tight, the obvious solution for Jonny Zazula was to house the band himself. Unfortunately, he and wife Marsha did not reckon on hosting an unruly rabble of heavy-metal maniacs. Metallica thought they could merely continue their usual drinking spree – from the plane, to the airport and then the Zazula house.

However, with next to no money they weren't able to fund much of a drinking spree and soon raided their host's drinks cabinet. They drank it dry, even guzzling the special wedding champagne the Zazulas had been saving. Without booze, Metallica were polite and respectful, but they couldn't seem to endure a single day of sobriety and weren't about to let anyone else's property or feelings get in their way. Jonny Zazula threw the band out of his house and forced them to shack up at the Music Building in Queens – a less than salubrious part of town.

'It used to be a furniture warehouse,' recalled James. 'It was eight storeys of rooms that had been turned into a rehearsal place and it was in this fucking really bad drug-infested neighbourhood. We had to live there! We had no transportation, no money, no food, it was pretty bad. The guys in Anthrax helped us out with a refrigerator and a toaster; they were practicing there too. There was nothing but fucking cold water in the sink.'

It wasn't just the spartan living conditions the band had to contend with, however. Lars was shocked to discover that the building seemed to be housing the dead alongside the living. 'On the second floor there's this huge ballroom which is perfect for getting a good drum sound,' he explained. 'The only problem is the place is fucking haunted, so I had to have someone else up there the whole time I was recording. My cymbals would start spinning, you know, shit like that. It was scary but I'd love to record there again.'

Though Jonny Zazula still believed in Metallica's musical potential, as individuals he felt little affinity for the band, finding these petulant young kids more than a little irritating. They drank, they cursed, and they were far less mature than average nineteen- and twenty-year-olds. As a consequence of this, he virtually banished the group from the control room whenever they weren't recording. They were merely permitted to go in, play their parts, then politely disappear. Luckily, the band were too naive to notice Zazula's distaste, and took their banishment from his home in relatively good spirit, assuming that it was simply a musical decision.

Zazula was controlling how his inexperienced charges sounded to the extent that he could make the record sound the way he imagined would sell best. Perhaps intelligently, Zazula removed any potential issues by marginalising the band. The group didn't like feeling shunned in the studio and were understandably curious to hear what the record sounded like. With a budget of just $12,000, and keenly aware of their penchant for drunkenness, Zazula was inclined to keep the group on a short leash. After all, they weren't used to the way things worked in a real studio and had next to no experience of arranging songs. At this early stage, Metallica were simply 'plug in and play' merchants with little appreciation for intricacies or perfectionism. Get drunk, rage and pass out was the order of the day. Only Lars could see beyond their present parameters and think of the future. As a consequence it was he who became most frustrated at being banned from seeing what really went on in a studio control room.

Zazula and co-producer Paul Curcio mixed the album, their results unsurprisingly leaving the band disappointed (perhaps more as a consequence of their lack of involvement rather than any serious aversion to the production). 'Cliff had all kinds of shit that he wanted to record on his bass and the producers would say, "Well, it doesn't sound right,"' opined James. 'Of course it didn't sound right! It wasn't fucking normal! But it's how we wanted to sound. Those guys were too fucking sterile. We were out there trying to create new sounds, and they were shooting us down from the beginning.'

Lars, ever the diplomat, was less critical, telling *Kerrang!*: 'We're really pleased with the way the album has turned out.' However, he would later joke to the same magazine, 'There's a credit on the back of that album that says "producer". I think you should erase that and put "coffee drinker"… I remember Cliff banging on the fucking studio door and this voice on the intercom saying, "Oh, you can't come in right now," and you could hear them listening to the mixes on the intercom!'

It's impossible to know how the pre-production recordings sounded. Clearly the band had updated their demo sound, but perhaps a lot of the credit for the overall feel of the album has to go to Zazula and Curcio. Doubtless, they could have trimmed the fat from *No Life 'Til Leather* and made it sound upfront and glorious. The songs were certainly there; they just needed coaxing and embellishing. Even in the beginning, Metallica were control freaks and their problem with the mix was simply that they were not the ones who mixed it.

What was under band control, however, was the rearrangement of their material. Armed with the same group of songs they'd had for many months, there was no time to write anything new, but they did seek to add extra parts to the demo versions and enhance the songs wherever possible.

Averaging over five minutes a track represented a rather grandiose statement from metal rookies, signalling early on that Metallica felt they were destined for great things. 'I think we've given the punters value for money,' insisted Lars to *Kerrang!*. 'I mean, side one runs at a staggering 25 minutes while the flip clocks in around the same. We used the first nine songs we ever wrote on this album and we'll use the next nine on the following one and so on. It's all part of Metallica's plan for world domination.'

With a slowly developing introduction, 'Hit The Lights' was highly reminiscent of the opening bars of Iron Maiden's 'Genghis Khan', but it set up a remarkable riff (also straight from the NWOBHM stable) and a yelp from Hetfield before the speed began. It was immediately clear that the production suited the material, bringing to life the potential only marginally evident in the *No Life 'Til Leather* demo.

It was obvious that Metallica had made a very wise decision in offloading Dave Mustaine. There was only room for one lead singer, one spokesman or even one lyricist – and his name was James Hetfield. Not only was Kirk capable of playing the same leads that Mustaine did, he embellished many of the guitar runs and threw in numerous new touches – a confident step from a shy kid who was merely a new addition to an established trio.

Hammett's extended solo was the focal point of 'Hit The Lights' – throwing in more NWOBHM licks and hard-rock stabs, before bringing the song to a crushing crescendo with the aid of Ulrich's titanic drum rolls. If he was a poor musician a year before, Ulrich was now demonstrating what a tremendously fast learner he was.

The lyrical matter to the track was a fundamental statement of Metallica's fast-living, metal-warrior lifestyle, which culminated with their short live set every night. The reference to 'sweet pain' was also a relatively poetic paean to the art of headbanging before ear-splitting amplification.

As 'The Four Horsemen' assaults the listener, the distinctive chug of Hetfield and Hammett's guitars presages thrash metal – not so much in terms of speed, but in the sheer power and brawny, defiantly harsh guitar tone. Ultimately it's a barnstormer of a riff perfectly suited to the mid-tempo crunch which follows. This was NWOBHM overlaid with Metallica's gruff, trebly style. There was simply no other band that sounded like this.

Though it was one of the band's catchiest songs and seemingly the most simplistic, there is more to the track than is immediately apparent. Firstly, it was a reworking of their demo track 'Mechanix'. In order not to plagiarise the Mustaine lyric book (he was still credited for his riff contribution) Hetfield had to quickly come up with new lyrics, which proved to be far more fitting than those on the demo version – which, in retrospect, now merely sounds like a bad cover version of 'The Four Horsemen'.

Although James wrote the lyrics in some haste, it is evident that he was writing from the heart. The song splices tales of biblical apocrypha with recountments of childhood angst. One can read between the lines and remember James's painful religious upbringing and the death of his mother. This is evident via lines such as, 'A sinner once a sinner twice/ No need for confession now/ 'Cause now you've got the fight of your life.' Likewise the song's valedictory challenge – 'choose your fate and die'.

For all its catastrophic intentions, 'The Four Horsemen' remains a resolutely positive song, filling the listener with images of four heroes coming to regain land, women and hope.

'Motorbreath' was Metallica's most obvious punk paean on the album, taking in the energy and simplicity of Motörhead and combining it with the dark savagery of the Misfits' early work. Billed as Hetfield's only solo credit on the album, the song urges everyone to live life at a fast pace, making the most of every day. It also cleverly combines the duality of fast cars (something Hetfield was very fond of) and the swift pace of life.

'Jump In The Fire' was one of the band's darkest tracks – seething with a seemingly satanic deference. Despite later controversies, there was little devil worshipping evident in metal during the early 1980s. Bands such as the darkly psychedelic Coven and prog-rockers Black Widow were overtly satanic in nature, yet they could hardly be lumped into the metal genre. The only metallic satanic artists of any significant standard were Lars's fellow countrymen, Mercyful Fate – a notable influence on Metallica, who subsequently provided them with cover song material.

Was 'Jump In The Fire' a lyrical tribute to their influences or yet another reference to James's past? Again, it is easy to ascribe dual meanings to the seemingly oblique references to devils, fiery homes and chiming bells, plus the more explicit lines such as, 'Now it's time for your fate and I won't hesitate/ To pull you down into this pit,' or 'Follow me now my child, not the meek or the mild/ But do just as I say.' If James was not exorcising demons from his past, then he at least put his fire-and-brimstone Sunday-school teachings to good use in creating a metal classic.

Above all else 'Jump In The Fire' is a tremendous track, one of the most underrated in the Metallica catalogue. Built upon two majestic riffs, each trying to surpass the other, the song is a mouthful of metallic glory. It was also one of the slower tracks on the album, with a pounding bass line erupting into the speaker synonymously with each drum thump. Despite the European influence on Metallica's sound there was a resolutely American feel to their approach, be it their stubborn personalities or the palpable Hetfield accent.

'(Anesthesia) Pulling Teeth' provided an opportunity for Cliff Burton to shine and to stamp *Kill 'Em All* with his unique sonic imprint. Metal bands seldom played bass solos live; they didn't record bass solos in rehearsal and they sure as hell did not include bass solos on their debut records. Were they insane? Hardly. '(Anesthesia)…' did not sound like one imagined a bass solo, it sounded like a bass played through a guitar amp, with more distortion than Lemmy's dirtiest nightmare and a disdain for all things commonplace. Regardless of the undoubted bravery of including this experimental track on an album of immaculate heavy metal, the song still had to be good.

Although the track furnished Burton with a showcase for his talents, neither he, the band, nor the producers saw it that way. Though the songs were long, it was felt Metallica needed a tenth song and that this track would break the album up and inspire a 'what the fuck was that?' response. Yet part of the reason Cliff was locked out of the studio control room was so he couldn't add anything deemed 'weird' to the already experimental song. A bass solo was one thing, but with more wah-wah than a Hendrix wet dream and a plethora of funny glitches and scrapes, Burton was allowed one take and that was all. ·

'Anyone who owns the *No Life 'Til Leather* demo will be pleased to know that most of the songs on the album are faster, especially "Motorbreath" and "Metal Militia",' asserted Lars. Equally importantly, the band also added a new track that was about as fast as they could get. After the brain-dizzying '(Anesthesia)…' the band upped the ante with the anthemic 'Whiplash'.

With a whirring riff reminiscent of a pneumatic drill, this 'Diamond Head on speed' jewel was almost over-simplistic in construction and lyrical meaning, yet perfectly illustrated the band's metal ethic. It epitomised their 'none more metal' attitude and need to drink, headbang and cause audio (and actual) mayhem. As many associates of the band have claimed, their rhetoric in their early years was to criticise and bemoan anything or anyone that was 'not as metal' as they were. This was in part borne of frustration at being in a minority of metalheads in their respective towns, but also because they were so young and metal-obsessed that they couldn't see beyond the musical limitations of the genre.

In regular drunken outbursts the band would mercilessly mock anyone they considered to be insufficiently metal. According to Bob Nalbandian, James and Lars would 'often criticise friends who were not listening to the heaviest, fastest metal'. 'Whiplash' was a stirring one-fingered epitome of those beliefs. Unsurprisingly perhaps, its roots were to be found in the NWOBHM – as Lars would later admit, saying of a particular Bristolian four-piece, 'Jaguar greatly influenced Metallica. In fact the intro to "Whiplash" was a direct rip-off from their "Stormchild" number, which appears on the *Heavy Metal Heroes* compilation. They were amazing.'

'Whiplash' was also notable for the rousing last verse which promised, 'We'll never quit 'cause we're Metallica.' As part of an EP, the song would feature on the first Metallica single released. It was stretched to breaking point with a throwaway remix of 'Whiplash' (called 'Neckbrace') as well as 'Jump In The Fire'. The EP, released in July 1983, made little impact except among established fans.

There were also 'live' tracks ('Phantom Lord' and 'Seek And Destroy') purportedly from the Automat in the Bay Area, but these were actually studio versions, enhanced with crowd overdubs.

Side two begins with 'Phantom Lord', another of the strongest tracks on *Kill 'Em All* – the title owing its provenance to the name of James's first serious band. The song was a supercharged remake of the demo track, seething with old-school metal venom. Undoubtedly the strongest tracks were those that carried a Mustaine co-credit, leaving some question over the lack of contribution from both Cliff Burton and especially Kirk Hammett. This is an issue the band would soon redress. More importantly, Hetfield and Ulrich held the creative reins so tightly that it was actually difficult for newer members to break in.

'Phantom Lord' was all about straight-up aggression, with the exception of the breakdown section a few minutes in, and a ferocity which belied their musical immaturity. This was a set of dynamics of which any veteran band would be proud, not least their beloved Diamond Head. Metallica's dual guitar assault clearly referenced Stourbridge's finest, and represented an unusual approach for any speed-metal outfit. It was only years later that other bands began to follow Metallica's lead and combine classic metal dynamics (largely inspired by Thin Lizzy) with breakneck speed.

By contrast, 'No Remorse' showed the limitations of the nascent Hetfield-Ulrich partnership, with just one rehashed riff too many and a spate of overwrought time changes which did little to augment the rather soulless tune. The less said about the lyrics the better, their immaturity evidencing a paucity of original material. Hetfield must cringe today when he reads lines such as, 'We are ready to kill all comers/ Like a loaded gun right at your face,' or, 'Swords are like lighting/ It all becomes frightening.'

But for every gram of disposable metal there were kilos of heavy brilliance. The future live favourite 'Seek And Destroy' may be overplayed today, but in 1983 this kind of catchy razor-sharp metal was a breath of fresh air. Indeed, this track is perhaps the best example of the manner in which Metallica combined their NWOBHM influences with a penchant for expanding the boundaries of metal. Pulsing with a swaying groove, this song was typical Metallica in the sense that it could not stay mid-paced for too long. Come the end of the second chorus, the band simply had to up the ante and head into a riotous speed romp.

Though, as stated earlier, the song was inspired by (and a little too reminiscent of) Diamond Head's 'Dead Reckoning', the main riff was still original and ultimately stuck in the consciousness. Yet the breakdown section (before the band heads into familiar speedy territory) was eerily reminiscent of several other Diamond Head tracks, especially the Ulrich drum sound – tight and snappy, awash with cymbals.

The lyrics may appear to be a juvenile take on typical metal themes of the 1980s but, as Fred Cotton explains, 'The contents were directly inspired by *The Warriors* [the 1979 film about New York gangs].'

'Metal Militia' was less direct in its lyrical inspiration, seemingly a mass of biblical fury cobbled together at the last minute. The song included some of the least inspired James Hetfield lyrics, and thankfully he would improve from here on. Lines such as 'the metallisation of your inner soul' would soon become a thing of the past. In terms of sheer speed 'Metal Militia' was also one of the band's fastest tracks, and again its simplicity was never to be repeated. Though abundantly brazen, 'Metal Militia' had to be one of Metallica's most fun tunes – simple, yet seriously effective and dowsed in thrash glory.

The sleeve for *Kill 'Em All* was as blunt as its title, some might say crude – though not as extreme as 'Metal Up Your Ass', the title the band had initially favoured, with the mooted front cover featuring a hand holding a knife coming out of a toilet bowl. Unsurprisingly, Megaforce did not approve and Metallica had to think of something less controversial. Thankfully the band approved of their new album cover and title.

'I really like the cover – the idea of a sledgehammer lying in a pool of blood may sound kinda simple, but it looks real neat,' enthused Lars. The sleeve was also notable for the quote on its reverse. The band, looking suitably young and grim, were underpinned by the sobriquet, 'Bang that head that doesn't bang.' The quote was attributed to an 'R. Birch' who, as Fred Cotton explains, was 'Lars's good friend'.

When Megaforce released *Kill 'Em All* they were not exactly optimistic about potential sales figures. Initially, Zazula pressed just 1,500 copies, but within two weeks they had pressed another 15,000 – all of which sold out straight away. The album would eventually sell over three million copies worldwide.

At the time of its release *Kill 'Em All* was a hotly anticipated slab of vinyl coming off the back of one of the greatest demo tapes in metal history. Therefore, it was bound to outsell the limited run of copies Zazula had expected. The whiff of expectation was rife in basements across the world and the media reaction to the album only exacerbated this. Every major metal magazine lavished praise upon the album. *Kerrang!* precipitated the rise of the thrash-metal movement when they focused on the sheer velocity of the LP. Malcolm Dome wrote, 'Mirror, mirror on the wall, who's the fastest of them all? Motörhead? Venom? Metallicaaaaaaaaarrrggghhh!'

Canadian metal author Martin Popoff later wrote, 'Nowhere previous had a band made such a beeline for eleven and just stayed there – riffs relentlessly carving and cramming full all the spaces once reserved for respites like filler, ballads, epics or party rockers. A hearty metal up yer ass indeed. Only Metallica could make it both a blessing and a punishment.'

Given the remarkable sales of *Kill 'Em All*, Jon Zazula decided to pair Metallica with his other biggest-selling act of the time, the NWOBHM stalwarts Raven. With their 1983 opus *All For One* fresh on the racks, Raven were establishing their name in both hard-rock and metal circles.

Combining both bands' respective album titles, Zazula named the tour 'Kill 'Em All For One'. Metallica were to support the Tyneside natives. In truth, by 1983 Raven were a decidedly unsophisticated band, more in line with the party-metal scene than either the NWOBHM or the early era of speed metal. They may have been experienced, but they had barely moved on from their early diet of 'meat and potatoes' metal.

By contrast, Metallica were light years ahead of their elders in terms of ability and songwriting nous. Their development from the band that recorded the *No Life 'Til Leather* demo tape, to the colossus who released *Kill 'Em All* cannot be overstated. Ironically, it was on the live stage where Raven came into their own, always putting on an energetic display and improving on the staid limitations of their studio output. Metallica meanwhile sounded more controlled in the studio and, indeed, *were* controlled – by their producers.

Onstage, at least early on, they were somewhat frantic and often their majestic material would be dowsed in a wall of noisy feedback and the snottiness of their onstage personas. Despite this somewhat naive approach, the band were still noticeably superior to their touring partners.

'It was an amazing tour,' recalled Raven bassist John Gallagher. 'There were the three guys in our band plus our three crew guys. There were the four guys in Metallica plus their three crew guys, a sound guy, a monitor guy and a tour manager all in a six-berth Winnebago and two trucks.' The Winnebago was past its sell-by date at the outset and eventually all but fell to pieces before the tour was over.

'The first three gigs were especially memorable as we had to take our tour manager to one side after three days and tell him, "We need a hotel room to sleep, or we're fucking going home,"' remembered Gallagher. 'Sleep deprivation! The Winnebago soon started to reek. We had some mattresses "obtained" from God knows where and lay them on top of the gear in one of the trucks and actually travelled like that most of the time.'

According to Gallagher, Metallica hopefully drew some benefit from the collective experience Raven had built through tough working-class gigs in northeast England. Though the Raven discography lists their first recording as their 1980 single 'Don't Need Your Money', they actually formed as far back as 1974, albeit in a different guise – their early gigs peppered with Status Quo and Deep Purple covers. 'I'd like to think Metallica learned a lot from us, especially about facing tough crowds,' observed Gallagher. 'The audience did not like them at the gig in Oklahoma, and it was painful to watch them somehow get through their set. We'd cut our teeth playing to punks and in working men's clubs in the northeast so we jumped on their tables and cajoled and shouted at the crowd and got them on our side.'

Indeed, Raven were familiar with crowd bust-ups, with Hells Angels often being present at gigs in their local clubs. Metallica took their Oklahoma lesson on the chin, despite being threatened with shotguns by the mountain men who did not take too kindly to such 'longhairs'.

Metallica and Raven then moved to the next state and another undeveloped part of America. Of the remote outpost of Bald Knob in Arkansas, James Hetfield remembered, 'There were more bugs than people. They set up catfish stands and that was about it. Our music was a little too rough for them, no doubt, but it was a good time.'

It was when Metallica returned to their home state that transportation issues finally reached crisis point. 'In California the Winnebago finally gave up the ghost in a spectacular fashion, the engine seized, there were flames in the cab and Lars was 300 yards up the road running before we even got out the door,' recounted Gallagher. 'To get to the next gig, both bands piled into the truck with the mattresses as it took a route up into the mountains. Through the hatch we could see a 1,000-foot drop. Lars, in his inimitable fashion, called out, "Kirk, I'm really scared, can I hold your hand?" We all looked at each other and exploded with laughter.'

Life on the Metallica-Raven tour was full of such unforgettable moments. 'There are so many memories,' remembered Gallagher. 'Staying the night in a little town right out of the twilight zone and seeing a waitress chasing the Metallica members down the street as they hadn't paid for breakfast… hanging out with Cliff playing our basses and trading riffs… Lars there, cutting the wires off his snare drum to change the bottom drumhead, as no one had ever told him they could actually be removed.'

As Gallagher recounted, stuck together in the pressure-cooker environment of the van, Raven were privy to Metallica's private personalities. 'Lars was very outgoing, always a million questions; James smiling and constantly with a beer; Cliff was very funny but came off as more together, mature, and Kirk, friendly but always looked tired and real young,'

In fact Kirk remembered things were often a little too cosy in terms of sleeping arrangements. 'We used to sleep four to a room. I had to share a bed with Lars. He used to take all the blankets. I would never sleep with Cliff, because he had really pointed elbows. Really bony. Actually, no one snores much. We drool a lot.'

When the Raven tour had come to a close Metallica did not rest on their laurels. Instead, they opted to build a domestic following and embarked on a number of shows from coast to coast, taking in Los Angeles, Chicago and New Jersey. With no established band to open for, Metallica were poorer than ever – they had no record company money besides the bare minimum for fuel and received just one meal per day.

'The only time I had money was when we went out on the road and had per diems,' opined Kirk. 'I remember, on our first tour, we got ten bucks a day on days off and seven bucks on a show day because we could always eat free at the gig.'

As winter temperatures plummeted, the band were unsurprisingly less than enthusiastic about the prospect of sleeping in their dilapidated tour van and would stay with friends or fans along their route. This had its disadvantages, as quite often the fans they would stay with would be so excited to have Metallica in their house that they would throw huge parties, inviting the whole neighbourhood while the weary Metallica members tried to get some much-needed rest.

Given that they were touring over the festive season, there were also numerous Christmas and New Year gatherings to endure. The band's most difficult obstacle was trying to find something to eat. Though they could often scrounge a few morsels from friends or fans, it was rarely nutritious and seldom provided enough fuel for a full day. In fact, hearty meals were so scarce that the band could often recall the one time they were treated to a full restaurant feast. On this occasion, a female fan paid for the meal but left before tipping and as such the band were accosted and bugged for the requisite gratuity. They grudgingly paid the extra few dollars.

By this time Kirk Hammett's friend and fellow guitar player, John Marshall, had been casually employed to assist the band in their technical guitar needs, which mostly consisted of keeping the guitars in tune and checking tones. He remembers of that particular day when the band walked out of the restaurant that the waitress 'freaked out, yelling and all pissed off. But we would barely have eaten that day if it hadn't been for that meal.'

However, the band were about to encounter a far greater problem. As 1984 dawned, Metallica continued their domestic trek while the weather grew worse with each passing day. During one stop in Boston, Massachusetts, Metallica were parted from their road crew. The crew had gone ahead earlier, travelling from New Jersey with the gear. But by the time the crew had arrived at the venue the severe snowstorms caused the show to be cancelled. There was nothing else to do but rent a room in a cheap hotel for the night and wait out the bad weather. Only John Marshall had the presence of mind to take care of the equipment however. Reasoning the cold weather could warp the guitar necks, he brought Hetfield's Flying V and Burton's red Rickenbacker bass into his hotel room. The next day, Marshall realised his foresight had been correct, as he woke up to see the band's van missing from the hotel parking lot.

Unfortunately it had the rest of the instruments and equipment still in it. 'Someone must have seen the guitars being unloaded the previous night,' concluded Marshall. 'The next day someone drove in from New Jersey to pick us up. We were all sitting in this sedan, with guitars under our legs, taking this five-hour drive back to New Jersey, and everyone was miserable because the gear was gone.'

The gear included the vaunted Hetfield amps, which held the tone for his *Kill 'Em All* crunch. Also missing was Lars's Camco drum kit and numerous other amplifiers and equipment (luckily Kirk had kept his own guitar with him in New Jersey). Hetfield was vexed by the crime, for which the Boston police had no leads. The Metallica frontman stated incredulously, 'If it was such a blizzard who the fuck would be out there? Hardcore criminals? Maybe the cops just took it away. Who knows? Maybe our gear's sitting in some police station somewhere.'

There were still three gigs remaining on the tour, so their old friends in Anthrax came through, loaning Metallica their stage equipment. The group soared through shows in New Jersey and New York before returning to play their cancelled gig in Boston. By now, the band was reconciled to their equipment being long gone and reacted with their typical gallows humour. Hetfield barked from the stage at the Channel club, 'If any of you know the fuckers who stole our equipment the last time we were here, please kill them for us.'

Megaforce Records did their part, eager to stabilise the band's already paltry finances, they announced news of the theft in the metal press and asked everyone to be vigilant. However, the gear has not been seen since.

Still, the theft hardly deterred Metallica from continuing on their *Kill 'Em All* assault and when the opportunity to support black-metal legends Venom came up, they jumped at the chance. They had previously supported Venom for a slew of shows on the US East Coast earlier in 1983.

All Metallica had to do to join the European jaunt was rent some equipment which was paid for by Megaforce. Like Raven, Venom were a three-piece from the northeast of England and steeped in NWOBHM tradition. They were also purveyors of black metal, a new take on the metal style which was an over-the-top run through speed metal with added anger and ferocity. Like Metallica, Venom were coming to the end of their tour for their previous album (1982's *Black Metal*) and were soon to be shut up in a small studio to record their next opus, which would become the 1984 classic *At War With Satan*.

The Seven Dates Of Hell tour saw Metallica play France, Italy and Germany before concluding with an appearance at the Aardschok Festival in Holland, where Venom headlined. This was some achievement given that on the very first gig of the tour James Hetfield had fallen down while the worse for wear and cut his hand open on the beer glass he'd been holding. In Holland the band played to some 7,000 punters at the festival, which was named after the Dutch word for 'earthquake'.

It is said that it was Metallica who most impressed at the festival, despite the eye-catching theatrics of the headliners. However, the early days for Metallica were all about diversity. They travelled from the heights of their biggest crowd to date, to one of their smallest. In Belgium the touring partners played together in a cafeteria on a stage made up of customer tables. As it was the last date of the tour Metallica's elders had a little treat for Lars Ulrich. They had filled his snare drum with talcum powder so the sticksman was covered in white smoke whenever he hit the snare – quite often considering the speedy nature of their material. Venom even played a trick on Cliff Burton, unhinging the table he had to perch upon, leaving the bassist in a permanent state of vertiginous imbalance.

Despite the stolen equipment, injured limbs and lack of food or decent shelter, it has to be said that Metallica's post-*Kill 'Em All* period was immensely successful and set the scene for their follow-up LP. The success of their debut album and its tours had created a buzz around the band, and it was shortly after their debut record that their fanbase had grown to the extent that it required proper administration.

K.J. Doughton, a friend of the band, was tasked with keeping the band's fan affairs in order and became president of the first Metallica fan club. 'I would attempt to answer the band's mail, send out T-shirts, and produce fan-club packets,' Doughton says. 'The band's first shirt displayed their logo, and the phrase "The Young Metal Attack" beneath it. This black T-shirt was manufactured in LA – probably by Lars – it came out even before the fan-club days, and is an extremely rare find. The second official shirt sold by the band also sported the Metallica logo, and accompanying phrase, "Metal Up Your Ass," on black.'

Doughton would go on to write the only authorised book on the band, 1992's *Unbound*, and he reveals the reason Metallica were such a success and why he agreed to run their fan club. 'To me, they represented everything that a metal band should be. Prior to Metallica, other bands passed most phases of the "evaluation" – but seldom did they integrate all the musical pieces. Venom had the wicked enthusiasm, Motörhead had the steamrolling, bulldog strength, and Iron Maiden had the intricate arrangements. But Metallica had it all.'

Torben Ulrich, despite his penchant for lighter forms of music, agreed with this assessment. 'One of the charms of Metallica for me was always that they handled the energy and still played in tune, which I felt was one of their strong assets. So, in that sense that was a charm, even if that word would not be one that would come quickly to my mind when trying to describe their music.'

In 1983, *Kill 'Em All* was the nearest thing a speed-metal band could get to a 'hit', and Metallica certainly enjoyed their time in the spotlight. Unwilling to rest on their laurels, however, they were about to blow their debut out of the water.

CHAPTER 6
SO LET IT BE WRITTEN

'We are a band with a little originality, quality songs and the ability to play our instruments so I'm sure we'll be successful.'
Lars Ulrich

Although extensive touring had taught Metallica a thing or two about life as a band, and just what they would have to endure to be successful, the overriding benefit was one of musical progression. It didn't take too many shows of simplistic, breakneck riffing for the band to realise their buzzsaw guitar sound and relentless speed ethic had to change if they were to have any longevity as a band. In hindsight, having their amps stolen may have been one of the best things to happen to the group. Certainly, if James had gone into the recording sessions for Metallica's second LP with the same equipment, their sophomore effort (*Ride The Lightning*) would likely have sounded stylistically closer to *Kill 'Em All*.

'The main difference between the two albums is we had Cliff and Kirk for *Ride The Lightning*,' Lars explained, 'and they brought a whole diversity and new musical edge to the whole thing. We wanted to try and do some different things, not to play "Whiplash" all the time, which we knew would get boring. We were really proud of the way *Ride The Lightning* came out. We were really thrilled with the sound.'

Achieving the desired sound was a troubling aspect of the preparation ahead of the second album. As Lars recalled, 'The initial sound problems were really due to all our gear getting ripped off just three weeks before we got to Copenhagen. For instance James had this one-in-a-million Marshall head that he lost and he had problems getting the rhythm sound that Metallica are known for. We probably went through every Marshall in Denmark, including all of Mercyful Fate's gear, before finding one that was right.'

Rather than returning home after their European jaunt with Venom, the band decided to hole up in Lars's home country and begin to lay the tracks they had been writing during the Seven Dates Of Hell tour. They weren't about to record their important follow up to *Kill 'Em All* with rented equipment. Initially, James Hetfield was hell-bent on finding the same sharp, crunchy sound he had employed for *Kill*

*'Em A*ll. However, this had clearly been a one-off tone specific to one particular amp. Wherever the band shopped for equipment, they could never quite recreate the *Kill 'Em All* sound. In the end, they settled for a more conventional heavy-metal guitar tone, far deeper and bass heavy. Unintentionally, by the simple act of changing amplification, Metallica would discover a darker, more mature sound.

Lars wasn't exaggerating when he spoke of the extensive search for an appropriate amp. 'They literally looked at every Marshall amp in Western Europe,' remembered John Marshall. 'They eventually found one that sounded good in some little Danish music shop.'

It would be logical to assume that the band chose to record in Denmark on account of Lars's background, but the truth was far more pragmatic. 'We did the album in Denmark basically because we were on tour there and we stayed because it was cheap to record,' said James. 'Flemming Rasmussen did it for very little money.'

This represented another fortunate twist of fate for Metallica. In picking an unknown producer who doubled as an engineer, they would end up creating a remarkably successful union, out of which came their three most revered albums. Flemming Rasmussen would oversee *Ride The Lightning, Master Of Puppets* and *...And Justice For All* – a glorious triumvirate still lauded by metal connoisseurs to this day.

Rasmussen was hardly thinking of his career when he accepted the production gig. He subsequently revealed that he had 'never heard of the band before. They were looking for a studio with a good in-house engineer, and had heard the work I'd done with Ritchie Blackmore and contacted me.'

The producer's first task was to address the issue of James's guitar sound. Rasmussen and Hetfield spent four days finessing the tone, which took a significant chunk out of precious studio time. Metallica had just a month to finish writing their material, rehearse it and record. 'We spent a lot of time trying to create the Metallica sound,' Rasmussen says, 'recording Lars's drums in a big empty backroom, and there was a sense of a common goal we were working to achieve. All in all a pretty good album if you ask me.'

Rasmussen also enjoyed the fact that Metallica went against the local vogue, stating, 'Everybody else was running round doing disco and shit, and I hated that. Most of the other people in the studio thought that Metallica was the worst piece of shit they'd ever heard in their lives, but I loved that.'

Ride The Lightning hums with a strength and consistency that was particularly impressive given that three of the songs were written between recording sessions in the studio. 'Trapped Under Ice', 'Escape' and the future live classic 'For Whom The Bell Tolls' were all thrown together in a matter of hours and added to the four demo tracks the band had already pushed into the metal underground in October of 1983. The material on the demo had been created just as the band finished their tour with Raven and included some of *Ride The Lightning*'s best material, from the title track and the original version of 'The Call Of Ktulu' (then known as 'When Hell Freezes Over'), to the burrowing, blinding ferocity of 'Creeping Death' and the album opener 'Fight Fire With Fire'.

The most noticeable difference from the demo work is in Hetfield's vocals, which are incredibly high-pitched, almost strained. The guitar work is frantic and solos are grossly overdone. It shows a great deal of potential, but in truth, the demo is more indicative of a typical thrash band. Credit must go to Flemming Rasmussen for really giving the band the space to flourish and get the most from their new material. Hetfield's vocals were to deepen for the LP recording, affording the songs additional gravitas, particularly when compared to the yelping youngster evident on the demo.

In demo form, the introduction to 'Fight Fire With Fire' was clumsy and lumpen, sounding more like a band tuning up than a professional introduction to a major album. Here, Hetfield's vocals were at their weakest, doing absolutely no justice to his eventual performance or his innate talents. Though the song was clearly recognisable against the finished version, the difference could not be more striking.

It should be noted, however, that the band were barely into their twenties at this point and as musicians, songwriters and artists they were still growing. Vocally, Hetfield wasn't even close to finding his full range and power.

Recalling Hetfield and Ulrich's receptivity to new ideas, Rasmussen observed that: 'They were pretty headstrong, but they were not un-moveable. Most of the time they were letting each other do their thing and kept out of each other's way, but on some things they were actually teaming up to get their way, like on solos, etcetera.'

The producer's biggest job was to focus the band on improving their individual performances and augmenting their existing material. It was clear from their instrumentation – aside from the often garish solos – that they were almost there. The demo version of 'When Hell Freezes Over' is almost note for note as it appears on the finished version on the album. With the arrangements arriving at the studio in good shape, Rasmussen directed his attention to honing the band's vocals and harmonies.

The Danish desk wizard has rightly received immense credit for his role in creating Metallica's most revered set of recordings. It is no coincidence he was at the helm for the albums widely considered to be their greatest. In fact, as they grew and matured as songwriters, and learned the intricacies of the studio environment, the group felt that they had accrued sufficient experience to work without the guidance of their mentor.

Rasmussen stamped his authority all over *Ride The Lightning*, but remarkably the LP sleeve will always read, 'Produced by Metallica, assisted by Flemming Rasmussen and Mark Whitaker.' Though Rasmussen was given full credit for engineering the album, it was puzzling to see him merely listed as assistant producer. The production was crucial to *Ride The Lightning* – both as a progression from the juvenile crunch evident on *Kill 'Em All* and as a tool to break the band beyond the thrash-metal ghetto. James subsequently acknowledged Rasmussen's influence, declaring that 'he introduced us to some stuff and we learnt a lot on that album. This is one of my favourite Metallica albums.'

'I think we're as happy as we could be,' Lars observed at the time of the LP's release. 'A few of the songs were only written just before we had to do the album, so I think we might have arranged them a little differently if we had had the opportunity to put them down on tape first, and then gone away and listened to them before doing the album. In terms of the songs, the production and the performance this LP is far superior to anything we've ever recorded. There's a lot more melody in *Ride The Lightning* material; the choruses are more out in the open and the arrangements are much better. We're beginning to broaden our horizons.'

Some years later, Lars observed that 'on *Ride The Lightning* we learnt that you could still be powerful, even if the pace was slowed right down, and now we've understood that you can still hit hard even when there's subtlety in the music'.

Although *Ride The Lightning* would draw cries of 'sell out' from sections of their earliest devotees, the writing was on the wall long before the finished LP hit the racks. Their four-track demo had caused ripples of panic in the metal underground. Most fans at the time wanted and expected *Kill 'Em All* part two, but if anything was plain early on in the land of Metallica, it was that this band coveted rebellion. The demo was a partial exercise in experimentation, with the likes of the sinister mid-paced title track and the epic instrumental 'When Hell Freezes Over', which technically represented a great leap forward for the band.

The song title was inspired by the extra-terrestrial entity Cthulhu that appears in horror/fantasy author H.P. Lovecraft's short story 'The Call Of Cthulhu'. Cliff Burton introduced the band to Lovecraft's fiction and the song is driven by Burton's languid bass, which carries a genuinely spooky tone. Most impressive are the sparse opening guitar parts, which evoke visions of a cold wilderness.

Despite this fairly standard metal action, rumours abounded that Metallica were going to commit the cardinal sin in thrash circles and record a ballad. Such rumours turned out to be well founded, and many fans were shocked and dismayed. As ridiculous as it may sound today, the inclusion of a ballad in any so-called thrash band's repertoire was taboo in the early to mid-1980s. This obsession with 'wimping out' would carry on until the thrash bubble burst as the 1990s dawned.

There were some thrash bands that would later bravely record ballads, Testament, Annihilator and Death Angel among them, but Metallica were the first. To give an indication of the snobbery regarding musical progression in thrash circles in this era, you need only look to Kirk Hammett's old band to see how deeply this mindset was entrenched.

Exodus prided themselves on rarely playing slow or demonstrating 'progression'. As for a ballad? That was out of the question. The group always emphasised that they were a straight-up thrash band who would never attempt to gain popularity by producing anything remotely palatable to the commercial mainstream. By the time of their 1990 album *Impact Is Imminent*, Exodus even proudly proclaimed on band T-shirts: 'Album number four and still no ballad!'

Metallica, however, had little interest in playing by anyone's rules – even those of the metal underground from which they had sprung. After all, many of their favourite NWOBHM bands – Diamond Head among them – weren't afraid to strip their sound down and create plaintive, melancholy material at times. Lars spoke with supreme confidence regarding Metallica's decision to write a mostly acoustic song: 'We're playing for ourselves and if we wanna do a ballad or whatever, we'll do a ballad.

If people don't like it, fuck 'em.'

According to Lars, the change in direction and the inclusion of more intricate material was due to Kirk and Cliff being in the band from the start of *Ride The Lightning*. 'Cliff was responsible for a lot of the things that happened between *Kill 'Em All* and *Ride The Lightning*... Cliff really exposed me and James to a whole new musical horizon of harmonies and melodies ... He was certainly a big part of how we got our chops together in the early days, our attitudes and musical vibe. He was a great part of the way Metallica turned out.'

Both Kirk and Cliff were now fully integrated into the Metallica line-up and their influence was felt throughout the material. Unlike some later Metallica albums, which were predominantly focused on the Hetfield-Ulrich partnership, *Ride The Lightning* saw the band as a fully functioning democracy, with much of the material Burton and Hammett offered being accepted. All songs featured at least one of the two new boys, and two of the strongest tracks, 'Creeping Death' and 'Fade To Black', credited both.

As much of *Ride The Lightning* was overtly heavy and dowsed in velocity, the cries of 'sell out' were all about the inclusion of 'Fade To Black'.

However, Lars had precipitated this reaction and signalled both his and Metallica's desire to avoid clichés early on. 'This ballad we're writing is pretty different,' he mused. 'There will probably be a few hardcores who will go, "What the fuck?" and be totally against it, just because they don't understand that you grow and mature. They'll want us to just keep playing open E chords for the next three years. But I think we'll gain a wider array of fans with this material.'

Although it is something of a cliché that women generally tend to prefer softer music, it was 'Fade To Black' that brought Metallica many more female fans than was previously the case. Furthermore, it wasn't just female fans who were drawn to Metallica by this unusual 'thrash' song. It was the first time mainstream metal fans had taken notice of a speed-metal act. This was the first indication Metallica were not simply a thrash outfit and had a wealth of crossover potential. *Q* magazine later acknowledged Metallica's broad appeal, stating that 'they broke with the conventions of thrash metal to record the genre's first power ballad in "Fade To Black". Even non-metal fans paid attention.'

'Fade To Black' can be viewed as a form of power ballad, albeit with thrash overtones. The mournful acoustic strumming that took up the main part of the song was in part inspired by their stolen gear and general despondency whilst on tour. James was also lamenting the loss of his amp, which had been a gift from his mother just before she died. Lyrically, 'Fade To Black' was a song written from the point of view of a person about to commit suicide, the lyrics representing his valedictory note. Both Ulrich and Hetfield would later say *Ride The Lightning* was 'about death' overall, telling MTV that they were 'obsessed with death at the time'.

The dark subtext of 'Fade To Black' left the band open to accusations of promoting a pro-suicide agenda, despite the fact that Lars would later attest many fans had approached him to thank the band for writing the song as it had actually prevented them from taking their own lives.

'"Fade To Black" was written to me in a letter and it was just poetry. I didn't even think it was a song, it seemed like a poem,' revealed Leah Storkson. 'James was always writing really deep stuff to me that blew me away and I knew it was just how he was feeling and it just turned into a song. It was just pure depression, depression, which I totally understood. I felt really bad for them; I didn't really know what they were going through, only what he was telling me.'

Although the sense of depression that underpins *Ride The Lightning* cannot be overstated, it is perhaps surprising just how low the band were feeling during the recording period, especially the Metallica frontman. 'When they went to Copenhagen and London to record *RTL* it was terrible – he was gone about six months,' Storkson recalls. 'That was very hard for both of us, as we were both young. The making of that album was brutal, they had nothing to eat, they sometimes had nowhere to sleep. They mostly slept on floors in sleeping bags and they ate scraps from people's refrigerators, and they just lived off the kindness of people. And it was apparent in all the letters he sent me which went on for about two years – just misery and frustration. He was starving and cold and lonely and depressed. It was like that on both sides, and on his end, possibly even harder, as he had none of the comforts of home anywhere in sight.'

Perhaps surprisingly, the recording of 'Fade To Black' had some lighter moments. The acoustic guitar used on the song had to be borrowed. Rather than simply playing with an undistorted electric guitar, the band insisted on using a genuine acoustic six-string. The trouble was that they decided this at three o'clock one morning. Enter local Dane Ken Jacobsen, who is thanked on the album as 'Ken "3 AM" Jack'.

'Lars and I had a mutual friend named Ken Anthony who worked at Bristol Record Store, [which] at the time [was] the only real metal store around Copenhagen,' Jacobsen recalls. 'We both went there to buy music. Ken Anthony asked if I could pick Metallica up at the airport when they arrived to record the *Ride The Lightning* record. I said, "Sure," and that is how we met.

'I had to go to Los Angeles in the mid- to late 1980s and somehow I met some people, including Ron McGovney, who went to school with James Hetfield and said that they used to be in Metallica. That was a little strange since I was so far from home. So they invited me over for dinner and some beers. When we had been hanging out for a while, lo and behold, Hetfield walked in. That was very odd.'

Jacobsen remembers the background to his place in Metallica folklore. 'My place in Copenhagen was a hangout for my band at the time, Dark Mission [Jacobsen was credited as Ken Jack on the Danish-American band's sole demo], and a bunch of other bands like Mercyful Fate, Maltese Falcon and Artillery. They knew they could depend on me and that's why they called when they were in a bind. Three in the morning was a little extreme and I'm sure it could have waited until next morning. But now I have a story to tell!'

'Fight Fire With Fire' begins – thanks to Jacobsen – with a plaintive acoustic refrain. This set a template that was later to be followed by many bands. Superficially incongruous, a ballad is still an elegant and novel way to open a thrash-metal album.

Of the thrash bands who've attempted to showcase their softer side since *Ride The Lightning*, many have opted for this kind of acoustic opener – everyone from Annihilator to Testament has used this tool, directly inspired by Metallica.

However, the band were used to thrashing and the opening track soon reached terminal velocity, topped by drums that teetered on the point of accelerating out of sight – you could hear Lars Ulrich's bouncy mannerisms infecting his snare hits. It was also apparent that Hetfield's vocals had taken on a new power, courtesy of the production, underpinning the frantic gnawing of the verse before the simple yet devastating chorus slowed the pace.

The addition of Kirk Hammett to the line-up had a particularly positive influence on the guitar interplay. It is arguable that Kirk was already a far better guitarist than Dave Mustaine. Hammett had immensely improved his technique in a very short space of time. Being fully aware of his shortcomings, after the tours for *Kill 'Em All*, Hammett had taken tuition with axe supremo Joe Satriani. The veteran New York six-stringer taught Kirk the principles of varying guitar styles including jazz, blues, classical and the fundamental techniques used by one of Kirk's guitar heroes, Jimi Hendrix.

The title track heralded the first appearance of Hetfield's new 'singing' voice. Up until now he had merely barked and yelped his way through a galley of hi-octane thrashers, but for the chorus of 'Ride The Lightning' he demonstrated a melodic understanding of basic heavy-metal dynamics. The result was a mix of creepy interplay during the verses, which rose to a thundering yet tuneful crescendo.

Metallica had evidently taken no notice whatsoever of their fans' reservations over the 'new' direction of their demo material. If anything, 'Ride The Lightning' was *more* polished and, in the opinion of some die-hard thrashers, more commercial. It was the last Metallica track to feature a writing credit for Dave Mustaine (though this only appeared due to the use of his opening riff), consigning the guitarist's association with the band's material to the past – or so they believed.

Lyrically, the track provided the basis for the album cover, which portrayed a bleak electric-chair setting, complete with coruscating bolts of energy. The cover was also the first appearance for Metallica's new-look 3-D logo, which would be imitated and usurped for years to come by many other metal bands, and eventually even trendy clothing companies.

'Ride The Lightning' is written from the perspective of a man about to be executed in the chair. For this, Metallica surely took inspiration from Iron Maiden's 'Hallowed Be Thy Name' (which appeared on their 1982 LP, *The Number Of The Beast*). This track also focuses on the last thoughts of a man condemned to die, and remains one of Maiden's most popular compositions.

'For Whom The Bell Tolls' would rightly become one of Metallica's best-known recordings – catchy, groove-laden and utterly brilliant. The song is led by a swaying Burton bass line and was perhaps the clearest indication (along with 'The Call Of Ktulu') that he was now a significant part of the band's songwriting process and destined to be a massive influence on their future direction.

The track was dynamic, free-flowing and awash with true heavy-metal components, from the high-end harmonic leads pitched by Kirk Hammett to the war-torn poetry of the lyrics, again inspired by the likes of Iron Maiden's 'Where Eagles Dare'. By now, Hetfield was emerging as a confident, inspiring lyricist and 'For Whom The Bell Tolls' represented his greatest accomplishment to date. He incorporated a series of memorable one-liners amidst a wealth of evocative poeticism. Lines such as, 'For a hill men would kill. Why? They do not know…' and, 'Crack of dawn, all is gone except the will to be,' provided effective depictions of the futility and brutality of war.

If 'For Whom The Bell Tolls' showed Hetfield's lyrical maturity, then 'Fade To Black' blew it out of the water. Forget the debates about Metallica going soft or assertions that the song is a musical masterpiece – the true beauty of the track is to be found in the words and the graceful way these were emotively spliced to the musical harmony. The emotion in Hetfield's voice was palpable on such lines as, 'Emptiness is filling me/ To the point of agony.'

'Trapped Under Ice' is one of the most straightforward numbers on *Ride The Lightning* and the nearest to clear-cut thrash on the record. Though entertaining, it was one of the album's least memorable tracks and a song Metallica would virtually forget in years to come.

Likewise, they did all they could to distance themselves from the unusual 'Escape', which certainly courted commerciality with its over-melodic, layered chorus. James Hetfield himself was particularly critical of the song in later years. Though it was certainly unusual for Metallica to write such a simple, rock-tinged number, the basic premise was certainly representative of Hetfield's outlook at the time. This rebellious song illustrated Hetfield's anti-authoritarian stance perfectly. 'No one to hear things that they say,' he sings. 'Life's for my own, to live my own way.'

'Creeping Death' stands as one of Metallica's most masterful works – a perfect blend of thrash fury and heavy-metal wizardry. Where other songs such as 'Seek And Destroy' have been over-exposed, 'Creeping Death' is a song which never becomes tiresome and, deserving of all its plaudits, stands as perhaps the ultimate Metallica song. To underline this suggestion, it is interesting to note the band have played this song live more times than any other track in their repertoire. They may have been touted as a thrash band, but there were no thrash bands in existence that could have penned a song featuring such an astonishing arsenal of heavy-metal trickery. Traversing the entire spectrum of metal, Metallica reference the NWOBHM, speed metal and basic rock. Like most of Metallica's best work, the outline was simple; they just built upon the foundations with lavish harmonies, frenetic fretwork and Hetfield's savage vocals, which tipped the scale of ferocity while carrying the melodious tinge he had recently developed. It was a wondrous combination of all four members' writing talents and rightly saw release as a twelve-inch single.

Lyrically, the song drew further parallels with Iron Maiden. The British metal titans would release *Powerslave* in 1984, and the album was bathed in Egyptian imagery and symbolism. 'Creeping Death' included references to 'pharaohs', though this seemed to be merely coincidence. Drawing upon the 1956 movie *The Ten Commandments*, the lyrics refer to the biblical plagues visited upon the Ancient Egyptians. The film also provided Cliff Burton with the song's title. 'When it got to the part where the first pharaoh's son is taken and the fog rolls in, Cliff said, "Look... creeping death,"' revealed James. 'And I was like, "Whoa, dude, write it down!" Sheer poetry!'

Though the 'die by my hand' refrain featured in the breakdown section of the song seems biblical in nature, it actually came from one of Kirk's old Exodus songs, which contained the phrase.

The B-sides to the 'Creeping Death' single gave rise to an ongoing sideline for the band – that of performing cover versions to epic standards. Often bands recorded cover songs for fun and merely replicated the original song verbatim, with most attempts paling next to the original version. Metallica, however, could breathe new life into a staid or poorly produced piece of work, wringing every last drop of untapped potential from the song. In this way, the band often made hitherto obscure tracks their very own. They re-ignited the rather tame Diamond Head track 'Am I Evil?', and scorched it into a blistering speed-metal frenzy. They also turned the anonymous Blitzkrieg's self-titled anthem into an altogether more confident, thundering beast.

Metallica's knack for making a song their own had been evident from their very earliest performances. 'Heavy-metal companies in Europe prefer to have "unavailable anywhere else" type shit on the B-sides of singles,' Lars shrugged. 'Now we're not a band who likes to submit our own songs solely for B-sides because we like to have them on albums. So we just went into the studio and knocked out a couple of cover songs. They're the only two cover songs that we still play at rehearsals or live for the seventh encore!'

Considering the band's development between first and second album, Lars observed, 'The difference with *Ride The Lightning* compared to *Kill 'Em All* is that it's not just one complete track like *Kill 'Em All* was, and not all the tracks are played at "Metal Militia" speed. The one thing we realised between the making of the two albums was that you don't have to depend on speed to be powerful and heavy; I think songs like "For Whom The Bell Tolls" and "Ride The Lightning" reflect that sort of attitude.'

Ride The Lightning would later be viewed as something of a concept album – revolving around the theme of death. It was true that many of the songs concerned the inevitability and fear or experience of death, but the band would reject any notion of there being a definitive concept. 'Most bands in this area of rock do tend to spit out banal words about Satan, death and rock'n'roll,' asserted Lars. 'And I'll admit that on *Kill 'Em All* we were equally as guilty... But we've developed a lot... For example, the title track deals with the electric chair and the fear it can generate; "Fade To Black" is about someone who gives up on life and "Trapped Under Ice" is to do with cryogenics. We have consciously moved away from the traditional clichés of heavy metal because if you stick with old images you're doomed to obscurity.'

'The songs were made out of what I call "the three Ds": drunkenness, depression and despair,' observes Leah Storkson. 'James didn't like Europe, he didn't like England. He didn't like the winter – he didn't like cold or darkness at all, for some people that causes a lot of fear. And of course they were in a foreign country and they couldn't speak the language. Except for Lars, Lars loved being there 'cause he's Danish! He was loving life – he was hanging out with all his old friends. But James really felt like an outsider. I'd made friends with Cliff and Kirk as well, and Cliff actually got to come home a couple of times for some reason during that time, but James never did. And of course they were starving and they were always fighting and arguing – making the album was really stressful. They weren't sleeping, all they were doing was getting drunk, I mean, how happy can you be? But the best songs came out of that time; I think it's one of the best metal albums ever.'

The disharmony and crippling cold, not to mention the lack of money, makes one wonder why the band persevered, particularly James. Storkson explains, 'The music – it was his life, it was keeping him together. The band had such conviction – I knew James, and he would never give up no matter what. He just believed so much in his music and what he wanted to do and it wasn't just like wanting to be successful. It 100 per cent was a case of, "This is my music and, goddamn, I have to get it out there."'

Lars's observations about avoiding metal clichés would prove to be wholly prescient, as Metallica's popularity would inspire hundreds of new thrash acts seemingly overnight. Most bands were destined for obscurity simply because they didn't seek to improve their songwriting or think of anything original; it was merely rehashing an existing band's ideas. Whereas Metallica always put an interesting slant on their influences, most thrash bands sounded like rank amateurs. 'I've noticed there's been loads of so-called thrash-metal bands coming through recently,' asserted Lars. 'Most of them just use "speed for speed's sake" techniques, thinking that fast guitar work is the only criteria for producing energetic performances. We're chuffed to have had such an influence on these acts, but what you hear from most of them is riff upon riff upon riff. They ignore the virtue of writing good material and at the end of the day it's the standard of the tune you're delivering that matters. To us, it's more important to record numbers that people can hum when they wake up in the morning. Sure, we enjoy playing fast but there's more to us than speed.'

The twenty-seventh of July 1984 saw *Ride The Lightning* released worldwide on Megaforce Records. Initial responses were good, with most fans convinced by praiseworthy reviews; in a four-K review *Kerrang!* described the album as 'one of the greatest, most original heavy metal albums of all time', praising the quartet's 'melody, maturity and musical intelligence'. *Metal Hammer* suggested *Ride The Lightning* was 'an enormous technical and creative advance', with Metallica 'hitting a formula too good not to develop further'.

Despite such positive press, it is interesting to note the album only initially made Number 100 on the *Billboard* chart. Of course, for a thrash-metal album, this represented remarkably good business and perhaps came as a surprise to Megaforce, even after the success of *Kill 'Em All*.

Given Metallica's huge commercial success just a few years later, placing so low on the *Billboard* chart may seem unusual. In actuality, in 1984 it was more remarkable that they even made the chart, and they were the first thrash band to do so. Eventually, *Ride The Lightning*'s sales would become enormous, hitting over 5.5 million units by 2009.

These rumblings of mainstream recognition were noticed by both Elektra Records and Q-Prime management. This agency was headed by the highly effective partnership of Cliff Burnstein and Peter Mensch and had been responsible for providing Brit rockers Def Leppard with a huge American fanbase, and would also propel Queensrÿche toward great success.

At a show in New York, Metallica were approached by Elektra's Michael Alago, who seemed interested in acquiring the quartet. 'Alago and a few other A&R guys were down in our dressing room after the gig,' Lars recounted. 'The next thing we knew, we were having dinner with them, and a couple of days later they were dealing with us.'

Michael Alago worked for Elektra from 1983 to 1990, and then again from 1996 to 1999. Asked whether he had been told to go out and find the 'next big metal band', Alago answers, 'No, I did not have any mandates on the types of artists to sign. Historically Elektra Records had been a very eclectic label and I think the A&R department wanted to keep that vibe going, so as long as we thought the artists had the guts, the charisma and the great songwriting talent, and had the elements of future stars, we wanted to be involved with them. The range was wide – from Nina Simone to Metallica.'

Alago remembers the show at the Roseland very well and the subsequent working relationship he would develop with Metallica. 'The gig was sold out and the air was full of electricity – the band kicked ass. I felt they were unique when I saw them, all four members were so charismatic and the songwriting was so powerful that I knew I wanted to work with them at Elektra. They were the most awesome band I had ever seen. James was just a natural-born, very charismatic ringleader onstage. They infused so many elements of musical styles that were so new to metal that I just knew they were going to blow the roof off the industry and go on to be the biggest band in the world.

'The minute the show was over I made my way to the back and said, "All of you are not to go *anywhere* but to my office tomorrow." And Cliff said, "Is there gonna be lots of beer there?" And I said, "Whatever you want. I'll order Chinese and you'll come." James and I, in the beginning, kind of didn't get along because we were definitely two different types of people. He was reserved and kinda intimidated by me at first. I mostly spoke to Lars in the beginning to discuss the band's work. Then at some party in San Francisco, with both our heads in a toilet bowl, we kind of bonded. After that, we got along famously, him and I.'

Alago reveals that Elektra were not the only label hot on the heels of the next metal sensation. 'That summer there were other A&R folks at major labels sniffing around, but I had the balls and the guts to make my way backstage and charm the guys and discuss the history of Elektra and we were all young at that point in time. We were all in our twenties and we all just kind of connected and, like I said, they were in my office the next day after the Roseland gig for some beer and Chinese food and the rest is fuckin' history.'

Alago would continue working with the band up to the release of ...*And Justice*

For All, and he describes his duties as follows. 'An A&R person is responsible for many things; from putting recording budgets together to making sure the material for the album is top notch. I worked on all facets of the records from art direction to giving advice on the songs, working with all the departments at the label from radio promotion to publicity. I just stuck my nose in every department and put my two cents in everywhere I could so that all my bands became a priority. I was a pain in the ass as well, but that's what I did and I think that made my job very well rounded and helped with the success of the bands.'

As the summer of 1984 drew to a close, Metallica had a remarkable album behind them and a new management team, plus a mainstream, major record label. The prestige of appearing on Elektra seemed to appeal to the band, as Kirk confirmed. 'Even though other offers were financially better, Elektra had a reputation of leaving complete artistic freedom with their acts. It was a pretty liberal label. They had a reputation for trying out new things that were pretty experimental at the time.'

While Q-Prime and Elektra certainly knew their business, the gushing reviews for *Ride The Lightning* were also in Metallica's favour. Many future classic albums are not often classed as such to begin with. A legend takes time to develop, but many magazines and fans alike were instantly convinced *Ride The Lightning* was a classic album. Though they were certainly far more of a thrash act, Metallica were already making a name for themselves as one of the bigger heavy-metal bands in existence, with only Iron Maiden and Judas Priest apparently capable of maintaining their popularity. The difference was of course that the likes of Maiden and Priest were well established over the course of many years in the business. Metallica were relative newcomers, yet already they were raising themselves to compete with the legends of metal.

CHAPTER 7

FOREVER TRUSTING WHO WE ARE

*'The conflict between Lars and James was not that big a problem,
as they were on the way up, and that is so much funnier than being in
the top and fighting to maintain your position.'*
Flemming Rasmussen

Throughout their career, Metallica would make a habit of downplaying their own talents as their obsession with perfectionism drove the band to see faults in their work that few others could perceive. In 1984, the band were not about to publicly brag that they had just made a classic record; to them it was just another stage in their creative and technical development.

By 1990, Metallica's lengthy list of achievements allowed sufficient perspective for James to assess the status their extraordinary second album in a wider context. 'Even though most people say that *Master Of Puppets* was the definitive Metallica album, I would probably take *Ride The Lightning* as my most favourite album,' Hetfield reflected.

Thus, it would take the frontman six years to articulate what most members of the press knew from the first. *Kerrang!* stated that *Ride The Lightning* was 'one of the greatest, most original heavy-metal albums of all time', while *Metal Forces* hailed the disc as 'a veritable feast of heavy-metal goodness'. At the end of the year Metallica won almost every possible accolade in the *Metal Forces* readers' poll, scooping 'Best Band', 'Best Live Band', 'Best Album' and 'Best Single'. Kirk was named 'Best Guitarist', while Lars snared the 'Best Drummer' award, with readers even predicting Metallica would have 'major success in 1985'.

From here on in, Metallica would win many polls in most major metal magazines. When they didn't win, they came very close.

The thrash movement was destined to build, reaching its peak in the latter part of the 1980s with a slew of talented bands and rapidly improving sounds and recordings flooding the marketplace. Yet in 1984 Metallica alone shone as a thrash band with a strong, mature sound. Where *Kill 'Em All* was more reflective of its time – all cheap amps, crunchy riffs and nasal, grouchy vocals – *Ride The Lightning* was a step towards the future, an evocation of the bigger budgets and more elaborate productions associated with metal's greats.

With a fantastic album in tow, and a new management team behind them, Metallica were booked to showcase their new material on a 26-date tour of various European venues. 'They were home for a little while and then they had to go again, to promote the album,' Leah Storkson remembers. 'Things didn't change that much though; they still had no money, they still slept on floors – maybe they had a hotel room which was a little bit nicer, but not much. Things didn't break for them for quite a while.'

As something of a warm-up before the European tour, Metallica played a secret show at Mabuhay Gardens in San Francisco on 20 July 1984. They were billed as 'Kill 'Em All' and supported by local thrash combo Die Sieger. Guitarist Terry Lauderdale remembers the gig well. 'Our bassist at the time, George Ritter, was managing a few bands, one of which was a band called Rude Girl, from San Francisco. He found out that Metallica had gotten their gear stolen in New York prior to coming to San Francisco and offered to let them use our gear if we could open for them. They were in town and wanted to play a gig. They wanted to keep it a secret that they were playing so they were billed in the local "Pink Section" as Kill 'Em All. It was a small club and saying Metallica was playing would have caused a riot! Well the secret show bill didn't fool anybody and the place was freakin' packed from front to back and top to bottom. When we were onstage there were bodies flying everywhere! It was a great show and a great time.'

Lauderdale felt privileged to be able to spend some time with Metallica, who he reveals were down-to-earth and friendly. 'The band rehearsed at our studio three days prior to the show so we got to hang out with them during that time. Our rehearsal space was located at Hunters Point Shipyard in San Francisco. We rehearsed in an old meat freezer! I drove James and Leah around San Francisco a few times. I sat and watched Cliff Burton mostly; he was really digging our bass player's huge Ampeg bass head. They were all cool and just really wanted to get up onstage.'

After the pressures of writing and recording new material so quickly, Metallica wanted to let their hair down in the most decadent way possible. It was here where the business end of Metallica would be eclipsed by the relentless mayhem that seemed to follow them to every gig.

The dichotomy between heartfelt, sober music and the juvenile antics of a gang of spotty youths was still part of the group's collective DNA. Simply put, though their material was maturing, the band, individually, were not. All they wanted to do was drink, and predictably there were moments of unnecessary mayhem and destruction. John Marshall, who was the only American member of the band's crew on their European jaunt, would tell K.J. Doughton of his bewilderment at the humour of his mostly English counterparts. 'English humour is very harsh and sarcastic,' he explained. 'Being the only American I got tons of shit. I was kind of miserable now that I look back on it. I even got pissed on in my bunk by a drunk lighting guy. I woke up thinking I was sweating but it turned out to be piss. He was really ripped and I think the other English guys had whispered to him, "Hey, go down to that American's bunk and piss on him.""

The offending lighting man, Tony Zed, was also alleged to have dowsed Kirk – according to James at least. 'Kirk will deny it to this day,' the frontman laughed, 'but I saw it. I think the guy got both Kirk and John. He had a lot of fucking beer in his gut!'

At the end of 1984, Metallica embarked on a European tour with yet another NWOBHM outfit, London trio Tank, who were best known for featuring former Saints and Damned bassist, Algy Ward. The tour was mostly memorable for the sheer volume of fans Metallica would play to each night – numbers were regularly over a thousand for each show.

The tour was also notable for the emergence of a new nickname for the band. In the crowd on one particular European stop, the band noticed a fan wearing a homemade T-shirt. As James later explained, 'The first time I saw it was some kid had done a shirt, with silk screens or paints at home. He had the *Kill 'Em All* album cover, except instead of "Metallica" it said "Alcoholica", and instead of "Kill 'Em All", it said "Drink 'Em All". Instead of the hammer with the blood, it was a vodka bottle dumped over. We thought it was pretty cool. We had shirts like that made up for ourselves.'

As 1985 dawned, Metallica moved closer to home, playing dates across the US as well as Canada. 'In 1985 they played a show at the Kabuki in San Francisco which was when I realised they were getting a lot bigger, it actually was just really trivial but I noticed it and it was very telling in hindsight,' Leah Storkson recalls. 'When we parked our car to get out to go to the gig, here was someone in front of me who had a "Kill 'Em All" license plate on their car. And I realised, "Wow – more than 2,000 people know who Metallica is?" 'Cause the venue held almost 2,000 and it was sold out and I was *shocked*. Later that night at my parents' house we had a huge argument. I realised that he didn't need to be bound to me any longer and I didn't think it was fair to him or me. And so I wound up breaking off with him. I'd see him at shows or parties with different girls. Rebecca got married to Kirk a year or so later. Time marched on.'

Metallica were headlining a run of shows with shock-rockers W.A.S.P. and underground metallers Armored Saint in tow (the latter would become most famous for offloading vocalist John Bush to Anthrax in 1992). Saint bassist Joey Vera often joined Metallica for bouts of vodka-fuelled lunacy across hotel rooms and bars throughout the States, and one incident in particular will forever remain in his mind.

'We were raging one night in Denver,' Vera recalls, 'when James came into my room wanting to try on my leather jacket. As he tried it on he walked towards the window saying, "This is a nice jacket. Let's see how it flies!" He tossed it out the window and it landed by the pool. We went down to retrieve it and when we were coming back up the hotel elevator we decided to pull out its emergency stop button. This set off an alarm. We tried pushing the button back in, but nothing happened. So the elevator was stuck literally between two floors, security was screaming at us to get out of the elevator, alarms were going off and James was going nuts. Then we crawled out of the elevator onto the hallway of the floor below. James picked up a fire extinguisher from off the wall and aimed it at me. He started fucking squirting it, there was fog all over and the sensors picked up that someone had shot off an extinguisher so the fire alarms started going off all over.

'I snuck back into my room and out the window police cars and fire trucks were pulling into the hotel parking lot and people were being evacuated outside in their pyjamas and underwear. A lot of people got pissed off because there was a convention in town and half the clientele packed up their bags and left. The hotel lost all kinds of money. James ended up having to pay a fine.'

Though Metallica bonded with Vera and company, it was a different story with W.A.S.P., who felt that they should be headlining. By all accounts Metallica and Armored Saint were hardly welcomed by the Los Angeles stalwarts. As K.J. Doughton wrote in *Unbound*: 'W.A.S.P. frontman Blackie Lawless treated the other bands with a reclusive indifference born initially of arrogance and later of embarrassment.'

Though W.A.S.P. were more in line with the LA party-rock scene than feral heavy metal, they didn't enjoy a wholly supportive crowd at every date, and this further divided Lawless from his younger touring partners. 'Some kid in the audience had a sign that said, "Blackie Ball-less sucks,"' recalled Armored Saint vocalist John Bush. 'Blackie spotted it and was getting pissed, so he spit on the guy. Then the guy conjured up this loogie from hell, and it nailed Blackie right in the face. Metallica and us were on the side of the stage roaring and he looked over and gave us this look of doom.'

From that moment on, Lawless refused to have anything to do with Metallica or Armored Saint. He took his precious behaviour one step further when the bands arrived in Canada. Arguing that W.A.S.P. were the bigger sellers in the country, Lawless was granted the headlining slot for all Canadian dates, leaving his band in the unenviable position of following Metallica every night. The move backfired and Metallica left the crowd drained, with W.A.S.P. unable to rouse the remaining audience. 'They got killed every single night by Metallica,' Bush observed.

Meanwhile, in England, Metallica were becoming the band of the moment. Loved by fans and critics alike, *Ride The Lightning* had proved so popular that the band were asked to perform at Castle Donington, the UK's premier heavy-metal festival. Audience figures were always sketchy but there was a headcount of at least 80,000 on the day, a record at the time.

The original adverts for the August 1985 'Monsters Of Rock' festival did not include Metallica, who were very much a last-minute addition. Despite this there were plenty of fans who travelled on that day specifically to see the fast-rising quartet. For once, Donington was blessed with perfect weather for the entire day, though this did not stop the local tradition of large bottles of urine being launched into the air at every opportunity, a delight that the bands were not immune to. Even the penultimate band, Marillion, were victims of the constant bottle-throwing, and when frontman Fish saw fans at the front of the muddy field being bombarded by projectile piss he proclaimed, 'Those of you who are throwing bottles, people down the front are getting hurt, so fuck off.'

'British audiences are strange,' Lars told *Metal Forces*. 'But once you've convinced yourselves that just because you're being bombarded with two-litre bottles full of piss, mud and ham sandwiches doesn't mean that they don't like you, and you've learnt to play your instrument while ducking and running away from things, then, yeah, it was great and good fun.'

James also remarked on one unsavoury addition to the expected surge of bottles. 'There's mostly demo tapes, flowers, flyers, underwear, bras and other crap that fly up there. At one of the Donington shows, we had pieces of pig flying up. Someone had slaughtered a pig and threw it up there.'

Bizarrely, Metallica found themselves sandwiched between a raft of lightweight hair-metal acts. Before them came Ratt – who were seemingly gob-smacked at being demoted to fifth on the bill – and to follow, a cornucopia of airy harmonies courtesy of Bon Jovi. In fact, this was Donington's least heavy gathering, with ZZ Top headlining and Magnum propping up an AOR-friendly bill. So flaccid was the line-up, James felt compelled to warn the crowd, 'If you came here to see spandex, eye make-up and the words "ooh, baby" in every fucking song, this ain't the fucking band!'

However, playing on a soft-rock bill did ensure Metallica enjoyed the attention of the more metal-orientated sections of the audience, whose only fix for testosterone-driven speed antics were the Bay Area quartet. The band duly delivered a watertight set that included the now familiar epics 'Creeping Death' and 'For Whom The Bell Tolls', as well as established crowd-pleasers like 'Seek And Destroy' and 'Whiplash'.

'We were out of place,' conceded Lars Ulrich. 'But it was all about proving ourselves, winning people over, but always, *always* doing it on our terms.'

Metallica's next major outdoor engagement came on 31 August 1985 at the Day On The Green festival, on home soil in Oakland, California. The venue was also the home of the Oakland Raiders football team, whom James had supported for many years.

Once again, Metallica were squeezed between a raft of soft rockers, including Y&T, Scorpions, Yngwie Malmsteen and Ratt. Fred Cotton travelled with the band to the gig and laughs that Metallica 'were billed under Y&T – go figure! But they crushed everybody, man – and in front of their hometown crowd, it was bad ass.'

'The crowd was fuckin' real good – real big,' Cliff Burton enthused. 'I was fuckin' real drunk. I guess we did okay. Fuckin' it's hard to tell when you're onstage, you know. You don't really know what's going on, you just do it and fuckin' find out what happens later.'

Writing for *Kerrang!*, Malcolm Dome spoke with some understatement, predicting, 'There's room somewhere around the top for this band if they can play those tarot cards in their possession with a modicum of foresight and devious intent. And whilst I worry about exactly how the band intend to mature and open out their appeal whilst holding on to the hardcore, on the day, Metallica were fun, pure 80-degree fun.'

Despite the success of the show, the build-up to the gig was anything but smooth. 'We were at El Cerrito, and everyone's talking about getting limos to the gig and James goes, "Fuck that, I want to go in Fred's truck,"' recalls Cotton. 'If you look at the thanks list on *Master Of Puppets* it thanks "Fred and his flippin' truck". We went down to Stetson Beach just to drink all day in my truck, but it was in pretty bad shape – I had to pump the brakes and everything. Lars and some friends are in the truck in front of us and we're road-racing, driving fast, you know, and we're coming down this part of the hill that goes to a right-hand turn and it's a blind corner coming up with just a sheer drop on the other side. And I slammed the gas, we were going to pass them, you know, and we got right up to the turn and saw oncoming traffic so I hit the brakes and they fucking locked up. We spun out on the side of the fucking hill and ended up with the back of the truck part way up the hill to where the back wheels were off the ground – they wouldn't turn so we couldn't get out of there.

'There's people up the hill shouting, "Hey, you guys need some help?" And we said, "We're alright." And he goes, "No, I think you need help." And he goes back to the house and calls the cops so we're panicking! We got traffic stopped now because of everything and I guess a couple of people a few cars back recognised James and they helped us put rocks underneath the wheels and we were able to get out of there.'

Although the band turned in a professional set on a day emblazoned with sunshine and a clear blue sky ('For Whom The Bell Tolls' and a Cliff Burton bass solo from this gig made the *Cliff 'Em All* video), drunken mayhem was never far away. 'I remember after that gig we were all feeling rowdy and shit,' Cotton recalls, 'and me and James went back and decided to take the fruit from the deli tray because each side of the stage was closed off so there were no people there. And I said, "Let's just take some fruit and go throw it at people!" So we took the deli tray and went out and started throwing it into the crowd and then we went into the parking lot – just to rage around and fuck with people.

'So we go outside the gates and stay out in the parking lot for a while and then we want to come back in and the security guard wouldn't let us in. They didn't believe that James was in the band 'cause he looked like a regular guy with ripped Levis and everything. So we had to go around where the cars are parked backstage and you look down and you can see all these limos and shit and then there's my fucked-up truck parked amongst all of them!'

Cotton also recalls the real story behind Metallica's famous dressing-room incident, for which James was blamed by promoter Bill Graham (who had staged Day On The Green as a series of summer concerts). 'We were drinking backstage and they had these little portable rooms with paper-thin walls. There was an air conditioning vent on one of the walls. We took a coat rack and rammed it through the air conditioning duct right into Yngwie's dressing room. He got all pissy about it but we didn't give a fuck.'

'We were throwing fruit and it would explode on this grating,' added James, 'a vent that would go into the next trailer, so the juice would spray all over whoever happened to be in there. So we were throwing all these things and eventually avocado was all that was left on the fruit tray, but somehow the avocados wouldn't go through. So we took baseball bats and kinda smashed the vent apart. Then we went off on the furniture. The whole trailer got demolished basically.'

Bill Graham was a legendry sixties promoter who had worked with bands such as

Jefferson Airplane and the Grateful Dead. Given the peace and love doctrine of his era, Graham was bemused by such violent actions. 'Bill didn't understand how we could treat things like that,' explained James.

Still in their home state, Metallica ended the year by playing a gig in San Francisco along with Exodus, Metal Church and Dave Mustaine's new band Megadeth, who had just released their debut album *Killing Is My Business... And Business Is Good!*

It was New Year's Eve and so Metallica – and James in particular – were even more inebriated than usual. 'James picked up a mic stand and threw it in the crowd and it hit this kid and it fucked him up, I mean he didn't mean to, he just threw it in the crowd,' explains Cotton.

Hetfield confessed, 'We were pretty fucked-up with the countdown and all the balloons dropping and everything. We were singing some fucking thing and we basically wanted people in the crowd to sing along but I couldn't get the mic off the mic stand to throw it out. So I took the whole mic stand and tossed it. The big metal base on the bottom cracked some kid on the head. I guess he wasn't looking or something.'

Fred Cotton recalls that the fan 'was on a gurney and had to get stitches. I remember [road manager] Bobby Schneider telling James, "Just whatever you do don't tell him you're sorry; just give him some free signed shit." But the kid had his mother with him and they sued the band for a lot of money, but it was settled out of court. After that they were telling James, "You know, you can't do that shit."'

Amazingly, throughout the run of live shows and regular drinking sessions, Metallica were hard at work writing new material. Less than a year after their greatest triumph so far, the band began composing songs that would appear on their third record, *Master Of Puppets*.

Despite this dedication to their music, the band continued to party hard, but it was Hetfield who was most affected by the constant hell-raising. The various potential legal issues and disapproval from promoters and management should have provided sufficient motivation to steer James onto a safer course. He was on the cusp of major success with Metallica and yet he could not shake off his inner adolescent. Some fifteen years hence, James would finally check into rehab for his alcohol and other unspecified addictions.

However, in 1985 James was at the height of his hedonistic excess, and it didn't help when he joined up with a side project known as Spastik Children. As the name suggested, this was no serious outfit – it was merely an excuse for a bunch of Californians to get drunk regularly onstage and play stupid songs for their own amusement. Initially the band contained Fred Cotton on vocals (though Fred was really a drummer), James 'Flunky' McDaniel on guitars and Rich 'Jumbo' Sielert on drums.

'James came back shortly after recording *Master Of Puppets* and he had a full beard,' Cotton remembers, 'and I told James about our Spastik gig we'd recently played and he goes, "Fuck, I wanna play."' The whole premise behind the band was to place musicians on instruments they didn't normally play, so Cotton suggested Hetfield could play drums. 'He's like, "Fuck, yeah,"' Cotton recalls, '"cause they had been over in the studio for so long he wanted to do something different.'

The other Metallica mainstay to join Spastik Children was Cliff Burton, who also sought some light relief from the intense sessions Metallica would endure while recording their third LP. Fred Cotton explains the night Burton fell in with the band. 'There was a Rush concert in 1985 and James called me and asked me if I wanted to go, we had a couple of all-access passes so we were straight in. Cliff Burnstein played in a softball league with Geddy Lee [Rush frontman] and that's how James knew them.

'So we get to go backstage after the show and it's kinda like "Uncle Rush",' he laughs. 'We were just young kids. We go backstage and there's no groupies or anything – it's totally quiet. We got the whole place to ourselves, and then Geddy Lee comes out in a robe with a glass of wine! We were just chatting to him and it was really cool. And the topic was, Geddy was breaking a lot of strings during the show and it bothered him a lot 'cause Rush are perfectionists. James is like, "It's cool, man, shit happens," and Geddy didn't understand. James is like, "No, it's good because it makes it real." The subject was having a perfect set, and I brought up the Spastik Children gig and everyone was cracking up about it. Cliff Burton looked at me with a straight face and he says, "Count me in, I wanna play." I said, "You can't man, we don't even have a bass player!" But James says, "Yeah, he should play – he makes retarded enough noises on the bass as it is."

'I just wanted to cause mayhem, get thrown offstage and have people think, "What the fuck?"' Cotton says, recalling the band's chaotic debut performance. 'Flunky wore a mechanic's outfit, I was going to bring a lawnmower onstage and so there's a drummer, a guitar player and me singing, no bass. It was just fucking hideous! And half of it was doing stand-up comedy in between songs. You know, I was so ripped I climbed up on the roof of Ruthie's Inn and stood on the edge of the marquee and started peeing on people, and I was a big guy, I was like a dump truck and I was having fun because I knew there weren't too many people who could stop me.'

For James, Spastik Children represented a means of escape from the rapidly growing Metallica circus and the ever-increasing pressures of success. The way Hetfield dealt with popularity was to attempt to deny it as much as possible. The side project's line-up was entirely fluid, and at one stage contained every Metallica member bar Lars Ulrich. There was also a place for 'Big, Sick, Ugly' Jim Martin at a few gigs, a close friend of both Cliff and James.

Spastik Children played very few shows, but when they did they just wanted to have a good time and be seen as a band in their own right, with no connection to Metallica. However, it rarely worked out like that. Fred Cotton would later join Piranha, who featured former Exodus singer Paul Baloff. It was the unfortunate intervention of Baloff (who sadly passed away in 2002 after suffering a stroke that left him in a coma) which alerted the media to James Hetfield's new 'project'.

'*MTV News* announced our gig and we were like, "What the fuck?" Because we always made sure not to exploit the Metallica name,' recalls Cotton. 'Something Paul Baloff did was release flyers about one of our gigs saying, "Spastik Children – featuring Metallica," and exploited the shit out of it.'

Cotton remembers that for the first time in Spastik Children's brief history, 'The whole place was packed. We were just like, "Fuck this."' The band did manage to perform such favourites as 'The Ballad Of Harald O' and 'Guys Like Farts'. In the *Adventures Of Zoe* fanzine, the eponymous reviewer observed, 'The crowd jumps up and down, screams, makes obscene gestures and runs around in circles. The band is totally drunk, everyone sings off-key, James, playing on Pigs' drum kit, spits beer in the air. As always, they do their encore in their underpants. Kirk said, "We wanted to do it naked but the clubs won't let us."'

The band were less than impressed with the sold-out crowd and the presence of MTV. James in particular needed to be placated by Cotton and convinced to play. 'We were pissed off about it,' says Cotton. 'So to fuck with people, I went out and found this half a joint – it looked like a cigar – and I get up on the drum riser and shout out, "Who smokes weed?" And everyone yells, "Yeah!" And I shouted out, "We don't," and I drop it on the ground and crush it. In the end we just walked offstage flipping everybody off.'

Perhaps part of Spastik Children's reluctance to be taken seriously was because musically the band were devoid of actual songs, and it was almost an embarrassment to be so closely under the spotlight, especially when those in attendance were often expecting to hear Metallica songs or at least tracks which were closely related. But Cotton admits, 'There's nothing there musically that you could be proud of, it's just fucking noise. It's really cool that it will always be a part of Metallica history, even just as a footnote, but musically, I mean, fuck – it would be ridiculous to put anything out. It's not meant for that. It's more for a side project – something to do on a Tuesday night to get drunk to.'

As always, alcohol played a vital part in the proceedings and it was this extra-curricular behaviour that would further justify Metallica's 'Alcoholica' pseudonym. 'My partner who worked in the chemical department at the local university brought this stuff down which said "Ethel Alcohol" on the bottle,' remembers Cotton. 'It's, like, 200 proof and on the label it says "for manufacturing use only". He brought two pints of it! There were probably twenty people around backstage and everybody got fucked-up and hammered on the shit and we still had a quarter of a bottle left over! Kirk took a straight shot of it and almost fucking choked. You put it on your tongue and you could feel it expand – it was brutal shit.'

Metallica had enjoyed a tremendously successful couple of years that would help shape their future career and personalities, even if they didn't realise it at the time. *Ride The Lightning* had been a phenomenal triumph, and with their new management and promotional teams behind them, Metallica knew they could become even bigger with their third album.

But first they would need to perfect and record the songs they had been working on. No one but the band themselves could have known just how stupendous those songs would turn out to be.

CHAPTER 8

OWNING THE GLOBE

'We're getting a good draw; it's a fucking hell of a lot of fun.
It is painful at first, our necks and lower backs really hurt.
But aspirin is a great drug.'
Cliff Burton

Ride The Lightning had been so immense that it was going to take something extraordinary from Metallica to equal the impact made by their second opus. Although the band shied away from praise, shunning suggestions that *Ride The Lightning* was an instant classic, they were savvy enough to realise it represented a huge advance on their debut. They assumed that the pressure was now off, but equally realised that their next set of songs had to be just as focused, tight and heavy as possible, while still retaining their newfound sense of melody.

Despite the huge strides the quartet had made, overtaking many of their peers with just a few notes of 'Creeping Death' or 'Trapped Under Ice', essentially Metallica were still a garage band. Lars revealed that the band still practiced 'a lot, by ourselves. Where me and James live, we have a sort of rehearsal place out in the garage. And I enjoy playing my drum kit by myself. If we have considerable time off, we still take lessons. Kirk is taking lessons right now, and the last big break we had I took some advanced drum lessons. Why stop learning, if you can keep expanding?'

Such dedication to self-improvement was a characteristic that set Metallica well apart from many of their contemporaries. Most aspiring musicians take lessons when they first take up an instrument. Sometimes those lessons inspire them and sometimes they opt to eschew lessons altogether and develop under their own aegis. But it was very rare for a group to record two spectacular records, draw lavish praise from all quarters and then stand back and say, 'Hey, wait a minute – we're still not good enough.' Some years later, James Hetfield would even take singing lessons.

Still, for all the tutoring available in scales, techniques and general fret or drum wizardry, the best teachers in the world cannot teach songwriting from the heart. This was something inherent to Metallica, and they hardly needed a tutorial to compose sumptuous melodies, dynamics and choruses.

'As compared to the last album, I think I'm surprised how each member of the band goes about playing their individual instrument,' observed Lars. 'I think all of us have really progressed as musicians over the last couple of years. We're always interested in soaking up as many influences and learning as much about our instruments as we can.'

All of the music the band had collectively absorbed over the last eighteen months would influence the quartet to varying degrees, but in truth there was no other band that sounded remotely like Metallica. This had been evident almost from the band's inception. By 1985 Metallica were operating in a rarefied creative zone that would see many fans subsequently identifying their third album as a high-water mark in the band's career.

Not only had they practiced night and day, toured the world and taken lessons to hone their craft even further, but Metallica also spent five months in the studio perfecting new material and spending most of their earnings from the *Ride The Lightning* period in the process. This again was wholly indicative of the band's intense dedication. There was no question of taking the money and running: Metallica wanted to plough their resources back into the band and into the process of constructing a masterpiece.

When German photographer Buffo Schnädelbach spent two weeks with the group at their El Cerrito base in 1985, he recalls that both he and pal Alexis Olson were 'banished from the garage where the band were rehearsing. I mean, we could hear some sounds coming out, but we couldn't actually go in there.' Then with a knowing wink, Buffo confesses, 'To be honest my English wasn't that great back then and I am not exactly sure if we weren't allowed in there because it was too small or because they were hiding their songs!'

Thanks to Elektra's backing, Metallica were afforded relative luxury during the recording process. 'Last album we all lived in a room the size of a small office,' explained Lars. 'And we had to take buses back and forth to the studio, and we ate really bad. This time, we were able to live in a nicer hotel, get a car and drive around, and it just made the stay a lot easier for us.'

Once again, Metallica were ensconced in Sweet Silence Studios – enabling Lars to combine his passions for both Danish culture and getting drunk. 'Me and James would go out drinking,' recalled the drummer. 'In late November, early December, they have something called Christmas beers, which is just an excuse for everyone to drink their Christmas sorrows away. It's twice as strong as regular beer. Every time we went out and drank these Christmas beers, James would start trying to talk Danish – completely pissed out of his face! Which all made for good fun.'

Lars would also remember this as the period during which he cemented his relationship with Cliff. 'We hung out a lot. We'd go out and play poker for eight hours straight after being up for 24 hours. We'd find a seafood restaurant that was open, eat raw oysters and drink beer then scream at the natives while we were drunk.'

Perhaps because of their partying, Metallica found the recording process laborious, and realised that, in striving for perfection, excellence would not always flow as readily as the beer. '*Master Of Puppets* was really focused,' insisted Flemming Rasmussen, who was again engaged to produce the album. 'We knew what we wanted and worked hard to get it, but it was very hard work. By this album we were pretty sure what Metallica should sound like.'

'Making *Master Of Puppets* was definitely a chore,' revealed Lars. 'The faster stuff came easily to us, so we tried to maintain an interest in it by incorporating variations in mood and tempo.' In fact, Lars felt the material was still connected to their thrash roots – only 'three years later and three years better'.

Despite this, there was no danger of this album drawing on the past just to please their listeners. The band had been unfazed by criticisms that *Ride The Lightning*, and 'Fade To Black' in particular, represented the band 'selling out' to achieve wider success. They knew where they were headed, and would not be diverted by external opinions.

'That didn't worry us at all,' asserted Lars. 'I mean, what are we supposed to do? Just cater for a specific 200 people or so for the rest of our lives? We are playing in a band that is growing musically and keeps getting new ideas and to us, as long as we're powerful and have that energy and feel for our music, then it doesn't really matter what tempo we play at.'

Tempo was the order of the day. If a band is supposedly part of the speed-metal sub-genre, there tends to be some expectation of velocity. Metal was expanding at a breakneck pace, and as the media's poster boys for the thrash movement, Metallica were expected to keep up.

Since the release of *Ride The Lightning*, there had been several significant developments in the thrash sub-genre. Kirk Hammett's former band Exodus hit the streets with the ferocious *Bonded By Blood*, which even today is considered a classic. Indeed, this was the album that – largely via word of mouth and underground fanzines – introduced the speed-thrash style to unsuspecting kids from the Bay Area to Europe.

Although it is not considered their best album, Slayer's *Hell Awaits* upped the ante in terms of speed and aggression. Even European bands were making a name for themselves, with the likes of Germany's Kreator releasing the incendiary *Pleasure To Kill* in 1986.

'Thrash metal to me is just open-E riffing for five minutes as fast as you can go,' an unimpressed Lars told a delighted *Kerrang!* (who had adopted a dismissive attitude to thrash from the outset). 'From a musician's point of view I don't really like that term. It implies lack of arrangement, lack of ability, lack of songwriting, lack of any form of intelligence. We do play very fast, but I think there's a lot more to our songs than just thrashing. I hate the mentality of thrash acts: all they want to do is play faster and faster. What does that prove?'

The attitudes of many of the bands in question, not to mention their fans, did little to persuade Ulrich that Metallica should confine themselves to the extreme end of the metal spectrum. 'These days there seems to be all these people that suddenly jump on something just because it's trendy, like going out and buying upside-down crosses, spikes and whatever and listening to certain bands because they're new,' Lars told Bernard Doe of *Metal Forces*. 'I just think there's something wrong with this whole underground thing; not necessarily the bands, but with these so-called true metallists... With the underground you're either thrash or you're posing and there seems to be no middle ground. It's all a bit worrying.'

It was the attitude of elitism from the speed-metal faithful that most irked Lars. Essentially he, and the rest of Metallica, felt they were frowned upon if they slowed the tempo for too long, and the quartet were hardly inclined toward accommodating any such criticisms. Almost to rile the die-hards, they protested at being called a thrash band, even though for the most part, this still held true. But they wanted no part of a scene with limitations and their main assertion was that *they* decided when to limit their material, not genre definitions or advocates of any particular, narrow style.

'You know, they never took out a thrash band in support,' says Buffo Schnädelbach. 'There was never a Death Angel or a Forbidden propping up one of their bills, and I think this is one of the reasons for their mainstream success. They distanced themselves from that whole scene and so it was easier for them to be accepted in commercial circles. It didn't go down well with certain people in the scene, however.'

Metallica completed work on their third album at the end of 1985. They returned to the US to spend Christmas with friends and family, rested their weary limbs, then sat back and waited. The album would be released three months later.

Much like its predecessor, *Master Of Puppets* was a completely unique take on heavy metal and for this reason – in spite of every declaration to the contrary – Metallica were slightly dubious as to how the new material would be received. Though they knew the songs were immensely strong and original, even the band's management Q-Prime were not prepared for the band being suddenly accepted by mass audiences. In some ways the disc was simply another Metallica album – if it sold well and took the band to new heights, so be it.

Better than anyone, Lars could see the bigger picture and he knew that if there were to be an album which globalised the Metallica name, *Master Of Puppets* would surely be the one. For the first time, the band had not been tied to a deadline, pressurised by a long list of repercussions should they fail to meet it. Thus, they were not only allowed to experiment, they could also meticulously search for their signature sound. '*Master Of Puppets* was really focused,' recalled Flemming Rasmussen. 'We knew what we wanted and worked hard to get it, but it was *very* hard work.'

Every aspect of the recording process was analysed and amended. It took several days just to set the gear up to their satisfaction, and several more to establish the right tone for each instrument. Only Cliff Burton was relatively relaxed, mainly due to his 'plug-in-and-play' approach. The process was gruelling and regularly demoralising, but *Master Of Puppets* would eventually prove worth all the hard work and perfectionism.

The album opens with a Spanish guitar flurry, introducing the monstrous 'Battery'. Any doubts as to whether Metallica were still a thrash band were instantly scotched by the time the main riff obliterated its mournful Spanish introduction. If this wasn't thrash or speed-metal then nothing was. The song contained every identifiable characteristic of the twin sub-genres: the deep, chugging open-E riffing, bass drums which announced that the attack was about to find a snare for accompaniment, and – the ultimate pay off for any thrasher – the blistering pace. This found its groove instantly before breaking down briefly into a simple refrain, before the tempo picks up again, this time accompanied by Hetfield's awesome larynx.

James's voice sounded crisp, clean and clear, and showed an undeniable improvement from *Ride The Lightning*. Ironically, there was a detectable sneer to his voice *à la* Dave Mustaine – particularly in the third verse. The frontman no longer sounded as if he were in a different room from the rest of the band – his delivery was upfront and precise. The twin assault of machine-gun riffage and thunderous drum salvos rolled on – an exercise in concussive sonics that runs for almost three minutes before there is any let up. Moulding their bludgeon into something altogether more tuneful, Metallica demonstrated the manner in which their range and use of juxtaposition had developed in the two years since *Ride The Lightning*.

Hammett's guitar bled deeply into the grooves before the band blasted their way back to the edge of metal meltdown. The lyrics were an assertion of Metallica's manifesto: 'Powerhouse of energy/ Whipping up a fury, dominating flurry/ We create the battery.' Despite the literal connotations of the lyrics, the real inspiration behind the choice of song title was far more prosaic. '"Battery" was about a club called the Old Waldorf on Battery Street in San Francisco,' Fred Cotton reveals. 'James loved that name for a street.'

The whirring, chrome riff that scrapes the speakers during the title track's introduction is a colossus of the genre, signalling the beginning of more than eight minutes of molten-hot metal. Rasmussen, who'd taken the helm once more, recognised the song's classic quality immediately. 'When we did the title track – it's a thing you kind of sense as a vibe in the studio – but as we had done three or four tracks, I knew this was at least as good as *Ride The Lightning*,' he recalled in an internet chat some years later.

The track was one of the few to include a writing credit for each member of the band – it needed a sizeable contribution from each of the quartet to create something so complex and faultless. 'Master Of Puppets' effectively encapsulated the album to which it lent its name, signalling the band's immense progression since 1984. They sounded wiser, more streamlined and able to execute the kind of epic material only metal giants such as Iron Maiden could effectively pull off.

Lyrically, the song's anti-drugs message was well ahead of the trend in metal that became fashionable during the early 1990s. Many artists would make concerted attempts to warn against the perils of drug use and record labels such as Roadrunner encouraged clean living. Their slogan was plastered on many albums from 1990 onwards: 'STOP THE MADNESS. Drugs are no fun, drugs endanger the life and happiness of millions, it must stop. We appeal in particular to the youth of today, stop the madness. There are better things in life.'

In 1986, however, such sentiments were rarely expressed. The 1980s would be remembered as a golden era for hedonistic hard rock and metal, when excess was the norm. Notorious for their alcohol consumption, Metallica were no strangers to prohibited substances either – which made Hetfield's assertions with 'Master...' all the more puzzling. While his close friends Kirk Hammett and Lars Ulrich were wont to partake in the chemical pleasures of life (specifically cocaine), Hetfield seemingly disapproved.

'If the name Metallica is in something the media portrays then it bugs me', James told the Metallica fan club. 'Why not say, "Hello, my name's Lars and I snort cocaine, thank you, goodnight." That's fine, that's fucking fine, but to say Metallica… that word "Metallica" means a lot to a lot of people, and when someone says Metallica is not drug-free, "We get up to things you don't know about," quoted to Lars or Kirk, that bugs me a little bit.'

'I think at the time James wrote the lyrics to "Master…", 75 per cent of the rest of Metallica all dabbled in cocaine use at a very social level,' Ulrich explained. 'Social. That song is written about people who have very addictive personalities and who aren't in control of their lives. Thanks to people like Dave Mustaine, Nikki Sixx or Steven Tyler, people think that rock'n'roll is either all or nothing. Nobody in this band has an addictive personality, and that goes for everything. The only one who doesn't do any drugs whatsoever is James Hetfield. But it's not that big of a deal, and it is possible that you can dabble with these things at a recreational level.'

According to Ron Quintana and Fred Cotton, 'Master Of Puppets' was inspired by one of the band's friends, Rich 'Skitchy' Birch, who was credited with the quote on the back of the *Kill 'Em All* album. Cotton reveals that the 'chop your breakfast on a mirror' line on 'Master Of Puppets' was directly inspired by Birch. 'One morning after sleeping on the couch, James, Lars and I were reading fan mail, and Rich stopped by on his way to work. He grabbed an Elephant beer mirror off the wall to chop a line of speed. He snorted it, said, "Thanks," and left for work. Funny shit. He was more into the punk scene, so he really wasn't around much but I did see him at the El Cerrito house a few times.'

'Rich Skitch was Lars and James's friend and had family problems and later drug problems, but was the nicest, truest headbanger you could ever know!' recalled Quintana. 'Rich influenced James to write "Master Of Puppets", but we all knew many others with worse problems than Rich had before that was written, and I don't think that was written about Rich's problem *per se*, but about society's problems.'

Sadly, the story of Rich Birch ended in tragedy, and Quintana describes the man himself and his relation to the metal scene of the time. 'Rich was a loud, crazy guy who totally got into music and hung out with a similar group of headbangers like me. We went to a ton of metal shows where kids would just stand around or raise their fist, which was weak! We would play air guitar, thrash into each other like pinballs and headbang or even pogo – punk was still big – at shows to the good bands. We learned to headbang by watching NWOBHM videos of English bangers. Skitchy was always crashing into us or poseurs if we weren't banging enough and yelling, "Bang the head that doesn't bang," or, "Roar for Uli [Roth]," or, "Roar for Schenker/Ritchie/Lemmy/Yngwie," etcetera. And instigating early metal pits. I helped him get a job at Record Vault where they did too much speed and used needles later. Rich died of AIDS from dirty needles.'

It's interesting to note that as Metallica wrote 'Master Of Puppets', a crumbling Megadeth were being split asunder by cocaine and heroin use. This gives the impression that perhaps 'Master Of Puppets' was a subliminal dig at their former bandmate.

The following track, 'The Thing That Should Not Be', caused *Metal Forces* writer Dave Constable to exclaim, 'Ozzy and Sabbath would have died to have written a riff this powerful. This song will bring the walls caving in; it truly is like being pulverised by a sledgehammer – the most ominous metal song ever.'

This was the slowest, most deliberate, hulking epic Metallica had thus far committed to vinyl; in fact the song stands among their most unusual and unique in the sense that they have yet to try and replicate its style. This style of metal, verging on doom, would have been embarrassing even in the hands of veterans of the genre. For this track, Metallica took metal into new realms, and pulled the trick off with aplomb.

Adding further originality, Kirk Hammett's solo is a preciously dank trawl along the fretboard. Though he is often best known for blazing, histrionic, high-pitched solos, it was this unexpectedly mournful contribution that marked him out as a nascent guitar genius.

Though nowhere near as long, it was as if this were Metallica's take on Iron Maiden's 'Rime Of The Ancient Mariner'. Metallica's own epic was inspired by Cliff Burton's passion for H.P. Lovecraft (also admired by Iron Maiden's Steve Harris), and he passed on a copy of Lovecraft's short story 'Dagon' to James Hetfield.

The omnipresent eerie darkness that permeated Lovecraft's work is much in evidence throughout 'Dagon', and Hetfield simply adapted the story into a set of lyrics that evoked images of giant fish-human hybrids. The singer would later observe that when the bludgeoning number was played live, those at stage front must have 'shit themselves as the bass bins rattled'.

In the context of the album, 'The Thing That Should Not Be' is one of the less instant compositions, but it is eminently notable for the impressive manner in which the band nailed a style they were otherwise unfamiliar with.

'Welcome Home (Sanitarium)' begins with one of the band's most famous guitar introductions, making it a truly memorable Metallica track. Indeed, Lars Ulrich cites it as one of his personal favourites. The languid ringing open-E chord and the harmonics of the opening notes were used to indicate time slowly ticking by.

By this point, it was evident that *Master Of Puppets* followed exactly the same trajectory as *Ride The Lightning* in the way its tracks were structured: fast opener, title track, epic track, power ballad, before picking up the pace again for the beginning of Side Two.

'Sanitarium' – as it would come to be more commonly known – was the true definition of a 'power ballad'. Although it featured numerous soulful and harmonious guitar licks, the track still managed to emit a bleak sense of heaviness. There were no syrupy radio-friendly sections or a soft, gradual chorus – this was fundamental power-metal balladry, which simply went from soft to heavy quickly and impressively. As the song hits the second chorus it erupts into a lyrical and musical mutiny – the rhythms mimicking psychological restlessness as Kirk's evermore frantic solos seek to represent the mental spasms of those trapped by insanity.

The track was partially inspired by the 1975 film adaptation of Ken Kesey's novel

One Flew Over The Cuckoo's Nest, which starred Jack Nicholson as a patient who rebels against the tyrannical rules of a mental asylum. 'The whole thing is about hanging out at places like that and being told that you're crazy and insane, and that this is your home, where you belong, and feeling inside that these people are wrong,' explained Lars.

As the song breaks down after the second chorus, there is a riff which some felt was similar to Rush's 1981 track 'Tom Sawyer'. Metallica have never confirmed or denied if they deliberately paid homage to the Canadian band, though Rush were thanked in the liner notes of the album. As previously mentioned, there were links to Rush through Metallica's management and both bands were well acquainted – any similarity would have been a respectful homage.

'Disposable Heroes' begins with a tumbling guitar break, underpinned by Ulrich's tom rolls which, according to Fred Cotton, owed their provenance to 'the old TV show *Hogan's Heroes*. The theme song starts with a snare-drum roll that James emulates with the opening guitar crunch on "Disposable Heroes".' The sixties comedy show – which featured the antics of a group of captured American GIs held by the Nazis – was also the inspiration for the song's title.

The song is one of the more instantaneous cuts on *Master Of Puppets*, particularly for old-school thrash fans, as it's mostly based around a pulsating riff and speedy chorus. Along with 'Battery' and 'Damage, Inc.', it is also one of the album's apparent contradictions, in light of Lars's comments regarding Metallica's standing as a thrash band. Drawing on lashings of open-E rhythms, it was difficult to argue that these were not thrash tracks. They were also arguably three of the four strongest songs on the LP.

One element which marks 'Disposable Heroes' out in comparison with most thrash epics is Kirk's melodic soloing, the guitarist also having a hand in the song's composition. His solo on 'Disposable Heroes' is far more reminiscent of basic heavy metal than thrash, bringing a classy veneer to the otherwise straightforward speed anthem.

The lyrics are more forthright than many of Hetfield's early songs, focusing on the futility of war and the young soldiers who are mere machine-gun fodder. It also ties in with the theme of the cover art – more so than any other song. The repeated line, 'Bodies fill the fields I see,' is represented by the crosses adorning the front sleeve and the lone helmet which perches atop one grave on the left. If anything, this particular theme is the most direct reference to manipulation (according to Hammett and Ulrich, this was the mooted 'concept' of the album) of all the song meanings. The puppet master is overseeing the graves, his strings attached to each individual cross. As Hetfield's desperate vocals assert, 'I was born for dying.'

'Leper Messiah' is often identified as the least powerful of all the tracks on *Master Of Puppets* and is perhaps notable more for its perceived lyrical meaning than for any musical element. Given the use of the word 'leper', many wrongly assume the song is fixated on peeling skin and rotten body parts. In fact, it is a cleverly constructed commentary on the rise of evangelism during the 1980s, mocking the television evangelists who implore viewers to send them money, in the belief that a grateful God will cure their ills or woes. The symbolism of an incurable leper is used to comment on the avarice of the TV preacher and his promise of heaven – 'Make a contribution and you'll get the better seat.'

After the album was released, Dave Mustaine incredulously stated, in any interview during which he was asked about Metallica (of which there were many), that the guitar parts from 'Leper Messiah' were rehashed from one of his old songs, 'The Hills Ran Red'. Metallica would later assert that, although the riff was drawn from the archives, it had nothing to do with Mustaine. This does seem questionable seeing as Mustaine had no problem with any material from *Ride The Lightning* – perhaps as he was credited in songs that featured his riffs. It is possible that at this time Mustaine felt at his lowest regarding his lamented exit from Metallica. Not only was he seeing his old band garner serious plaudits in the press, but he was also fighting cocaine and heroin addictions. He later described this period as 'the worst in my life'. His upset at being marginalised by his former friends was later explored in the documentary *Some Kind Of Monster*.

The song is, in fact, decidedly weak compared to the rest of the material to be found on *Master Of Puppets*, and certainly sounds more like an earlier composition.

Like its antecedent, *Master Of Puppets* featured a lengthy instrumental track. 'Orion' demonstrates Metallica's remarkable musical prowess, not to mention their ability to keep such a track interesting for over eight minutes. There wasn't another metal band around who possessed this capability. Even Iron Maiden failed to achieve it with their 'Losfer Words (Big 'Orra)' track from the *Powerslave* LP, and that was less than four minutes long.

Though Burton would receive only a partial songwriting credit, the number was chiefly his idea and he dictated the arrangement of the track, dominating with swollen bass chimes and lengthy finger movements. Despite the Hetfield-Ulrich accreditation, Lars would concede the idea was Burton's, telling *Metal Forces*, 'Cliff came up with a very different-sounding piece to anything we'd done before. To me it sounded like a Swedish folk song! And we really liked listening to it and playing it, so we just based the whole song around that middle part.'

The central part of the song is the gorgeous bass solo, which fields intermittent guitar bullets while propelling the track toward a memorable, stunning climax. It was hard to believe that elements of the song before and after the bass breakdown were assembled from other ideas. The original demo for 'Welcome Home (Sanitarium)' featured an ending that was scrapped and inserted into 'Orion' as intermittent solos. Even within the web guitar solos, there was space for more Burton brilliance. 'There's a little bass solo in "Orion"; it's right next to a little guitar solo,' Burton explained. 'No one will probably be able to tell that it's bass, but it is.'

'"Orion" is actually bits and pieces of other songs thrown together,' admitted Lars. 'The bluesy, moody part in the middle was originally the tail-end part of another song, but we felt that it was so strong that it could be the basis of an instrumental as words weren't really needed. So we built the whole song around that middle part and as an instrumental I think it works really well.' Writing for *Metal Forces* magazine, Dave

Constable enthused, 'Someone write a film for this track; it deserves one.'

Cliff Burton was again instrumental in the instantly recognisable beginning for album closer 'Damage, Inc.'. 'It's about eight or twelve tracks of bass, a lot of harmonies and volume swells and effects and stuff,' he disclosed. 'I would hesitate to call it a bass solo; it's more just an intro, but it is all bass.'

The lulling introduction gives way to one of the band's most striking speed anthems – basic, yet devastatingly effective. The song was a flurry of expletives, snarling fangs and flashy speed-thrash elements – all from a band who would not admit to being thrash. 'Damage, Inc.' is relentless, a potent stab of thrash few could compete with, all the while spilling melodious guitar grunts and overlaid by a riff wrenched from the lowest reaches of the fretboard. It was a vicious, clear-cut ending to an album of immense depth and originality. It was also a well-timed sign that the band could still kick it when they so desired, that if you thought this band couldn't still play fast and precise, the proof was blindingly apparent.

The art of the concept album was a term generally applied to progressive rock, though it had originated much earlier in the works of everyone from Frank Sinatra to the Beatles. Though Iron Maiden would dabble in this united theme for their 1984 LP *Powerslave*, concept albums had fallen into disfavour in metal circles during the mid-1980s. But with the puppeteer/gravesite cover art for *Master Of Puppets*, Metallica were assumed to have created a concept based on a premise most critics could never figure out. This resulted in the band facing continuous questions, as the press – especially *Kerrang!* – attempted to discern a unifying thematic concept behind the album.

'Personally I would say the "master" of this whole thing is fate,' mused Cliff. 'Manipulation,' interjected Kirk, 'various forms of manipulation, which can go into entirely different subjects which we could talk about for hours.'

In a fan-club interview Lars appeared to concur, saying, 'There are many songs on this record that explore manipulation. "Leper Messiah", for instance, deals with people being manipulated into sending these people money, thinking they'll be able to meet God sooner, or meet God better.'

The truth was that these were merely concepts that had floated into Metallica's lyrical cross-hairs in an organic fashion. Vastly different subject matter lay at the heart of each song, yet most could be said to tie in with the theme of manipulation – if you stretched it far enough. The band would never admit it was a concept album, quite simply because it wasn't – it was merely a reflection of society's ills and a mélange of other influences, be they *One Flew Over The Cuckoo's Nest* or an H.P. Lovecraft yarn. 'We don't plan concepts,' insisted James. 'We didn't write *Ride The Lightning* about death, or *Master Of Puppets* about manipulation. That just happens.'

Still, the idea that this was a specially created, in-depth conceptual piece generated a mystique around *Master Of Puppets* and drew people into Metallica's world just that little bit faster. The initial reaction did not instantly propel Metallica to number one metal band in the world, but even upon its first release there wasn't a bad review to be read. 'Before 1986 is through they will be one of the biggest, if not *the* biggest, true metal bands in the world,' *Metal Forces* predicted. '*Master Of Puppets* is the best metal album I've ever heard.'

Indeed, the LP was so good that even the band's families were impressed. 'You know, we had never really been exposed to heavy metal at all; it was so new to us,' explained Cliff's father, Ray Burton. 'When *Ride The Lightning* came out I said, "Oh!" I thought it was the best album in the world, you know. I was all scared and I said, "Cliff, how can you do a better one than that? It's impossible to do a better album." And then they came out with *Master Of Puppets*!'

Released on 21 February 1986, *Master Of Puppets* instantly hit the *Billboard* Top 30 chart and was quickly certified gold – Metallica's first album to reach this level. It was also outselling their previous albums at a ratio of three to one. Metallica were finding new fans by the day, and their success was only set to increase.

Above: *Lars, Cliff and James enter into the spirit of the Netherlands' Aardschok Festival, 11 February 1984.*
Below: *James and Lars in Poperinge, Belgium in 1984, during the Tank Tour.*

Right: *James pictured in 1984, just after the release of* Ride The Lightning.
Below: *The infamous El Cerrito pad in San Francisco.*
Opposite above: *The four horsemen photographed in 1983, enjoying copious amounts of beer and hair.*
Opposite below: *Hetfield banging on the snares for Spastik Children.*

Opposite above: *James sits contemplative on a beach north of San Francisco, 1985.*
Opposite below: *James, Lars and Fred Cotton show their enthusiasm for candid photography.*
Above (left to right): *Lars, Fred Cotton (Spastik Children), James and Andre Verhuysen (founder of the Dynamo Festival).*

Opposite above: James and Kirk during one of their many European shows in support of Master Of Puppets.
Opposite below: Cliff at the El Cerrito pad swapping four strings for six.
Right: Cliff poses in front of a dramatic lightning-torn backdrop, January 1985.
Below: James and Kirk pay tribute to Metallica influence Glenn Danzig with Misfits and Samhain T-shirts.
Next page: A publicity shot dated 1 January 1986.

CHAPTER 9

WE'LL NEVER QUIT 'CAUSE WE'RE METALLICA

'I often think, now much more than ever,
how much of a character and personality Cliff actually was.
He was just one in five billion people on this earth, and we will never,
ever even be tempted to come up with anyone like him.'

Lars Ulrich

With the release of *Master Of Puppets*, Metallica started to enjoy crossover success. Despite this, along with Slayer's *Reign In Blood* the same year, they precipitated an explosion in the burgeoning thrash-metal movement. Metallica began to revel in acceptance from more mainstream circles. Many music fans who otherwise shunned heavy metal, much less thrash, had a soft spot for Metallica once *Master Of Puppets* hit the racks.

When metal fans played the album in front of their college friends who favoured the vapid soft rock of U2, the metalheads would be amazed to discover that their friends actually dug it. *Master Of Puppets* became the in-vogue platter of 1986 and the heavy-metal album that was acceptable to accept. Be it the sheer latent power of the band in full flow, or the way in which they juxtaposed melody against brutality, *Master Of Puppets* captivated an ever-expanding demographic.

The mid-1980s saw the development of clear lines of demarcation between higher and lower forms of metal. The big guns who had long established themselves – be it straightforward metal giants such as Iron Maiden, Dio and Judas Priest, or the faux-metal spandex rock of Mötley Crüe and Twisted Sister – were part of a relatively small pack indulging in quality rock and metal records. Their songs had melody, anger, balls and, occasionally (as with Maiden), brains.

Their contemporaries often failed to match this standard. While many metal devotees would attach themselves to the likes of Malice, Lizzie Borden or Armored Saint, there was still a clear distinction in quality. Although these bands wrote the odd decent song, they were unable to match Metallica in terms of consistency. Where Metallica's 1980s work has aged well, much of the work produced by lesser bands during the period sounds decidedly dated.

By virtue of their habitual use of sensational imagery, or ridiculous, overblown lyrics, the likes of Crüe and Dio were the chief reason metal seemed destined to remain a fringe genre. It required a certain reckless abandon to devote oneself to heavy metal and a desire to separate from the mainstream, even if that meant an adolescence of loneliness and introspection.

However, Metallica blew these conventions and restrictions to smithereens. Certainly, Lars Ulrich believed his band could transcend regular boundaries – stylistic and monetary alike – and it's true that he held the vision for Metallica's potential long before *Master Of Puppets* arrived.

Aside from their tremendous arsenal of songs, what was it that so endeared Metallica to legions of non-heavy-metal fans? For one thing, despite the convoluted nature of some material and their penchant for hefty time changes and lengthy musical statements, the band succeeded in imbuing this with an air of simplicity that was readily accessible.

All Metallica album covers to date had been basic affairs, which spoke volumes despite the vulgarity of the artwork. *Master Of Puppets* was fronted by an almost pleasant visual image, which carried a greater (albeit subtle) depth than previous Metallica covers. There were no demons, no inverted crosses (rather a Christian-friendly batch of crosses), no ridiculous mascots, no blood, gore or guts – it was merely clear, concise imagery. It was also housed underneath *that* terrific 3-D logo.

The album's main back-cover photo was a reflection of the fact the band did not take themselves too seriously and, despite their status as metal gods, were more than game to poke fun at the genre, or at least carefully distance themselves from its limitations and negative connotations. Clearly they knew how to have fun. Without the need for spandex or copious amounts of leather, they made skinny jeans look cool.

On the inner sleeve, the band were pictured as typical twenty-somethings ensconced in a drinking den (the El Cerrito pad) complete with huge stereo and the staples of an unwholesome diet. Within this setting – not unlike a college dorm room, or a sixth-form common room – the subliminal connotations of youthful exuberance were evident to record buyers.

Metallica appeared so 'normal', yet the back sleeve of the LP belied this. In a scene from a festival the band had played at a gargantuan football stadium, thousands of rabid fans were visible as Ulrich stoked the masses. Here was a band that had developed their craft and gradually increased their fanbase but still called a glorified trailer home.

Fred Cotton remembers, 'On the coffee table in front of them on the photo, there was a newspaper headline that read, "Hudson Has Aids," referring to Rock Hudson the actor. The record label cut it out.' Strangely enough Elektra weren't quite so picky about the stream of expletives that adorned the fake warning sticker on the album cover. Included to poke fun at the glut of Parental Advisory indicators which now festooned many rock and metal records, Metallica's parody (in the shape of a stop sign) read, 'The only track you probably won't want to play is "Damage, Inc." due to the multiple use of the infamous "F" word. Otherwise, there aren't any "Shits", "Fucks", "Pisses", "Sucks", "Cunts", "Motherfuckers", or "Cocksuckers" anywhere on this record.'

Formed in 1985 by the wives of several high-profile Christian fundamentalist Republicans, the Parents Music Resource Center (PMRC) was a high-profile pressure group responsible for these ubiquitous warning stickers. Their intent was 'to educate and inform parents' about 'the growing trend in music towards lyrics that are sexually explicit, excessively violent, or glorify the use of drugs and alcohol'. To this end they introduced the concept of the 'Parental Advisory' warning sticker, which would be placed on the front of any album that featured 'explicit' lyrics.

This could mean anything from profanity or blasphemy to references to sex or violence. It was promoted as being a musical equivalent of ratings for movies, and in order to appease the influential religious right and ensure that their product remained available in mass outlets, record labels played safe and began stickering anything remotely incendiary or ambiguous.

The PMRC's self-generated controversies failed to affect *Master Of Puppets* in any discernible fashion. Several vastly different publications have cited the disc as the 'greatest metal album of all time', from *Time* magazine to the *Metal Rules* website. The album would also quickly develop a reputation that extended far beyond any narrow genre definitions, and saw *Rolling Stone* include it at Number 167 of its '500 Greatest Albums Of All Time'.

Unlike modern-day Metallica – for whom the promotional machine kicks in with each new release, the internet spreads the musical message like wildfire and there are numerous videos to promote new material – in 1986 publicity outlets for a so-called thrash-metal opus were few. There were no promotional videos and the singles released from the LP received barely any airplay, and therefore had little chance of hitting the charts.

Metallica's obvious potential for mainstream popularity alerted the management behind Ozzy Osbourne and it was decided that the quartet would be the perfect support act for the ex-Black Sabbath singer on his 'Ultimate Sin' tour. This came at the height of Osbourne's debauched years and the singer was so blitzed on the tour he can no longer remember much of what happened. It was later claimed in the book *Metallica: The Frayed Ends Of Metal* that, 'Ozzy was said to have had a mean temper when loaded, and one night Lars got a hint of it. Drinking with Ozzy, Lars asked if for some reason Ozzy washed his hair after the show. Somehow, Ozzy was insulted by this. Briefly, Lars thought the bizarre incident might have them kicked off the tour.'

'I would walk past their bus before shows and hear them playing old Sabbath songs, and I thought they were making fun of me,' recalled Ozzy. 'And they wouldn't talk to me and always kept their distance, and I thought it was really weird. I asked their tour manager about it and said, "Is this their idea of a joke?" And he said, "No, they think you're gods."'

From Metallica's point of view, the tour was an opportunity to present their material to a wider rock and metal demographic. Essentially, they were still regarded as a thrash band, despite accusations from the sub-generic purists that they'd sold out. Given Metallica's rampaging live set, it was a brave move by the Ozzy camp to allow the band to assail his crowd ahead of him. To Ozzy's credit, he allowed Metallica full use of the stage and facilities at every venue. They were allowed to set up their complete stage set nightly, bringing the *Master Of Puppets* cover art to life for the crowds. Unlike some support bands, they were not sabotaged by the headliner or forced to play through a PA at half-volume. This was the big league and they were treated with respect, almost as if Ozzy and company had already accepted them as a major band. This was especially unusual given the musical climate of the time. There was generally an established divide between regular heavy metal, glam and thrash.

These three sub-genres all co-existed; yet more often than not they featured a separate fanbase. No self-respecting thrasher would admit listening to Poison, just as a Dokken fan would not usually express a fondness for Slayer. The Ozzy-Metallica spectacle was a huge step, not only for Metallica's career but also for the mainstream acceptance of thrash metal. Some would say it was even the point at which thrash lost its edge.

Of course, Metallica did not consider themselves a thrash band and never had. Certainly, they often played fast, lending credence to their representation of speed metal, but that was merely a preference, and one that was intermittent – unlike most thrashers. It is ironic that *Master Of Puppets* would be regarded as a thrash masterpiece when the very band that would be credited as defining an entire genre in 54 minutes openly expressed distaste for the style. Equally ironic was the fact that *Master Of Puppets* introduced the wider metal public to thrash – though they may not have appreciated the genre, they were evidently fans of Metallica.

However, the enjoyment derived from a successful tour with Ozzy would quickly be replaced by a feeling that it was almost too good to be true. Though the band were often out of their heads on booze, they still realised that they were privileged. 'What happened in 1986 was it was the first time we got out to Middle America,' Lars told MTV. 'The big reason it did get out there was Ozzy Osbourne. Metallica and Ozzy in arenas all across America, and especially Middle America. It was the first time that Metallica penetrated into those layers, the first time we showed up on the radar screens. I guess we know that this band is starting to get genuine success, because not only have we got two bottles of vodka per night on our dressing-room rider, but this isn't the cheap stuff we've been used to – rather it's Absolut!'

The Ozzy tour signalled the end of Metallica's association with the thrash underground. As if proof were needed, the mainstream metal tour showed the band had outgrown their Bay Area roots. 'The San Francisco people felt that Metallica had sold out way back when because we felt we helped make them what they were by being supportive,' asserts Leah Storkson. 'When they got big and supported Ozzy, they basically turned their backs and said, "See ya." But in reality they just wanted to get their music out there and they didn't care what anyone thought of them, they never have and they never will. They wanted to play with bigger bands, and get their name out there.'

Lamentably, Metallica's good fortune was about to change. Cliff Burton's earlier suggestion regarding the concept of *Master Of Puppets* seemed prophetic, as fate began to deal the band one blow after another. It was almost as if the album carried a curse.

Skateboarding had long been a means of relaxation for James. While the band were stationed in Evansville, Indiana, he came off his board, breaking his arm in the process. Skateboarding injuries can be particularly damaging and for Hetfield the injury was so severe that the singer required sedation and a night's stay in hospital. The band were forced to take to the stage that evening to announce they could not play the show. The crowd were less than understanding, booing and chanting 'Bullshit!' several times over.

Fred Cotton remembers that Metallica's management subsequently 'made James sign something that promised he wasn't going to skateboard anymore. I was with him the second time he did it. We were skating in an empty swimming pool up at Oakland Hills. It was the first time James had ever skated in a pool and he was just getting way ahead of himself. He had all the arm guards and shit on, but you know he's tall and lanky and he got a little too vertical, and as soon as he came down into the bottom of the pool you could hear a snap. It was me, him, [artist] Pushead, Kirk and someone else I can't remember. I drove James to Highland Hospital, which was just a shithole place, but it was the nearest hospital. We were well and truly in the ghetto. It sucked; I would rather die than go there!

'The nurse had this huge q-tip, ten-inches long, and it was a compound fracture so there was a cut on his forearm. She said, "I have to just make sure what this hole is from." And she took it and stuck it in his fucking arm and he's like, "Aaarrrgh, what the fuck are you doing?!" She let his arm go, but she's still holding it by his elbow so it just flapped over right in the middle of the forearm. It was pretty nasty; he almost kicked her in the face. They had him hooked up to an IV and I was clowning around calling him Intravenous De Milo!'

Concerned by the possible repercussions of cancelling the whole tour, Metallica (along with a still groggy Hetfield) hastily met with their management to decide on the best course of action. The group were warned that cancelling the tour would cripple them financially and potentially damage their relationship with fans. So Hetfield came up with a plan: he would handle vocal duties whilst a replacement guitarist would assume rhythm duties. Several high-profile names such as Anthrax's Scott Ian were considered, but preferring to keep matters in-house, the band decided on their friend John Marshall, who was the obvious choice, as he knew the parts to every song.

On the way to their next date in Nashville, Marshall played guitar along to the *Master Of Puppets* tape by way of a warm-up, but nothing could prepare him for the intense reaction of the Metallica crowd. Marshall would later join Seattle power metal crew Metal Church, but in 1986 he had zero experience of playing to a large, enthusiastic audience. A shy, gangly individual, John felt ill at ease performing in public despite his mastery of the guitar. The public realised there was an additional guitarist playing James' parts, but where was he? The answer was in a makeshift den next to the PA system, some distance away from the band. Many cynically presumed this was a stipulation made by Metallica and also the reason they picked an unseasoned performer. Such cynics suggested the band couldn't bear to share a stage with a 'new' member.

A few songs into their nightly set, Hetfield would introduce Marshall, explaining to the crowd who was playing rhythm guitar. The replacement six-stringer would walk out onto the stage, wave at the audience, and return to his hiding place. The chief reason Marshall ensconced himself in a safe spot side-stage was simply because he was too nervous to stand up front, feeling the scrutiny of thousands of pairs of eyes as he moved his fingers on the fretboard – and one thing he certainly did not want to do was make a mistake.

Unbeknownst to Marshall at the time, Lars Ulrich had some reservations about him taking over Hetfield's guitar duties, though the drummer had little choice but to accept the substitution. After a few gigs, Ulrich was satisfied the arrangement could work. Though not noticeable to the fans, the material did sound marginally different with a stand-in guitarist, and after so long playing together the core members were equally nervous about making changes or even how to end certain songs.

After five more gigs with the still uneasy Marshall, Metallica took a month off, fully expecting James's arm to heal in time for the European leg of their tour. Yet as the tour approached, his injury was still a problem and the band realised they'd have to bring in John Marshall once again to save their live performances. The guitarist was still unsure about full stage participation however, this time skulking behind one of the crosses in the *Master Of Puppets* set.

Eventually, after some persuasion from Cliff Burton in particular, Marshall found the courage to appear onstage alongside his sometime bandmates. 'I didn't move around too much 'cause I was really scared,' the reluctant stand-in admitted. 'I also felt kind of obligated not to do too much, since I was just there to play guitar.'

Despite the financial benefits of doubling his duties as both roadie and replacement rhythm guitarist, Marshall was eager to return to his main job after twelve more European dates. By now Marshall, a diabetic, realised his health was suffering and just a couple of months later he would leave the Metallica team altogether. Before that, however, he would witness the return of James Hetfield on guitar, at a show in Stockholm, Sweden on 26 September. 'They just fucking slaughtered,' Marshall enthused after watching the band return to full strength.

Sadly, where this date should have been memorable for featuring Hetfield's triumphant return to the guitar, it would become known as the last gig that Cliff Burton ever played.

After the Stockholm gig, the band set about drinking and playing cards, drawing from the pack to determine who would sleep where. Metallica's tour bus was then little more than a glorified van with makeshift beds bolted to the sides of the vehicle. Their curtains were actually pieces of cardboard taped across the fragile windows. Whilst drawing cards, Burton picked the ace of spades and decided he would swap bunks with Kirk, reasoning his was the best bed available.

Thus, by some strange quirk of fate, Kirk Hammett avoided death by a mere playing card – one that happens to have been mythologised as the 'death card' at that.

The band and assorted crew then retired to their bunks, with the long drive overnight to Copenhagen ahead of them. The trip was overseen by an English driver who'd been onboard for the entire European jaunt. It was early morning and the roads were frozen with black ice – not unusual for that part of the world during autumn – making for treacherous driving conditions. As the driver felt the bus swerve into the right-hand lane of the dual carriageway, he steered hard left in a vain attempt to correct the vehicle's trajectory. As he did so, the bus dragged on an unseen patch of ice and turned virtually full circle.

There were many injuries to both band and crew. Tour manager Bobby Schneider shattered two ribs, whilst Lars Ulrich broke his toe. Kirk Hammett sustained a black eye. Guitar tech Aidan Mullen and drum tech Flemming Larsen were both trapped under the crushed bus for three hours while firefighters worked to remove their battered bodies.

Everyone on the bus had been numbed by the crash and it took a while for all to recover their bearings. Kirk was the first to stumble clear, through an emergency exit. He was shocked and horrified by the sight of Cliff Burton lying lifeless under the right side of the vehicle. Cliff had been sleeping in one of the top bunks and as the bus began to topple he was thrown halfway through the window. As the bus slipped onto its side the young bassist was crushed by its full weight and killed instantly.

Gradually realisation dawned among the band and crew, standing in the freezing temperatures in nothing more than what they'd worn to bed. 'I remember Bobby Schneider lying next to me as they were taking our blood pressure and stuff, and saying, "Cliff's gone you know,"' recalls John Marshall. 'All of a sudden the reality of everything hit me. Right then I looked above at the ceiling and thanked whoever was up there that nobody else had been seriously hurt and that it hadn't turned out even worse than it was.'

As the driver, who had escaped unscathed, went to pull at the blanket still covering Cliff, both Hetfield and Hammett strained to stop him as a mark of respect. Worse was to come when the rescue services began to pull the bus into an upright position. Suddenly the winch holding the bus snapped and the vehicle once again fell onto Burton, eliciting howls of anguish from all who were watching. Hetfield trudged off into the distance, still in his underwear, in search of evidence of any black ice, oblivious to the sub-zero temperature.

Although he had somehow avoided physical injury, James felt the impact of Cliff's accidental death most profoundly. 'One thing I remember was when our tour manager Bobby Schneider was saying, "Okay. Let's get the band together and take them back to the hotel." I'm thinking, "The band? No way! There ain't no band. The band is not the band right now. It's just three guys."'

In the hotel room Hetfield released his anger and hurt the only way he knew how – by lashing out. Screaming at the top of his lungs, he smashed two hotel room windows. Everyone immediately hit the booze – despite the fact it was still early morning – in a desperate attempt to block out the pain and shock.

John Marshall would later relate that he and Kirk had been so shaken by the day's events that that night both slept with the light on in their hotel room. Such actions were the product of trauma, what would today be called post-traumatic stress, where the mind essentially draws in on itself and tries to find its way back to the safety of the womb or, at the very least, in comforts provided as a child.

Likewise James Hetfield, who had felt closest to Cliff, dealt with the loss in the way a mother might mourn for a lost child. He took to the streets of Copenhagen outside the hotel and in a drunken haze began screaming for his dead friend. Kirk later recalled, 'When I heard that I just broke into tears.'

Despite the fact the band self-medicated with alcohol as a coping mechanism, the incident was the beginning of a realisation that Metallica were not invulnerable. 'There was a sense of recklessness during the 1980s, we'd get up and start drinking at 2:00pm, be drunk all through the show, get offstage and drink until we passed out,' explained Kirk. 'That went on for months and months, both on tour and off tour. It was like nothing could harm us or tear us apart. The world was our playground and we were going to push everyone off the slide and swings and take them for ourselves.'

Cliff's death grounded the band in a reality they'd not experienced since adolescence. Suddenly, they felt their actions had consequences and their small, exclusive bubble had burst. It forced the band to grow up, and from that moment on, things would never be quite the same again. The trio would soon return to their homeland, devastated from the loss of a band member and – more importantly – a close friend.

Fan-club chief K.J. Doughton was inundated with flowers and condolence messages at his San Francisco base. 'I can't remember how the news first reached me. It seemed surreal. The permanency of his death was numbing. The band had dealt with problems before, but never like this. I recall their equipment truck being stolen in Boston, during a 1983 tour. Lars was devastated. But when Cliff died, it was like his world had stopped.'

Metallica's world did stop, albeit for a much shorter period than many would have expected. Most fans would have understood a longer hiatus or even if Metallica had never toured again. Rather sensibly, however, instead of just curtailing their travels, the band decided from then on they would travel by air whenever possible. The experience of that bitterly cold morning in 1986 continues to haunt them, to the extent that Lars now wears a Saint Christopher (the patron saint of travellers) pendant to bring him luck when the band is on the road.

Ironically, Cliff had never enjoyed travelling too much. Though he loved playing to a new crowd every night, the bassist was happiest in San Francisco. 'Cliff was a home person,' recalled Fred Cotton. 'He was always at home.' Indeed, it was Cliff who had persuaded Metallica to move to the Bay Area in the first place, so desperate was he to stay close to everything he held dear.

Though Metallica were not the household name they are today, and Burton was perhaps the least talkative member of the quartet, his death attracted widespread coverage. It was not only San Franciscan newspapers and TV stations that alerted the world to the death of the 'most headbanging bassist' in existence; the tragedy made commercial news around the world. The outpouring of sympathy encompassed a multitude of music genres and the kind of media factions that normally shunned heavy metal.

For once metal was in the news for something other than dangerous lyrics, satanic messages or vulgar cover art, and it was impossible to find anyone with a bad word to say about Cliff Burton. The overwhelming feeling, from the mainstream and underground alike, was that this was a true tragedy, where one of the good guys was gone. Such excessively friendly sentiments are normally expressed when someone passes on, by those unwilling to speak ill of the dead. Yet the same positive expressions were common *before* Cliff's death. He was simply a quietly spoken, easygoing guy who did nothing to invoke anyone's wrath.

There are many clues and insights into Cliff's personality from those who knew him well. 'He never acted like a big shot, one bit,' his father Ray remembered. 'In fact, he really disliked anybody with that attitude.'

'He never considered himself a star,' concurred Jan Burton. 'He said, "I'm just a good musician, but I'm not a star." He was a star, but he wouldn't recognise himself as that.'

Despite their lack of direct interest in heavy metal, Cliff's parents remained staunchly proud of their son's achievements, but even more so they were contented with the kind of person he became. 'There are no prouder parents in the world,' asserted Jan. 'Nowhere is anybody prouder of their son. His achievements definitely. But the kind of person he was along with it never changed, which I think we're even more proud of. He always used to say, "Thank you, mom and dad, for everything. Thank you for the support throughout the years." He never got bigheaded.'

'He had a pretty serious type of personality,' Fred Cotton remembers. 'He was honest and hated fakes. You never heard Cliff talk shit about anyone, but he spoke the truth to you if you liked it or not. He never worried about anything and he always seemed to have the answer if you had a problem. I was having a bad week once and Cliff told me, "Fred, it looks like you need to go do some fishing." I went fishing and it did help.'

Jim Martin, a close friend of James Hetfield and Cliff Burton, whom he also went to school with, remembers Cliff as 'pretty much an inspiration for me, he showed me that it could be done'. Martin went onto huge commercial success with his band Faith No More. 'Lots of people around me were telling me, "How many guys do you think are going to make a mark as a musician? Forget about it, just do it for fun. Get a trade going or something like that." He just went ahead and did it, you know? Despite the attitude most people have. So it was like, shit, I really guess it can be done.'

'I felt that he was an extraordinary young man, and the fact that he was my son made it all the more satisfying to me,' Ray explained. 'He set his goals and made the choices of how to obtain those goals, and he did it. He felt that with Metallica there was a possibility of success. He stated that, "Every once in a while we may fall on our face, but we insist on doing what we wanna do." "We" was not "I". It was always "we". He always took the other three fellows' points of view. I felt it was a very empathetic organisation. He certainly had some bad times, especially on that first tour when they went back east. But it didn't stop him even when everything was stolen except three guitars. He still stayed in there and persisted. I can only admire and love the kid, along with Kirk, James and Lars. They were a marvellous team. He was doing something he definitely enjoyed and got that fulfilment from his job. It's just too bad that his part of it was terminated.'

Just as the Metallica fan club received a deluge of condolence messages and gifts, many fans were considerate enough to address Cliff's parents directly and pass on their sadness, respect and ultimately, a positive slant on the tragedy. 'Many of the letters,' Ray relayed, 'have said that his memory will live on.'

Many memories of Cliff recounted his mellow yet rebellious nature. 'One time Cliff was staying at my house and I told him I just got rear-ended on the Bay Bridge,' recalled Kirk. 'The next day I couldn't turn my head, I had whiplash! It hurt to stand up straight, to walk, to talk, to laugh. I couldn't drive so I asked Cliff to drive me to the hospital and that drive was the most painful, excruciating ride I had at that point. Cliff drove like a madman, swerving all over the place, screaming Misfits songs at the top of his lungs, banging on his steering wheel that was broken in four places all with me howling in pain because I couldn't keep my neck still. At one point I said, "Can't you drive a little more carefully? My neck is killing me!" At that point he just looked at me and shouted, "Pussy!" After that I tried not to ride with him too much, only when I had to.'

'We were writing *Master Of Puppets* and driving around in his green Volkswagen to photo sessions,' remembered Lars. 'Cliff would just pound this Misfits stuff, drum on the dashboard, and make everybody fucking nuts. And Cliff wasn't the best driver to begin with.'

Dave Donato, who can be seen smoking pot with Cliff in the *Cliff 'Em All* video, remembers Cliff driving to Misfits tunes almost incessantly. 'I don't think I ever saw music move Cliff the way the Misfits did,' he says. 'When Cliff drove to the pier he would play the Misfits. He would headbang and drum on his steering wheel, to the point of breaking it. There were pieces of it to drive with – he had it all duct-taped together. Whenever he played his Misfits tapes he just went wild. Just like fucking yelling, screaming, spitting and headbanging. The Misfits were a great moment in his life. I think he enjoyed the Misfits more than anything else, period.'

Donato recalls that he, Cliff and Jim Martin were 'inseparable' from 1980 up until Cliff died. 'We were never bored,' he recalls, 'but we never really "did" things. We went to places and hung out. We laughed and laughed. I think the best way to describe our friendship was just that it was so spontaneous. It was like it was in a make-believe world. There was always something going on, but nothing planned. We fed off each other quite a bit.'

Indeed, Donato moonlighted as a drummer and, along with guitar contributions from Jim Martin, the trio formed a number of offshoot bands in downtime from their day jobs. One such band was known as Agents Of Misfortune. 'We got together some of those tapes that we made in the hills,' remembers Martin. 'We just took sections out of 'em and figured out how to play it. And we strung them together. They give you twelve minutes. So most people do three or four songs in twelve minutes, we just did one huge one. We were the only guys around for miles. We'd play this really weird shit and record it. Cliff's mom heard some of the tapes and she goes, "You guys sound like fucked-up weirdos!"'

During Metallica's European tour with Anthrax, whilst in London, Cliff Burton and Anthrax's Scott Ian were hanging out when they were arrested as drug kingpins. 'The police captain called us into his office and apologised,' Ian remembers. 'He said that in America we'd probably have been treated even worse. Cliff told him that in America the police don't stop you for having long hair and that most US cops can tell the difference between a cold pill and a Quaalude, and that they spend their time tracking down real lawbreakers like jaywalkers.' This type of anecdote sums up Cliff's straightforward, no-bullshit nature.

Yet there are few better memories to cherish than the three Metallica albums adorned by Cliff's bass prowess. He was the first heavy-metal bassist to address the instrument as a lead. Cliff could literally play anything on the bass guitar. He routinely produced licks and backing that many would have considered out of place in any other band. Sometimes even the Metallica members were wary of utilising such seemingly leftfield accompaniment, but ultimately they trusted the 'major rager on the four-string motherfucker' (as Dave Mustaine had dubbed Cliff).

The band enabled Cliff to express himself freely and it always complimented the overall sound in a unique and complimentary manner. Which other bass player incorporated harmonics, classical fills, heavy distortion and thick wah-wah effects?

'We never would have written guitar harmonies or instrumentals or songs with very intricate melodies and orchestrations without Cliff,' admitted James. 'We wouldn't be where we are today without him. We still talk about what Cliff would think and what he would have added.'

Cliff Burton was in a league of his own and this, along with the most admirable, charming traits of his personality, means legions of Metallica fans will always believe his memory lives on. In October of 1986 the remaining members of Metallica spoke with Jan and Ray Burton regarding the future of the band, if there even *was* a future. The verdict was unanimous: the band should not even think about quitting. More than anyone, Cliff would have expected them to continue. The sentiment was reinforced in some spiritual way at the funeral; Cliff's masterpiece 'Orion' bathed the close friends and family gathered together that day in the inextinguishable light of his talent.

Fred Cotton recalls that it was not only Cliff's parents who encouraged the band to continue. 'Jim Martin's brother Lou also made it a point to drive that home to them. Jim and Lou's family owned a ranch up in Maxwell. Cliff was cremated and everyone close to him – his family and closest friends – went up to Maxwell to spread his ashes. That day we did a memorial for him and planted a tree. Everybody took turns holding some of his ashes in their hands and saying a little something.'

Those closest to Cliff would deal with the funeral and the realisation of his death in their own unique way. 'At the end of the day, all the family and everyone left but me, James and Jim,' remembers Cotton. 'We stayed up there to get fucked up, we were all real drunk and we went out in Jim's 4x4 truck and I'm thinking, "This is fucking nuts," and I'm standing at the back of his truck beating on a plastic fucking barrel.

'We're four-wheel driving on these crazy roads just looking to shoot anything that moves,' he says. 'We shot a bunch of rabbits. I put 'em in the back of the truck and we got back to the cabin and put 'em on this totem pole. I decided I was going to do a ballistics test on all the different rifles so I hung the rabbit and I'd take each rabbit and shoot 'em point blank with each rifle and I can't remember which one it was I grabbed but I got this one gun and shot that motherfucker and this thing just exploded! I mean it shot guts all over me, all over Jim, all over the side of the cabin.'

Despite the fact that he could never play with the band again, James, Kirk and Lars felt that, if they continued, they would honour Cliff's spirit more fittingly than they would by simply retiring. As Kirk would later say, 'If we had hung it up, Cliff would've been so pissed off.'

Besides, 'Whiplash' was always there to remind them of their *raison d'être*: 'We'll never stop, we'll never quit 'cause we're Metallica.'

CHAPTER 10

SHELLSHOCK

'The spirit of this band has always been about fighting on,
against all the shit we've always run into. Cliff, more than anyone
else in the band, would have been the first guy to give us a kick in
the ass, and wouldn't want us to sit around.'
Lars Ulrich

The pain of Cliff Burton's loss was still affecting Metallica members on a personal level. James Hetfield took it hardest and would struggle for many years to deal with the fallout from the accident. Yet the harsh reality was that if the band were to continue, they needed a new bassist. The search for Cliff's replacement should have helped assuage their feelings of bitterness and pent-up frustration. Yet, from the outset, it seemed the band never truly wanted a new member permeating their tight unit. Hetfield, Ulrich and Hammett had belonged alongside Cliff Burton and the remaining trio had expected Metallica to always consist of this four. To enlist a new man felt awkward from the get-go.

Nevertheless, more pressing financial concerns took over, with Lars Ulrich doing his utmost to mask the pain of Cliff's passing and move the band on efficiently. Along with the Q-Prime management team, he entered into negotiations to acquire a new four-stringer. Recruiting a friend or some other reliable acquaintance would doubtless have been the band's first choice, minimising the upheaval and, equally, avoiding a stream of faceless auditions with strangers. Unfortunately, they would find it difficult to snap up a quick replacement and so the band would be subjected to the indignity of amateurish fans trying out.

Brian Slagel described the initial moves to find a replacement for Cliff Burton. He states: 'A few weeks after Cliff died Lars called me up and told me they needed a bass player. I told him the obvious choice was Joey Vera of Armored Saint. He was the first guy they called but he didn't want to do it. I had numerous conversations with Joey and he said that even though the offer was great, Armored Saint had a dream to fulfil. I think Metallica understood why. So Lars asked me to keep my eyes open for other bassists, and to send any noteworthy tapes to San Francisco.'

Bizarrely there were no other clear contenders for the role and the band had to put the word out that auditions were available. Overall, almost 60 hopefuls passed through the band's small studio. Sadly, there was little talent on show, as Fred Cotton remembers. 'I watched every bass player they auditioned, except for Jason!' Cotton laughs. 'I mean, some guys wouldn't even make it through half a song. I was in the sound booth hitting the record button 'cause they wanted to record every bass player. I would put down little notes next to their names. This one guy was definitely on something so I drew a little syringe to represent a junkie!'

Ultimately Metallica felt they, and specifically Cliff Burton, were not being paid enough respect. Yes, there was the opportunity to join a massive band and they could understand the applicants' excitement, but the lack of sober, professional musicians angered the band. 'It was hard for them, especially James,' Fred Cotton explains, 'they had Cliff's gear set up for the guy to come in and plug into.' Indeed, this was perhaps the hardest aspect of the audition process: glorified fans with little ability to their names were in Metallica's working environment playing their late bass player's equipment. The cruel nature of the search was beginning to dawn and the realisation was almost too much to bear.

As James would later say, 'Those auditions were weird – fans were coming up and auditioning. Some fans would just audition so they could say, "I auditioned for Metallica," and that shit got old real quick. There were people outside with recorders going, "Here I am, I've just auditioned with Metallica." Needless to say a few tape recorders and faces got smashed! Those people were just taking advantage. If they were real fans why would they want to waste our time?'

Only a few of the potential replacements were of the standard required for Metallica. Aside from Jason Newsted, who would eventually be offered the role, there were memorable moments from both Troy Gregory and Lääz Rockit's Willy Lange. Gregory was a word-of-mouth suggestion and would later join Flotsam And Jetsam (ironically replacing Newsted) before hooking up with industrial thrash merchants Prong. Gregory recounts: 'The audition had its sombre overtone because these cats just lost their pal. Well-known or obscure, it comes down to what sort of noise you are making with whoever you are in cahoots with that makes for a wonderful moment or a god-awful time. I did enjoy myself that day though. I got two free cans of cold soda pop out of them as well.' Gregory asserts that he did not audition as such; he was just in the right place at the right time. As he states, 'Understand that I did not have an audition. I drove there with a guy I knew at the time that had an audition set up. I just wanted to see San Francisco. I didn't even have a bass with me. I ended up talking to a guy at the studio there who suggested that I try out and lent me a bass. I was behind seven other bassists when a Metallica rep announced that they were only going to see one more person that day and that would be it.'

Gregory recalls the fateful moment he snagged himself some jamming time with the metal giants. 'I announced from the back of the line that, "If these fuckers don't audition me, they would be making a grave mistake!" The guy laughed – I think his name was Aiden – and told me to hold on a bit while I got dirty glares from the other guys waiting. He came back and told me to come in. I introduced myself to Lars and Kirk sitting on a couch; they told me to go plug in and they would join me soon.

James came in and helped me figure out the crazy amp set up. We played "Master Of Puppets" and "Welcome Home (Sanitarium)".'

Though Gregory was not used to Burton's control settings and golden-toned amp, he gave a good account of himself – not bad for someone who did not even know he was going to audition. Metallica seemed to appreciate the laidback nature of the Detroit native and, as he remembers, the band weren't finished with just the two songs.

'We talked for a bit and Lars gave me his number, since I did not have a phone,' Gregory explains. 'When I was leaving in the parking lot they ran out and asked me to come back in. I did and we ended up playing a bunch more of their tunes. I suggested "Trapped Under Ice", which we started until James forgot the chords. Kirk found this to be very funny. They were all very nice to me; I was nineteen but looked fourteen and at the time didn't drink. I spoke with Lars on the phone a few times and was going to fly back to San Francisco when Lars told me that they decided on someone. I was invited to their first show with him at the Country Club in Los Angeles. I would run into them every few years after that.'

Clearly, when they felt respected, Metallica returned the compliment. The second favourable audition had been with Lääz Rockit's Willy Lange. He was a founding member of the Californian metalheads, who stand as one of the earliest thrash acts. In the same year Metallica released *Ride The Lightning*, Lange and company unleashed their debut album *City's Gonna Burn* on Target Records. Along with the likes of New York's Overkill, Lääz Rockit were a good few years ahead of most smaller thrash bands, who were to release their debut albums post-*Master Of Puppets*.

At the time of Lange's audition with Metallica, Lääz Rockit had released two hi-octane thrash LPs, *City's Gonna Burn* and *No Stranger To Danger*. Lääz were in the process of recording their third album when Lange received a surprising phone call.

'I got a call from Metallica's road manager Bobby Schneider,' Lange says. 'I was still really bummed out because Cliff was a good friend; we had known each other since we were kids. He was and still is my favourite bassist. Besides, he was super cool. I decided to give it a shot just to plug into his Boogie set up and jam with the boys. I had no expectations other than to have fun. Testament's studio was right next door to Metallica's so [Testament bassist] Greg Christian and I warmed up together. I saw quite a few bassists I knew, but since I had known the band for a long time I really wasn't nervous. James and I used to hang out. The band as people were, and still are, really cool.'

Lange remembers the scorching temperature on the day, despite it being October. 'It was a super hot day so when it was my turn I went in and ripped my shirt off,' he says. 'We thrashed through "Master Of Puppets", "For Whom The Bell Tolls", "Damage, Inc." and "Ride The Lighting". It was fucking amazing. The boys dug the audition and shut it down for an hour and we sat and rapped.' Though Lange was characteristically calm and collected on the day, he dared to dream when he heard back promptly. 'The next day I got a call from Bobby and he told me to learn the whole set,' Lange remembers. 'He told me it was between me and another guy. That was the best week of my life up to that point. We had a lot of mutual friends and everyone was telling me the job was mine.'

However, Lange recalls a change in atmosphere the second time around. 'When it came time for me to audition again and I got to the studio, the vibe was a lot different,' he says. 'There were Flotsam And Jetsam stickers everywhere so I knew who the other guy was.' Unfortunately for Lange, by the time of his follow-up with Metallica the band had already decided their new member was going to be Flotsam And Jetsam's Jason Newsted. Lange was unaware of this at the time, however.

'We played the whole set then went out for dinner and a few drinks,' Lange remembers. 'James and I got trashed but Lars and Kirk were a bit quiet. The band had some shows in Japan in a week or so, so I knew they had to make the decision soon. I got the news a couple days later. I was really bummed. For years and years I would wake up from the same dream: I was *in* Metallica playing a show or hanging out and then I would wake up. Fuck, I was almost in the greatest band ever.' Lange recalls the time his nightmare finally ended. 'These dreams lasted years and years until Lars asked me and a friend to come to their HQ and listen to *St. Anger* in 2003,' he says. 'We hung out while Lars and Bob Rock did a little work then we went to a bar in San Rafael and closed it down. After that we went back to HQ and listened and talked. Lars then said something that made the nightmares go away for good. He said looking back that he wished they would have picked me.'

Once again, the recruiting of Jason Newsted was due to Metal Blade's Brian Slagel. Though his label was home to Flotsam And Jetsam and he had reservations about fragmenting the line-up, Slagel felt his old friends in Metallica deserved the best bassist he could find. He believed that man to be Jason Newsted. Based in Arizona, Newsted was surprised to receive a call from Lars Ulrich, the drummer in his favourite metal band.

'I was pleasantly surprised and decided that I couldn't let the opportunity of a lifetime pass me by,' Newsted later recanted. 'Cliff was a god: I didn't sleep for a week practicing.' Newsted would, in 2003, explain just how his burning ambition to join the band was sparked. 'When I found out Cliff had died I had this epiphany watching and just thinking and I was like, "I'm going to be the dude. I'm going to do it. If they're going to go on then I'm the man. I'm going to do it." And from that minute on I wasn't going to let anybody else get it.'

Like Willy Lange, Newsted had two auditions, both of them extremely promising. Apparently there was something more behind this kid's enthusiasm – and it wasn't just the severe expression fixed on his baby-faced features as he furiously banged his head. Newsted's performance was marked out by intense fervour and respect, giving the distinct impression that this meant more to him than any of the others who'd tried out before. And, indeed, it did mean more to him. Auditioning for his favourite band, in place of the bass player he most admired, Newsted's reverence was absolute.

On 6 March 1985, Newsted had attended a Metallica concert in Phoenix, Arizona. He later recalled the occasion with typical enthusiasm: 'Front row. Right in front of Cliff Burton, worshipping. Drooling. Banging madly. Fourteen bucks for a shirt, which was all the money in the world at that time. We only went to see Metallica. As soon as Metallica was done, we walked out. They just crushed it, and we knew everything they did by heart.'

With the second audition over, Newsted was ready to undergo the next phase of his initiation into the group and testing of a different kind. Lars recalled, 'We played all day and then went out for a meal. And then we went for the big test, which was obviously the drink test. Somehow, and I swear it wasn't planned, me and Kirk and James ended up in the toilet together, pissing. So we're standing there at three in the morning, out of our faces, all of us in a line and not saying anything, and I just said without looking at anybody, "That's him, right?" And the other guys said, "Yeah, that's him." And that was it!'

Jason Newsted carried a quirky, slightly eccentric air which no doubt endeared him to his new bandmates. He was also a leader; a strong character with the conviction and self-belief to make a name for little-known thrash act Flotsam And Jetsam – a group of nobodies he'd turned into serious contenders with the well-received debut album *Doomsday For The Deceiver*. Even today this is considered a cult thrash classic, not least because of its epic title track. Nevertheless, much like his new bandmates, Jason felt Flotsam And Jetsam were above the limitations of the strict genre. In a 1987 interview Newsted echoed Lars Ulrich's sentiments regarding thrash. 'We're more of a power metal band than a thrash metal band,' he commented. 'We do play fast, but we're more into the melodic side of things and our music is much more refined than thrash. With thrash you can't hear what's going on and it's just like, noise. With what we play – US power metal – you can hear the melodies and all the other subtleties. I thought the best description of us was "thrash with an IQ". Yeah, that's just how we feel.'

In an interesting similarity with Cliff Burton, Jason also revealed his love for classical music and broad musical palette. 'We do listen to a lot of thrash bands – I mean, I really like the Crumbsuckers – but that's not all we listen to,' he divulged. 'I like listening to classical music a lot, particularly Paganini and Bach, and I also like people like Stanley Jordan, Al Di Meola, Dixie Dregs and John McLaughlin – so I have a lot of influences coming in at me. I might listen to Bach one minute and Slayer the next.'

Newsted's early life was far removed from the glitz and glamour of the music business, however. He was born Jason Curtis Newsted on 4 March 1963 in Battle Creek, Michigan and grew up on a horse farm. Like James Hetfield, Jason was raised by strict Christian parents in a family-orientated environment. 'I was a farm boy,' Newsted later confirmed. 'My father and I raised Arabian stallions on our farm. I rode all the time, and I did the circuit horse shows, all that sort of crap. My parents were very hard workers. They always set a real good example, "go-gettedness". My dad would always say, "Take the incentive and don't sit around waiting for something to come around. You gotta get to it and take advantage."'

When he was fourteen Jason's family moved to the wonderfully named county of Kalamazoo and Newsted began attending Gull Lake High School in Richland. The move was something of a culture shock, but it was here his passion for music would blossom. As he later offered, Gull Lake was a 'different kind of high school with a lot of real rich kids. I started getting into trouble and I didn't like school anymore. I started listening to a lot of music and buying records. I had a couple of jobs making pizza and whatever and I'd save up and just buy records.'

Newsted's musical passion was further buoyed by the fact that his family now lived just five miles from Gibson Guitars' Michigan factory. Unsurprisingly, Newsted took advantage of living near to one of the world's most renowned guitar makers. 'I ended up getting a little Gibson amp and bass, because of Gene Simmons of Kiss,' he said. 'Myself and three other kids would pretend to be Kiss – I liked Gene the best.' Newsted was also heavily influenced by the revered Motown session musician James Jamerson, as well as Metallica's associate, Geddy Lee of Rush.

Jason eventually caught on to the NWOBHM and furthered his bass knowledge. 'My brothers were heavily into Motown but when they left for college I started finding other music. Heavier stuff like Motörhead and Tygers Of Pan Tang. I can remember getting very serious about the bass: I'd have it sitting in its case every night after I was done playing it. And I can remember dreaming about some day becoming a successful rock musician. I guess that's an experience a million people have had.'

As he improved on bass, Jason joined a local cover band called Gangster. Their guitarist Tim Hamlin passed on a wealth of new techniques to Newsted. Jason became more serious about music, quitting high school and moving into a house with his new bandmates. Gangster took a road trip and ended up in Arizona – a place Newsted would call home from then on.

Once established in this desert base, Newsted soon drifted away from his mentor Hamlin. At a local record store he saw an advert placed by drummer Kelly David-Smith, who was searching for musicians to jam with. The two soon decided to form a serious band together, with Newsted impressed by his new friend's percussive set-up. 'Kelly had this huge drum kit with cymbals and double bass. We'd jam away in his dad's den,' Newsted recalls.

Eventually the two would recruit several musicians to form DOGZ. By 1983, the band would be playing under a new name – Flotsam And Jetsam. Like Metallica, Flotsam got their first break on a *Metal Massacre* compilation. Their track 'I Live, You Die' appeared on *Metal Massacre VII* in 1986. Slagel was impressed by what he'd heard and signed the band to Metal Blade. Backed by the label, they released *Doomsday For The Deceiver* that same year.

Jason's ex-girlfriend Lauren Collins recalls the burgeoning of Flotsam And Jetsam. She remembers meeting Newsted for the first time. 'I saw Jason play in Flotsam at a river bottom party, and some clubs,' she says. 'I thought he was really cute. I remember the night we met very well. They were playing a show at a bar called the Bootlegger. I walked in and saw Jason onstage, and I think we made eye contact. I think he said something like, "There's some really good-looking girls in the audience," and looked right at me when he said it. I was flattered. After that set, he came over and said,

"Would you ever consider going on a date with me sometime?" Of course, I said, "Sure!" That's how we met.'

Lauren remembers finances being limited for the young couple, and Jason's attention focused mainly on the band. 'We mostly went to Flotsam shows,' Lauren says. 'We didn't go out a lot because back then money was tight and I was in college. He spent most of his free time writing or practicing, so time was limited, too. Sometimes we went to the Bootlegger and the Mason Jar because Jason got in free. We just hung out a lot at the Flotsam apartment on Camelback Road. We drank a lot. We used to get yelled at by Jason and Ed [guitarist Edward Carlson] to keep the noise down. It was funny!'

Lauren recalls Jason's strong work ethic and conscientious lifestyle, but despite his attempts to make it big with Flotsam And Jetsam, he still found time to be a gentleman. As she explains, 'He had a job picking up electrical waste at different construction sites when we were dating. I remember him waiting outside my house every weekday morning in that huge truck waiting to see me off to school. Every day he had at least one rose for me. It was and still is the sweetest thing anyone has ever done for me! I really miss his thoughtfulness. But I was only seventeen and not ready for a very serious relationship. I always wondered where he got those roses: I think he stole them from my neighbour's house!'

Newsted was a supremely dedicated musician and businessman, devoting every waking moment to his band. Like Lars Ulrich, he was one artist determined to make a living from his music. 'He spent nearly all of his free time doing promo stuff,' Lauren says. 'But he also worked really hard at the music. They practiced a lot back then, so his real free time was very limited.' However, Lauren is of the impression that Jason never actually believed he would make it. 'He worked so hard at it. I knew that he was special and my heart always said he would go far. I don't think he could fathom back then just what was going to happen and just how famous he would be,' she affirms.

Lauren, however, never stopped believing in her boyfriend. Although they split up shortly before Newsted's big break, she felt pleased for Jason nonetheless. 'I knew it! I knew he would make it big. I was very, very happy for him. I thought, "He has no worries now." And I believe I was a bit sad, because I knew I wouldn't see him much anymore.'

In a strange move, Troy Gregory took over from Jason in Flotsam And Jetsam. He explains: 'I think a few of the Flotsam folk had issues; the drummer [Kelly David-Smith] would always remind me that he wished Jason was still in the band. So I was like, "Okay then, get him back." It was a year or so after Jason joined Metallica that I ended up being offered the Flotsam job. Their history or previous band members were of no concern to me. In truth I accepted the job with Flotsam before even hearing them. They had a European tour already lined up and I wanted the travel. It is no secret that it wasn't really my thing. I had no idea what was in store for Flotsam; I knew that I would not want to stay very long in their group because I prefer doing my own music. I have been in over 30 bands since I was ten. Flotsam was a short but fun chapter in my life. That's it really.' Gregory spent just under four years in the band, but it was this period which diminished much of Newsted's hard-working legacy. Flotsam And Jetsam became forever synonymous with being the band that provided Metallica's new bass player, and little else.

Unsurprisingly the band were peeved at their leader's decision to change allegiance, but few among them could have questioned his motives. Though resolutely dedicated to Flotsam And Jetsam, the lure of Metallica proved too strong for Jason. 'Metallica was his favourite band,' Lauren remembers. 'I remember making out with him in his truck outside my dad's house and listening to Metallica! I can't listen to Metallica's first album anymore; it brings back too many memories. I believe he had a Metallica sticker in the back window of that truck too.'

Newsted recalled the upheaval after he announced his decision to quit Flotsam And Jetsam to his former bandmates. 'It was a pretty weird night,' he said. 'I handed everything over. I had piles laid out of all the fan-club stuff, the money and such, and I just handed it over. I went, "Here you go, man." They asked their questions about songs, copyrights and so on, and I gave them all the answers I could. I told them I hoped they understood what I was doing and to know that I would always be behind them. And I still am behind them, to this day.'

Five years after his arrival in Arizona, Jason Newsted played his final gig with Flotsam And Jetsam on Halloween 1986. Before their next album – 1988's *No Place For Disgrace* – Flotsam And Jetsam released an Elton John cover, 'Saturday Night's Alright For Fighting', upon which they were dropped by label Roadrunner. This led to three further lukewarm albums (showcasing a new, more progressive, less thrashy sound) for MCA before they were dropped once again due to poor sales. Thus the band returned to their roots and signed with Metal Blade, where they stayed for several years.

Jason Newsted's first show with Metallica was at the Country Club in Reseda, California on 8 November 1986. His second gig was the following night at Jezebel's in Anaheim. Unusually for Metallica at this stage, they were not only billed as a support band – tagging along with Metal Church – they were also besieged by technical problems. It was a baptism of fire for Jason Newsted, but he coped well, as Lars Ulrich later explained. 'On the second song of the set, "Master Of Puppets", the power went out three times,' Lars said. 'The only thing that didn't go out was the bass amp, so I just continued playing drums acoustically along with Jason. All the kids were singing. It was brilliant.'

Jason Newsted had been selected for the job of a lifetime and was warmly embraced by Metallica fans worldwide. He had been at the helm of a straight thrash band with a strong reputation in the metal underground, and thus his addition to the Metallica line-up revived the band's credibility with speed-metal fans everywhere. There was certainly no animosity from fans, no reservation that 'their' band now featured a different bassist from the hallowed Cliff Burton. Metallica, however, dealt with their new bandmate very differently.

CHAPTER 11
NEW KID ON THE CHOPPING BLOCK

'Jason's a little gullible at times, which makes it kinda fun.'
Lars Ulrich

'There was some misguided frustration over Cliff's death. He's taken from you and another person is put in his shoes, playing out of his amp 25 days later. What the fuck? It was my dream come true, man.' These are the words of Jason Newsted, reflecting on the disturbing treatment he received as the newest member of the Metallica clan. To begin with, the tricks played on Jason may have seemed light-hearted enough. But, though it started as harmless fun, the motives for plucking at the new guy's feathers were deep rooted. Of course, the surviving band members were still grieving for the friend they'd lost.

Though Cliff's name will always be intertwined with Metallica's rich legacy, the simple fact remains that the band's subsequent treatment of his replacement had nothing to do with musical direction. It was not related to Jason's musical prowess, which has always been exemplary; neither was his attitude – one of marked professionalism and reliability – at fault. And regardless of a dearth of writing credits for Newsted on their next album (*...And Justice For All*), Metallica were appreciative of Jason's writing style and ideas. He was easy to talk to and laidback, perhaps *too* laidback. For, with each effort to ingratiate himself to his new group, Newsted became an easy target for all their pranks.

James joked, 'We've told everybody that Jason is gay, and the first thing anyone says to him is, "Is it true?"' Lars then revealed that, 'In order to ease Jason into the band we charged everything to his room. He just treated everyone to a nice night out.' Lars was also amused upon their arrival in Japan for a series of tour dates: 'In Tokyo all these kids gave us gifts. Jason didn't get any though – they thought he was part of the road crew. So he had a temper tantrum. Poor guy. Maybe we should have got him a T-shirt with the statement: "I'm Jason, dammit, gimme a gift!"'

Public humiliation turned out to be only the beginning, however. Later on in the schedule, comprising five sold-out shows, the band took time out to visit a local sushi bar. It was on this occasion that they convinced an unsuspecting Jason to eat a sizeable ball of wasabi paste, the ultra-hot and spicy accompaniment. Numerous other pranks were played and often referred to as 'hazing', despite the fact that these so-called initiation rites continued well into Newsted's Metallica tenure. 'In Japan, after I had been in probably two weeks at that point, we went to have sushi,' Jason said of the infamous wasabi incident. 'It was my first time having sushi. And they're all talking about it. And the first time I probably ever had sake too. And the big beers and everything are just flowing. They all somehow collectively convince me that the green stuff, the wasabi, is mint ice-cream. "You should have a big spoonful, man," they said, "because it's really good for in between the meals and stuff." And I took a spoonful of wasabi and that was the beginning of the night.'

Kirk Hammett would later recall a night of typically childish antics at Newsted's expense. The guitarist explained, 'We had been drinking until four in the morning, then went to visit Jason. We called the doorman and said, "Hey man, our friend's in there choking on his puke! We have to get in there!" We kicked the door in, turned the bed over on Jason, sprayed shaving cream everywhere, threw his money all over and took his ghetto blaster. He didn't say anything. It was really funny.'

Newsted was understandably reluctant to rock the boat with his newfound bandmates. This, after all, was the gig of his dreams. Though he certainly didn't enjoy being the butt of every infantile prank, he believed it would not continue for long and simply endured the initial jibes. He later reasoned, 'They did the bullying to see if I could handle it. If you're going to fill the shoes of Cliff Burton you have to be resilient.' Almost instantly the press coined the term 'Newkid' for Jason, and he lived with this tag for many years. It was not until the turn of the 1990s that Newsted would finally feel fully integrated into the band's line-up. By this time he had attained something close to equal standing with more established members of Metallica. Yet in truth, throughout his tenure with the band, Newsted would experience an infuriating array of hypocritical snipes – the full extent of which will be revealed as we delve into the remainder of Metallica's story.

Despite – or maybe even thanks to – their replacement bassist and his thrash credentials, Metallica were enjoying a continuing surge in popularity. Continually playing in support of *Master Of Puppets*, the death of Cliff Burton had brought their name to the lips and hearts of many hitherto unconverted metal fans. All over the world, their music was reaching ever-growing audiences of Metallica devotees, as the Japanese tour confirmed. Lars Ulrich explained: 'The tour in Japan had different vibes than elsewhere because you don't use buses on the road. Instead, after every gig you stay at a hotel and then travel during the day on a bullet train. Also, there are no support acts – ever. You take the stage cold, which is weird, and the shows start early. You get onstage by 6:00, and are done by 7:30. In addition to all this, most of the kids in the audience are female. All these twelve-year-old girls follow you around like you're in Bon Jovi or something.'

Soon after Metallica were back on home soil, with a string of sold-out dates scheduled in the States and Canada. This time round, Metal Church would be playing in support. These shows were important stepping stones for Metallica on the path to mainstream success, but will remain memorable to one musician for an altogether more unfortunate reason. As Metal Church's then bassist Duke Erickson recounts, 'A lot of places we played in Canada were hockey rinks. Sometimes the ice behind the stage would be left open. We'd borrow skates and skate around. I remember playing hockey once and Lars was skating toward me with a hockey stick in his hand. He didn't know how to stop and ended up nailing me in the face.'

Injury was also to afflict James Hetfield, when the Metallica frontman broke his arm for the second time. The band were due to perform on *Saturday Night Live* soon after, but had to cancel at the last minute. Metallica's semi-official illustrator (through the mid- to late eighties), Pushead, was with Hetfield when the fracture occurred. In 2002 he revealed, 'James was really excited and asked me a lot of questions. I showed him some lines, and soon he was ripping it up. Then it happened. James somehow lost his balance coming down off the transition into the flat around the drain and fell backward. His wrist snapped and the bone was protruding out from his wrist brace. That basically ended James's skating career, since it affected his main career.'

With James effectively out of action, the band decided to convert Lars's two-car garage into a much-needed rehearsal space. Lars's new house was just across the street from the boys' old El Cerrito pad. 'I had a pretty big garage,' Lars reasoned. 'And, after all, the first three albums were written in a garage. Let's face it, in attitude, anyway, what more are we than a garage band?'

Jason had already completed a similar project back in Phoenix while he was still with Flotsam And Jetsam (a throwback to his days in construction), and so Lars immediately enlisted Newkid's services, allowing the bassist to take charge of the conversion. Displaying immense enthusiasm, Jason was often up and working on the garage before Lars even opened his eyes. At ten o'clock every morning Newsted was to be found with a team of buddies, putting the band's $4,000 budget to excellent use, tirelessly hammering and building. 'We couldn't really write shit without James so we ended up talking about things. We thought we might as well try and move back into a garage, so we found a suitable place back home and soundproofed it properly and everything,' Lars said. 'I came down to help out every day when I woke up; about 2:00pm James would come over and do whatever he could with his arm being broken, and Kirk was out doing his toy shopping!'

Indeed, Kirk was something of a toy aficionado, amassing a huge collection of comic books and a vast array of plastic toys. In an interview in 1986, Hammett explained how his newfound wealth had enabled him to invest in long-coveted items. 'Now I get to buy the comics I've been wanting since I was a little kid,' he said. 'I can pay more attention now to my hobbies. When I was younger I played with toys and they were a lot of fun. But why should anyone say that should end because you're older? There's absolutely no reason why that should end. I mean, it might appear to be an immature kind of thing to do, but if you think about it, what's so immature about wanting to have fun?'

To soundproof the garage walls, Newsted brought in rolls of disused carpet from his old apartment, though these had an unfortunate side effect, as he later told David Fricke. 'At first, you didn't notice it. But once the carpet was in the room, the stench hit you,' a horrified Newsted recalled. 'Huge spill spots, beer stains that used to be on people's floors. I tried to create a little air-conditioning system in there; it never really worked. But we spent a lot of time in that garage rehearsing those EP songs for a month before going into the studio to cut them.'

Once the conversion was complete the band had only a few weeks to wait before James was ready to play again. By this stage they were eager to recommence jamming and began hammering through a variety of cover songs. As the three Metallica mainstays jammed, Jason Newsted manned the controls, duly recording everything they came up with. Eventually the band were nailing some of their most obscure metal favourites, covering the obligatory Diamond Head and even pulling some Holocaust and Budgie numbers out of the hat. Though not so familiar with the material as Ulrich and company, Jason was soon jamming along regardless, leaving the tape set permanently on record. Before long inspiration struck and the band found they'd hit upon the perfect idea.

'It had nothing to do with albums or anything,' Lars said of their extended jamming sessions. 'We were really happy with the garage, it was a stylin' place and we started to jam and play covers again, just to break things in. That was when we decided that it might be fun to record and release the whole lot as an EP.'

Altogether the band refined five coherent songs from Newsted's recordings and the result was a mixed bag to say the least. In part-homage to Cliff Burton they recorded and segued together the two classic Misfits tracks, 'Last Caress' and 'Green Hell'. Tribute was also paid to Diamond Head – naturally enough – with one of Ulrich's longstanding favourites, 'Helpless', and two other NWOBHM cuts, Budgie's 'Crash Course In Brain Surgery' and 'The Small Hours', originally penned by Holocaust. Killing Joke's 'The Wait' seems a particularly bizarre inclusion, twisted by Metallica into an infinitely heavier, creepier affair. In the end, this peculiar track did not feature on every version of the final EP (in the UK the song was left off in keeping with British restrictions as to the length of an EP).

'The Wait' emerged from the band's intense desire to record underground anthems of the NWOBHM, despite the fact that some covers never quite fell into place. Previous attempts included Paralex's 'White Lightning', Gaskin's 'I'm No Fool' and even a version of 'Signal Thunder' by the Japanese group Bow Wow. While concentrating his efforts on the Paralex tune, Kirk Hammett found himself struggling with a guitar break in the song. So, he reverted to the eerie riff from 'The Wait', a song the band knew well. As the other members joined in with the riffage, it became clear that this was another track to be put down on tape.

'We went out of our way to make sure we had a bunch of weird shit to work on,' Lars later admitted. 'We've taken some strange things that these other bands did and given them the full Metallica treatment! We've thought about doing something like this for a long time, but we've never really had the opportunity before. This is still a fucking Metallica record; we just weren't responsible for writing the songs.'

Pushed by *So What!* (the Metallica Fan Club magazine) to provide some explanation for these 'surprising' choices, Lars remained defiant. 'Isn't that the whole integrity of this fucking band, to do different shit?' he countered. 'We've always tried to avoid following what everyone else is doing. It's a challenge to come up with things that are original. It's not easy, but that's part of the fun.'

The 25-minute collection was given the title of *Garage Days Re-Revisited*, though it is often called *The $5.98 EP: Garage Days Re-Revisited*. Metallica were adamant that no record store should be allowed to charge more than $5.98 for their new release, even if this meant plastering the intended price across the front cover. Once a CD version of the EP was released, the title was changed to *The $9.98 EP: Garage Days Re-Revisited*.

The EP's artwork also adds a special something to the release, introducing a raw, authentic punk-rock vibe. Featuring crass handwritten notes by James and deliberate misspellings of band members' names (James became 'Jaymz', Jason was 'Jasun', etc), along with a multitude of goofy photos, this was a rare piece of unbridled Metallica tomfoolery.

The songs came together effortlessly, providing a perfect introduction for Jason Newsted, who was referred to as 'Newkid' once more in the liner notes. Lars told *Metal Hammer*, 'We've taken a whole bunch of strange shit recorded by some other bands and breathed death into them! We went into the studio four days ago, laid down the tracks and now we've got a couple of days to mix the thing. I mean, we didn't fuck around here! Straight in, bang, bang, bang and out again, no shit!'

For once Lars was not exaggerating; indeed, Kirk Hammett recorded his guitar parts for the EP in just three hours. The recording process may have been somewhat relaxed and, in essence, an extended practice session, but the sheer weight of the cover versions blew most listeners away. Inspired by relatively weak and tinny-sounding originals, few would have believed this lacklustre material could be injected with such violent, vibrant energy.

Standout cuts include the roaring 'Crash Course In Brain Surgery' – complete with crushing bass introduction – with the vamped-up punk adage of 'Last Caress' and the less instant, but supremely fast, 'Green Hell'. Though original Misfits frontman Glenn Danzig would go on to produce a series of stunning albums under the Danzig moniker, the Misfits' early material was well written yet terribly produced. Hetfield and his associates dragged these early eighties classics screaming into the modern era of studio production with a clean, confrontational new sound – adrenaline-fuelled and clear enough to hear every last word. With 'Last Caress' the effect was particularly powerful, since the lyrics penned by Danzig are hardly sensitive.

The song opens with an immediately controversial statement: 'I got something to say/ I killed your baby today.' The words only become more provocative, with Hetfield barking: 'I raped your mother today/ And it doesn't matter much to me/ As long as she spread.'

James would later say, 'There was a huge comic element to the Misfits. They got their whole being from comic books and monster mags. But I loved their amazing, almost poppy hooks. They were smashing guitars and singing about some horrible stuff – in these pop songs.' Hetfield also acknowledged Misfits frontman Glenn Danzig as a tremendous source of inspiration. 'Glenn was singing some cool shit,' James later said with genuine admiration. 'He was a major influence when I was trying to become a real singer, getting that yelling/singing sound down. Most of the other punk bands – there were no notes. The Misfits had notes.'

Despite its questionable sentiment, 'Last Caress' is laden with instantly infectious hooks, revealing Metallica's reckless thirst for rebellion. Besides, it was easier for them to get away with such controversial lyrics when they weren't their own. Slipping into a breakneck rendition of 'Green Hell', the track ends with a short tribute to Iron Maiden, in the form of a few tuneless bars of 'Run To The Hills'. 'Lars had learned this drum bit,' Hetfield later recalled. 'He kept playing it over and over, and we just kind of goofed on it at the end of the track. It was nothing against Maiden. It was just a way to take the piss out of metal and, in a way, to take the piss out of ourselves.' When Maiden recorded Montrose's 'Space Station No. 5', frontman Bruce Dickinson quipped, 'Here comes Metallica in the rear-view mirror,' by way of response.

The EP was a glorious initiation for Jason Newsted, who relished every minute of the recording process. 'It was a fucking blast, man,' he said. 'You walked into the room, set up your amp the way you would live, put a microphone in front of it and played the song. We recorded it there and then, mistakes and all.'

Charting Newsted's integration into the line-up, the tone of the album was fun rather than formal. But given its innovation, many of Metallica's fans latched onto the EP and eventually it would sell a million copies in the United States alone. It may have comprised other bands' material, but the concept behind the EP was an entirely original one – something no other metal band had done before. Fan club chief K.J. Doughton would later remark, 'The *Garage Days Re-Revisited* EP was an unusual idea. After that record came out, every band decided to release an "all-covers" EP.'

Many bands may have copied the idea, but few could mimic Metallica's trademark cover treatment. Regardless of the song, Metallica brought maximum intensity and raw energy to each cover track, providing an electrifying new rendition of the original in every instance. This is a habit they have continued throughout their career, amassing a collection of increasingly diverse cover material.

As the day of the EP's release drew nearer, Lars underlined the irony of the band joining a major label while preparing to unleash their most subversive material yet. 'I think it's great that this will be our first release under our new European deal with Phonogram Records,' he explained. 'And just in case people are dumb enough to think that landing a deal with a major label means we're about to change our ways and play things safe, we've decided to do the most off-the-wall thing we could, which is this EP.'

In celebration of their new line-up and return to live gigging after James's accident, Metallica once again accepted the offer of a place on the Monsters Of Rock tour. The first stop was London, where, two days before the Castle Donington-based festival, the band played a secret show at Oxford Street's 100 Club. Billed as Damage, Inc., few fans failed to realise that this was Metallica, and the 250-capacity venue was besieged by a few thousand eager punters, most of whom managed to squeeze in on the night. The set was light-hearted and decidedly informal, with the atmosphere of an extended practice session and a somewhat sloppy Metallica still struggling to adjust to Newsted's place in the live unit. Jason himself was feeling the intense heat of the club, nearly fainting from the stifling temperature at one stage of the performance.

He did not fare much better when it came to Metallica's heralded appearance at Castle Donington. They featured on a mixed bill alongside heavy-metal legends Dio, glam-rock darlings Cinderella, soft-rockers Bon Jovi, old rivals W.A.S.P. and fellow thrashers Anthrax. Metallica played a varied set, revisiting old tracks they later regretted with a few choice cover versions thrown in. They also displayed their penchant for the grandiose, opening with a rendition of Ennio Morricone's 'The Ecstasy Of Gold' (taken from the film *The Good, The Bad And The Ugly*) for the first time. However, even this failed to lift their damp set. As *Kerrang!* later observed, 'Metallica were the band everyone was waiting for. But they seemed under-rehearsed. There were times when they seemed on the verge of collapse.'

Speculation was rife, with members of the music press considering a range of reasons for Metallica's poor performance, from the still-green Newsted to the suggestion the band had not yet recovered from the death of Cliff Burton. *Kerrang!* even mused that the presence of Bon Jovi's private helicopters, circling overheard throughout Metallica's set, may have been a distraction.

Lars Ulrich later admitted, 'It was a transitional period, what with the whole Cliff thing. I remember Jason wearing some really goofy pants. He looked silly. We played "Phantom Lord" and "Leper Messiah", which we hadn't played in ages. I remember looking over at Iron Maiden's Steve Harris on the side of the stage. He winced. I realised we shouldn't have played those songs.'

Metallica were not helped by the terrible quality of the sound, blown around on the windy August day as easily as an empty crisp packet. The band endured a barrage of piss-filled bottles and were happy when it was all over. The experience didn't prevent them from appearing at other European dates on the Monsters Of Rock tour, however. This transitory period was essential for Jason Newsted and, as the band played on, he began to feel more comfortable. For this leg, Metallica were joined by the hard-rock quartet of Kingdom Come, Dokken, Scorpions and Van Halen. During this period, *Master Of Puppets* hit platinum. Van Halen frontman Sammy Hagar commented that Metallica were going to be 'the new kings of rock, just you wait and see'.

Despite winning obvious admiration from the headliners, Metallica still felt they were the odd band out, for obvious reasons. Kirk Hammett explained this perception, saying, 'We're the underdogs. We haven't had a Top Ten hit, and we look like a bunch of bums out there. Amidst all this glam and this huge production, we're going to stick out. But that's what we're here for – and that's what put us here in the first place.'

It was surprising Metallica could perform such a professional set, given their propensity for alcohol-fuelled antics at this time. The heavy drinking habits of the band's Cliff Burton era did not change one iota once Burton was succeeded by Jason Newsted. If anything, Metallica were drinking more than ever. James later said, 'They were the Jägermeister days. I am still hearing stories about it, like that I slugged Lars, but I don't remember any of it. We were drunk the whole time. We were very much into drinking and having a good fucking time. That was the pinnacle of all the debauchery, drinking, fucking and general insanity.'

Lars Ulrich later intimated that regular stadium gigs were affecting their nerves and drinking was the antidote. 'Basically, at that time, we used to start drinking when we woke up,' he explained. 'We'd get the gig over by three o'clock, and then we'd have eight or nine hours to drink. It was awesome. That was our first exposure to big crowds, like, 50,000 people every day. We were just drunk basically all the time. There are pictures of us at the top of Tampa Stadium with our pants off, flashing everybody. It's four o'clock in the afternoon and we're already drunk off our asses. The not-giving-a-fuck metre was peaking.'

Despite this haphazard approach to live performances, their sets were becoming stronger. For a so-called thrash-metal band, to be appeasing crowds who were in attendance to see soft-rock acts was some achievement.

With the dates completed Metallica were ready to return home to San Francisco and begin work on material that would comprise their fourth studio album. Before this, however, at the end of 1987, they released a video tribute to Cliff Burton. Entitled *Cliff 'Em All*, the hour-and-a-half-long compilation drew upon a fan-friendly collection of bootleg material as well as clips and snippets of the man himself. 'It's really a look back at the three and a half years that Cliff was with us,' the official Metallica promotional material read, 'and includes his best bass solos and the home footage and pix that we feel best capture his unique personality and style. The quality in some places ain't that happening, but the feeling is.'

There were numerous handheld performances, such as a spirited version of 'Master Of Puppets' played by the band at Long Island in support of Ozzy Osbourne. At times the camera focuses entirely on Cliff, capturing some impressive moments including Burton's second gig with the band. This occasion finds him tearing through a performance of '(Anesthesia) Pulling Teeth' before the rest of the band join in, segueing into a riotous 'Whiplash'. The material generally displays the innocence of a band of young, spotty kids, with little consideration for anything other than getting smashed and having a good time. Showcasing performances that were raw verging on feral, the video manages to capture the development of the band after Cliff's first year, as demonstrated by faultless renditions of 'Fade To Black' and 'For Whom The Bell Tolls'.

Lars would later admit that *Cliff 'Em All* was 'real primitive' in parts, but described how this was entirely intentional. 'It's something that the whole band felt was cool,' he continued. 'Because the way a typical kid in the audience sees a show is similar to these one-camera bootlegs, zooming in on whoever in the band he wants to, then fucking banging a little bit so the thing's a little bit out of focus. And when some fucking drunk guy next to him falls into him, for five seconds you see a bit of the ceiling or a bit of the chair he's sitting on. That kind of thing makes for a really cool vibe. It's hella-Metallica.'

Cliff 'Em All marked the end of an era and remains a popular element of Metallica's back catalogue today. It signalled the closing of one stage of the band's career. Now they were ready for rebirth.

CHAPTER 12
BITTERSWEET SYMPHONY

*'We're no different from our fans. We see the world like other people.
We don't live in mansions, and we're not hiding behind fences and making
our own pretentious fantasy world with chicks and mountains of drugs.
We live in the real world, and the real world's an ugly place.'*

Lars Ulrich

Throughout their career to date, Metallica had been known as a band who liked to up the ante, breaking every convention and generally creating a shit-storm of controversy wherever they could. With subversive leanings which were virtually pre-programmed, this state of affairs seemed natural for the band. Even if they'd desired it any other way, it could never have been avoided. Metallica did not set out to create a contentious, technical mesh of hi-octane metal with ...*And Justice For All*, but this was the outcome. Once again, contradictions loom large over the band's story.

Metallica did not intend to devote months to the recording of their album, especially since they'd written the songs for ...*And Justice For All* in just eight weeks. Yet, despite their experience recording *Master Of Puppets*, they couldn't avoid the lengthy studio process this time around. They did, however, learn from the miserable experience of recording *Ride The Lightning* and *Master Of Puppets* in Europe. For their fourth album, Metallica opted to record in Los Angeles. Once again they hired Flemming Rasmussen to produce and engineer the album, flying him over from his Copenhagen base in February 1988 to stay until May that same year.

Rasmussen would later describe the project as 'hard and a long, tough haul. I came in on the session after a month, and they had nothing on tape when I got there. So there was a lot of work to do and I had to be back in Denmark after four months. They wanted a dry, upfront sound and we put a lot of work into getting the sounds. In the end that album has probably influenced all metal albums since, with the sharp clicking bass drum especially.'

Yet the band never intended to record with Rasmussen: ...*And Justice For All*, as it would soon be titled, would be the Dane's last album with the band. In fact, Mike Clink was the engineer they initially hired for the project. Having struck big as the producer of Guns N' Roses' 1987 debut, *Appetite For Destruction*, Clink's services were very much in demand. At Metallica's request, he took the helm for two more cover recordings: Diamond Head's 'The Prince' and Budgie's 'Breadfan', both destined for use as future B-sides. Once the job was complete, Clink went to work on two Metallica originals. The first tracks they attempted to record were 'Harvester Of Sorrow' and 'The Shortest Straw'. But once Clink had laid down drum tracks for these two titles, the band decided the collaboration wasn't working and called up Rasmussen. As James explained, 'We started that album with Mike Clink as producer. He didn't work out so well, so we got Flemming to come over and save our asses.'

Sessions were scheduled at One On One Studios, which James remembers as being 'really great. It wasn't one of those warehouse-y places where all of a sudden Frank from Death Killers opens the door and says, "Sounds good, dude!" We needed to have a big control room so everyone could be in there and feel comfortable listening. Most of the stuff we did was in the control room. We'd record guitars and eventually vocals in there. Getting away from home was almost a necessity for us. We had to get away from the distractions – the buddies, the parties, the phone calls. But as soon as you get to a new town, there's new bars, new friends, new hangs – especially in LA! It got a little crazy there for a little while.'

...And Justice For All begins with a fade-in stream of high-end guitar, but opener 'Blackened' takes a mere 40 seconds before launching into a scathing thrash attack. The impact of Lars's drumming is instant, sounding loud, upfront and punchy, with a distinctly audible bass drum click. This would be the scourge of the album for many. The song soon settles into a groove before launching back into the main riff, followed by a titanic, catchy chorus. This was the sound of a band who had found their musical niche, showcasing a distinctive style which was all Metallica's own – instantly recognisable, but never predictable. Despite the questionable percussive element, there is no disputing the infinitely listenable quality of the backing; feet cannot avoid tapping along. Keeping time in a live environment has proved difficult for Lars Ulrich – especially at the dawn of the 1990s – and his drumming style has oft been criticised. On ...And Justice For All however, each track is buoyed by his effortless timing – nowhere more pronounced than on 'Blackened', a track riddled with off-kilter time signatures.

Metallica also started a trend with the song's original lyrical content, creating a barrage of copycats in turn. Dealing with the environment was a unique choice for a metal band in 1988 and, of course, Metallica were the first prominent act to address this burning issue.

'Death of Mother Earth [...] Blistering of earth/ Terminate its worth,' Hetfield barks, referring to the topical subject of the hole in the ozone layer over Antarctica.

Thrashers followed his example in their droves and ozone depletion became the 'in' subject as the 1990s dawned. Nuclear Assault wrote 'Critical Mass', Annihilator penned 'Stonewall', Sacred Reich produced a number of environmental tracks – including 'Crimes Against Humanity' – while Testament famously released 'Greenhouse Effect'. All of these efforts were derived from a single Metallica song.

As usual, Metallica were not about to pontificate on this issue: it was simply a topic which sparked their interest. 'It's just about all the shit that's going on in the world right now,' Lars said, 'and how the whole environment that we're living in is slowly deteriorating into a shithole. This is not meant to be a huge environmental statement or anything like that: it's just a harsh look at what's going on around us.'

The title track was one of the longest Metallica had yet penned, and an ambitious trawl through several complex ideas and structures, most notably the main riff, which is set to another off-kilter rhythm, courtesy of Lars's pliable drumming. As the man himself commented, '"…And Justice For All" is a little different for us in that the main riff is centred around this weird drum beat that I came up with in rehearsal one day. It's not even a straightforward kind of beat, it's more like a sideways type of thing with a lot of tom-action and stuff, but it sounded cool so we used it.'

'…And Justice For All' certainly marks this album out as a darkly pessimistic endeavour, far bleaker than any of the band's previous efforts. But this is perhaps understandable, given the fact it was the first new material written since Cliff Burton's death.

The inspiration for the title of the song, and the album, was the 1979 film of the same name, directed by Norman Jewison and starring Al Pacino. The subject matter of the film is closely linked to the lyrics, as Lars would describe. 'It's about the court systems in the US, where it seems like no one is even concerned with finding out the truth anymore,' he said. 'It's becoming more and more like one-lawyer-versus-another-type situation, where the best lawyer can alter justice in any way he wants.'

Yet, behind the lyrics of the song – and perhaps the album as a whole – lies another potential implication, dealing with personal freedoms being taken away on many different levels.

This theme is developed further with the oddly-chosen single 'Eye Of The Beholder'. Indeed, it seems unlikely that this track, the band's own seditious stab at the sanitised mainstream music industry, was selected for any of its musical merits. The stop-start assault of guitar riffs is particularly vicious, almost military, yet Hetfield breaks into a cleaner voice for the chorus, brilliantly underscoring the song's message: 'Independence limited/ Freedom of choice/ Choice is made for you my friend.'

This referred to the onset of the Parents Music Resource Center (PMRC) in the mid- to late 1980s and, more specifically, a case involving Dead Kennedys frontman Jello Biafra. In 1985 the Dead Kennedys had released their *Frankenchrist* album, adorned with artwork that was immediately branded obscene.

The front cover itself was a swipe at the Illuminati, featuring a photograph of a Shriners Parade (a gathering of powerful Freemasons). Yet, hidden away on the inside sleeve was the truly contentious image: a poster version of 'Landscape #XX'. This painting by cult Swiss artist H.R. Giger features rows of penises engaged in sexual intercourse. The band faced charges of distributing harmful matter to minors. Hauled into court for this offence, Jello Biafra had his apartment raided by government agents. In the end, neither Biafra, the Dead Kennedys nor their label Alternative Tentacles (owned by Biafra) were convicted, although the offending inner poster was withdrawn from subsequent album pressings and Alternative Tentacles driven near to bankruptcy from the legal costs. But, masked by the high-profile case, the reasons for record-company executives' distress were perhaps altogether more commercial: namely lyrics which portrayed the industry machine as the vacuous sham it truly was. The *Frankenchrist* album showcases some of Biafra's most inspired lyrics, in the form of the vitriolic 'MTV – Get Off The Air'. 'My job is to help destroy/ What's left of your imagination,' Biafra whips mockingly.

This was a view shared by Metallica, of course, who had shunned such mainstream compliance – with a back catalogue of singles which could hardly be considered commercial, they were yet to make a video, and the obvious connotations of the Spastik Children gig, where Hetfield memorably pushed MTV away, had not yet faded. In one telling line of 'Eye Of The Beholder', Hetfield quips, 'Limit your imagination, keep you where they must,' no doubt referring to the bland, saccharine entertainment inflicted upon every viewer of mainstream television.

Reflecting on the Biafra trial – in which the Dead Kennedys frontman acquitted himself impressively – James Hetfield pondered the most fundamental questions of the case. 'What do you think is art? What is pornography? What's brilliant? Just what's in your head? You can't express yourself the way you want. It's kind of scary. I mean, you've got a choice – if you don't want to look at it, don't look at it.'

Despite the glaring flaws of the legal system, Lars also made the ambiguous claim that 'people can interpret the lyrics any way they want, and we're always careful to say in interviews that we're not trying to tell anybody what to think or how to feel about any particular subject. If there is one thing that we're trying to say, it's, "Be independent, don't listen to anyone – don't listen to *us*."'

This was a viewpoint shared by James Hetfield, who would later reiterate, 'People can take what they want from it; that's what it's all about.' Yet, with such intensely personal lyrics, it seems likely the frontman would have approved of anyone able to relate to his own bile-soaked rhetoric. Indeed, empathy for others is precisely what's required for 'One', the very next track featured on the album.

Inviting the listener inside the soldier's tortured mindset, this thrashy power ballad is amongst Metallica's most memorable material. Beginning with the eerie sounds of the battlefield and a slovenly clean guitar doused in bleakness, the accomplished track remains one of Metallica's greatest musical triumphs. Building into a crescendo similar in stature to 'Fade To Black', this was a dank trawl through power-ballad territory. With some truly beautiful guitar solos in the build-up, and behind the verse, the song once again revealed Hetfield's expressive vocal range, allowing him to delve into his emotive side. The second chorus gives way to an exquisite dual guitar refrain, before Lars flashes his double bass brilliance. The machine-gun riffing at this stage is blisteringly brilliant as the lyrics, revealing the true subject matter at play. 'Landmine has taken my sight/ Taken my speech/ [...] Taken my soul/ Left me with life in hell,' barks Hetfield.

Though 'Fade To Black' constitutes a single, colossal crescendo, 'One' took the climax a step further and remains blinding in its ferocity and potency, weaving in and out of guitar consciousness with a series of stunning melodies and leads, underpinned by a rhythmic attack that is positively feral.

The lyrics were inspired by Dalton Trumbo's haunting novel *Johnny Got His Gun*. Trumbo had based his book around the true-life story of one survivor of the First World War. To Trumbo's horror, the soldier had lost all his bodily senses, but none of his mental faculties – leaving him a prisoner, trapped within his own broken body. Lars explained, 'It's just about someone who is basically a living brain. It's about what sort of thoughts you would have if you were placed in that situation. It's actually a lyrical idea that we had a couple of years ago, but we never got around to using it before.'

The seven-minute-plus epic was released as a single, adorned with a suitably reflective cover of a floating skull and bandage-swathed torso, and accompanied by the band's first ever music video. Unsurprisingly, listeners seized upon the subject matter immediately, lauding Metallica as anti-war campaigners – a righteous label that the band themselves were keen to resist.

'The other day in Italy,' Ulrich told one magazine, 'there were these two guys just drilling into this whole thing about "One" and anti-war, making a statement of peace for the kids: "You guys care so much." I was telling James about this afterwards. We were laughing, "Why do people make such a big deal about it?" And James turns around and goes, "All it is, is a fucking song about a guy who steps on a landmine."'

It may seem hypocritical for the band to have made a video after openly criticising the vacuous contemporary culture of MTV, but they were determined it should be done their way from the very outset.

'We almost shot a video for "Welcome Home (Sanitarium)",' Lars revealed. 'But at the end of the day we just asked ourselves, "Why? What's the point?" We thought if we ever do get round to doing one, it would have to be completely different from your typical bullshit video that you can see on MTV's *Headbangers Ball*, because we don't want to be associated with all the other shit that's on there. On MTV, every video is the same: walking down the street in high heels and then playing to 500 people in a club. Everything is so faceless with no care gone into it – boring!'

On 6 December 1988, the band set their gear up in a warehouse near LA's Long Beach Arena. Though footage of the band playing was a stark, simplistic black-and-white affair, the clips from the movie adaptation of *Johnny Got His Gun* made the video particularly special. There were liberal inclusions from the film; so much so that many felt the power of the music was diluted. As such, Metallica made two versions of the video: one with the film segments and one without. 'I think the band was a little taken aback by how much of the movie I put in there,' Michael Salomon, who co-directed the video with Bill Pope, commented later. 'It's a very complicated story and to do it with just one or two sound bytes here and there wouldn't have made it. Basically, every time there was an extended guitar intro or guitar solo or anything like that, I covered the whole thing up. But I think they realised that for this particular clip, the story element was more important.'

Despite their seemingly strict attention to detail, the directors missed two important mistakes when editing the material. Firstly, the song begins with whirring helicopter blades, yet there were no helicopters involved in the First World War. To contradict the lyric stating Johnny was left limbless due to a landmine, the film depicts him as the victim of a mortar attack. Lars was finally forced to concede, 'Okay, there are a couple of historical inaccuracies. But this is not merely our interpretation of *Johnny Got His Gun*. We had the idea to do a number about someone totally cut off from reality kicking around for a few years before the book provided the catalyst. So these errors are really irrelevant. If anything, they just point up the fact that the song and the film/book aren't completely interlinked. And I don't think they spoil the effect of the video.'

Even for Metallica, 'One' was grave and the bleak essence of the video initially frightened MTV producers. In one memorable exchange, Metallica's co-manager Cliff Burnstein was informed by an MTV executive that the only way 'One' would be seen on television would be on the news. But by 20 January 1989 MTV could no longer ignore the dark lure of Metallica's first video and aired the clip on their late-night programme *Headbangers Ball*.

Very quickly, 'One' became the show's most requested song and was ultimately awarded Number 38 on *Rock On The Net: MTV's 100 Greatest Music Videos*. Though the video's popularity sat uncomfortably with Metallica, the band were still appreciative of the success of their first foray into the visual medium. Ultimately, as long as they had control over their own material and artistic direction, Metallica were satisfied. As Lars later admitted, '"One" proved to us that things we thought of as an evil aren't as evil as we thought – as long as we do it our way.'

Back to the album and, following on from 'One', 'The Shortest Straw' marks the beginning of the LP's second side. Lars Ulrich's own fondness for this track was revealed in 2009. According to the drummer, '"The Shortest Straw" is Metallica at its absolute best. I think that the lyrics are among the best that James has ever written.' Certainly, the track marks a return to subversive form, continuing the theme of one of James's own pet peeves. It was Lars who explained the basis for the song, however, saying, 'It deals with the whole blacklisting thing that took place in the 1950s, where anyone whose view was a little out of the ordinary was immediately labelled as a potential threat to society. There were all these people in Hollywood whose views didn't fit in with the mainstream, and they were all shoved out of the entertainment industry because of their beliefs.'

Built upon a stirring coupling of riffs, 'The Shortest Straw' is muscular, but little else, afflicted by a chorus that fails to ignite. Despite Lars's own opinion of the song, he was forced to leave it out of the band's live set thanks to James's reluctance. 'We've played it a few times,' Lars would later shrug, 'but there is a lot of singing in that song and every time I go, "Let's do the fucking 'The Shortest Straw'," it feels like James kind of backs away because I think there's so much singing in it. That's one I wish we would throw out there a little more often.'

With its creepy semi-acoustic introduction and deep, breathless entry into a complex metal groove, 'Harvester Of Sorrow' provided another chilling single. Unusually for such an oppressive song, it made the UK charts and was reluctantly played by mainstream radio DJs as part of their weekly run-down of the chart in full, albeit in a severely edited form.

Unlike most other tracks on the album, 'Harvester Of Sorrow' is primarily built around a single riff – arguably one of Metallica's most powerful ever. With a hulking, beastly Hetfield conducting proceedings, this was one enigmatic cry against the 'American Dream'.

As Lars cheerfully recounted, 'The song is about someone who leads a normal nine-to-five type of life, has a wife and three kids, and all of a sudden, one day, he just snaps and starts killing the people around him.' The 'let the beatings begin' line was inspired by an unusual source, however. Fred Cotton revealed: 'James and I were on a Bill Cosby kick at the time. In his stand-up video, *Bill Cosby: Himself*, he tells of chaos at home where the children are about to be punished by his wife. She announces, "The beatings will now begin," and that's where James got that line.'

'Harvester Of Sorrow' was released with two additional cover tunes Metallica had recorded as B-sides with the assistance of Guns N' Roses producer Mike Clink. The quality of these tracks remains undisputed. They had a slightly different vibe to them – courtesy, in part, of Clink's production – but also the low-slung, one-take glory of songs the band already knew by heart. 'Breadfan' was certainly close to the original Budgie version – in spirit, if nothing else – though musically speaking, it seems head and shoulders above the 1973 track. Fuelled with modern metal aggression, Metallica's version no longer sounded rooted in NWOBHM nostalgia, unlike some of their previous cover efforts. The track also ended with a bizarre aside spoken by James Hetfield ('Mummy, where's fluffy?'), with various effects used to disguise his voice. 'Breadfan' started out as an enduring mix-tape favourite, selected on one of the incessant listening sessions Hetfield and Ulrich had enjoyed whilst driving around Los Angeles in search of a suitable studio. Thus Metallica came to record two Budgie tracks in the space of a few years – a move which did not go unnoticed by the members of Budgie, all of whom were now in their forties. By a strange twist, the same night Metallica played in Cardiff, touring in support of their ...*And Justice For All* opus, Budgie vocalist and bassist Burke Shelley found himself working the venue as a stagehand. 'To add injury to the insult of our cover versions, his fingers got caught in a roadcase on the load out,' Lars recalled sheepishly. 'I think he broke his thumb.'

For Lars, the decision to cover Diamond Head's 'The Prince' was one of 'loyalty' – it may have been a predictable choice, but the song itself was anything but ordinary. 'The Prince' provides a blistering archetype for any band updating an otherwise staid hard-rock staple, blitzing it into the form of a future metal classic. Played at supreme speed and glossed with volumised guitars as well as Hetfield's crunchy sneer, the irresistibly infectious result bounced through four and a half rampant minutes. The dual guitar breakdown, which occurs three minutes in, constitutes some of the finest melodic interplay the band have ever produced. Diamond Head guitarist Brian Tatler expressed his gratitude for the Metallica tributes which regularly appeared on wax. 'I never made any money in Diamond Head, we never even recouped our advances,' he commented in 2008. 'But when Metallica recorded our songs we finally got some proper money. It's helped me and Sean [Harris, vocals] no end – it's enabled me to buy a house.'

'The Frayed Ends Of Sanity' is a veritable jewel of a track – even on an album loaded with such lavish gems – but, perhaps because of its infectious melodies, has been overlooked by Metallica's more image-conscious fans. Certainly, the fact that the band parodied a tune from *The Wizard Of Oz* for the introductory riff added nothing to the song's credibility.

Still, for such a simplistic, catchy number, 'Frayed Ends...' still delivers a dizzying array of technical drum beats as well as a concoction of Hetfield's ever-frantic trademark vocal lines. The upbeat yet paranoid mindset of the song's lead character surely influenced future Megadeth single 'Sweating Bullets'. This song appeared on the band's 1992 album *Countdown To Extinction*. Lyrically the song addresses the intriguing condition of dissociative identity disorder (in which the subject displays at least two separate personalities), with Dave Mustaine spewing such lines as, 'Well, me... it's nice talking to myself/ A credit to dementia.' With eerie echoes of the same paranoid state, 'Frayed Ends...' contains a myriad of references to darting eyes, hot sweats and uncontrollable tremors; the firm belief that 'something' or 'someone' is after you, when the reality of what's inside your head is far more terrifying. As Hetfield affirms towards the end of the song, 'Myself is after me.'

Cliff Burton receives a writing credit for one song only: the nine-minute-48-second-long instrumental 'To Live Is To Die', the band's haunting tribute to the bassist. Musically the song is imbued with Cliff's own spirit, opening with a plaintive refrain played on classical guitar and deepening into full metallic swing. Then there were the words, written by the man himself. Tellingly, these were scant, but carried a cryptic weight, subtly portrayed by Hetfield in an almost unrecognisable accent.

For such a lengthy, multi-faceted instrumental track, 'To Live Is To Die' moves at a swift pace, belying its extended running time (approaching ten minutes), before fading out once more, down to the classic guitar's mournful voice – seemingly paying one last tribute to Burton. It was a fitting lament for a man missed by all who knew him.

Few could have predicted the onslaught which interrupted the closing chimes of the instrumental, however. Unleashing their most ferocious song to date, Metallica ended *...And Justice For All* in the absolute frenzy of 'Dyers Eve'. Built around a ridiculously fast riff, this song had already been deemed too difficult to play on many live occasions. Unusually for the band there was no chorus as such; in the absence of any conventional structure, the track constitutes a relentless barrage of guitar and vocals, with fleeting breaks in the speed. Even when the pace slows, however, there's little respite for the listener. To experience this song is something akin to audio strangulation.

Though Lars always insisted that the lyrics were fictional, the subject matter seems quite transparent. 'It's about this kid who's been hidden from the real world by his parents the whole time he was growing up, and now that he's out there, he can't cope with it and is contemplating suicide. It's basically a letter from this kid to his parents asking them why they didn't expose him to the real world and why they kept him hidden for so long.'

However, the apparently fictitious narrative is virtually indistinguishable from the true events of James Hetfield's own childhood. Indeed, the lyrics read like a page torn from the frontman's bitter biography, and the venom he injected into every word was a rancorous personal diatribe.

'Dear mother, dear father,' Hetfield begins, 'What is this hell you have put me through?/ Believer, deceiver/ Day in, day out, live my life through you.' There is no question the words are based around Hetfield's lingering resentment against his parents for the way he was raised, the oppressive doctrine of Christian Science still ringing in his ears. The final verse is perhaps as enlightening as anything Hetfield has ever revealed regarding his upbringing. 'Undying spite I feel for you,' he spits, 'living out this hell you always knew.' Indeed, it is this untapped vein of resentment which marks the song out as such a special recording. Providing a blistering finish to the album, this remains Metallica's fastest ever song.

The title, however, was taken from an unexpected source. In the 1970 movie *Little Big Man*, starring Dustin Hoffman, the character of Hoffman's grandfather observes ominously, 'Today would be a good day for dying.' While James was working on the lyrics for what would become 'Dyers Eve', Lars recalled the phrase and suggested Hetfield write the song from the perspective of someone who was essentially writing his last letter before committing suicide the next day. Something in this concept appealed to James, and so the title evolved.

The band's sessions were almost at an end by the time the song was completed, and at a length of 5:13, the track meant the album was too long for a single LP. The record company warned Metallica against releasing a double album purely for the purpose of accommodating this last track, but on this point the band were immovable. Consequently, all vinyl versions of the album were sold as two-record sets.

Essentially *...And Justice For All* was more of a concept album than any of Metallica's previous efforts. Though written on differing subjects, the ambitious song structures and megalithic riffing constitute a whole composition – and one that demands to be heard as such. Indeed, this is the only way to grasp the full magnitude of the band's missive. Certain songs – namely 'Eye Of The Beholder', 'To Live Is To Die' and the convoluted title track – seem to belong together. Could these tracks have ever been split over separate recordings? For many devoted fans, the idea is virtually unthinkable.

'It's definitely one of those albums you need to spend a lot of time with,' Lars ventured upon the album's release. 'It's not the sort of thing you can put on in the background and then go and cook breakfast or have a wank. You have to listen to it because there's so much shit going on in the songs. If you don't pay attention it won't sound anything more than a bunch of riffs. But this is the first time there have been no compromises, either song-wise or time-wise.'

Despite featuring some of the band's most accomplished current material, *...And Justice For All* received a frosty reception from fans and critics alike. The most grievous complaint concerned the almost complete removal of the bass from the mix. Following the new bass player's first recording with Metallica, it was becoming apparent that this was not the same band fans had previously known. Indeed, the bass lines were barely there; vaguely audible with headphones and considerably strained ears, and even then only in certain parts of particular tracks. Whereas few other contemporary metal outfits were reliant on a prominent, strident bass, this had previously been Metallica's calling card. With effortlessly warm, leading bass runs from Cliff Burton, the four-string had played a prominent role in many of their best-loved tracks. Now, it was suddenly absent from the mix. Was it a case – as many assumed – of Jason's failure to integrate himself as a trusted member of the band? Or was it rather the band paying Cliff Burton the ultimate respect in masking all his successor had contributed to their sound? The latter scenario seems most likely.

Newsted was barely credited for his written contribution to the album, with a solitary appearance as co-writer for 'Blackened', even though he put forward many tapes of riffs and song melodies. Despite this, in 1988 Jason claimed that 'it's getting more comfortable for me to offer up ideas to Metallica'. He also spoke with admiration for his new frontman, saying, 'James Hetfield especially is really a genius when it comes to writing. It really amazes me sometimes. He can come up with the heaviest, chunking riffs, and then turn around and do something so pretty it makes you tingle. These guys are the upper sect of classy musicians.'

Flemming Rasmussen says there was 'no comparison' between Cliff and Jason. 'Cliff was a one-off, there's no one like Cliff and I don't think they tried to find a replacement,' he ventures, 'but a new bass player. Jason was technically better but music is about feelings, and Jason had to find his spot in the band. Jason had other qualities than Cliff so the end result was a bit different.'

Regarding the sound of the album and the lack of bass in the mix, Rasmussen defends the dramatic new balance. 'I thought it sounded pretty much like what the goal was during the session – dry, upfront sounds. But it was very clear to hear that it was a drummer and a guitar player who had assisted in mixing the album!'

Rasmussen was privy to the original bass lines, all of which were subsequently quietened in the studio. 'It's true Jason very much mimicked James's lines,' he explains, 'but I think the key point to the lack of bass on …And Justice For All is the lack of attention to the bass in the mix. The bass recordings were top quality, both in the playing, and in the recording.'

Lars later reasoned the absence of bass 'was just the right thing at that time. There was no secret master plan or special agenda. James and I ran Metallica with an iron fist and as a result that record was all about the two of us. That's how we wanted it, that's how we heard it and that's what we felt was best. I have nothing bad to say about anything we've ever done because 99.99 per cent of the time it's been the right thing. Whatever you want to say about this band, be it good or bad, that's one thing you can never take away from us.'

Perhaps a flippant comment made by Newsted in an issue of *Metal Forces* shortly before the band started to prepare …*And Justice For All* had something to do with his reduced playing time. Newsted was quoted as saying, 'I think the material is starting to get tighter because I play with a pick. No disrespect to Cliff at all 'cause he was a killer bass player, but the finger-picking style he adopted tended to drown the sound a little.'

Still, on some level at least, Lars Ulrich appeared to appreciate the new bassist's input, though the drummer was often guilty of contradictory statements and actions. 'The main difference between Jason's and Cliff's writing is that Jason tends to write a lot more with the guitar in mind,' Lars told one reporter, 'whereas Cliff's stuff was always really weird and off-the-wall. If anything, I think that Jason's stuff is a lot closer to James's and my songwriting than Cliff's shit ever was.'

On 25 August 1988 ...*And Justice For All* was released, becoming the first Metallica record ever to enter the *Billboard* Top Ten. By Halloween of 1988, the album would be certified platinum. This may never have occurred, however, had Lars had his way with a certain tongue-in-cheek album title. He later admitted they were thinking of calling the album, 'Wild Chicks And Fast Cars And Lots Of Drugs'.

As for the iconic album sleeve, Lars admitted the artwork was not entirely original. 'Anyone who's got *Shock Tactics* by Samson will know where we ripped off the sleeve design for ...*And Justice For All,*' he said. 'Er, let me put it this way, I would be lying if I said that I didn't look at this cover when we were thinking of ideas for our own sleeve!'

Though the band were obviously proud of their album upon release, others were not so sure. Music For Nations founder Martin Hooker, who had overseen the release of the first three Metallica albums in the UK, confessed his own disappointment. 'I was totally gutted when I heard it because I was obviously hoping that ...*And Justice For All* would go huge and take the back catalogue with it,' he said. 'When I heard it I almost wept and it didn't do nearly as well in the UK as it should have done given that the band had three consecutive gold records over here.'

Gem Howard, who also worked for MFN, added, 'I hated that record – it sounded awful; the bass was non-existent and the drums sounded like biscuit tins. Just goes to show how majors can fuck you up because they can't give you any advice, because they don't understand what you are about.' The normally dependable *Kerrang!* were similarly underwhelmed by the LP, but acknowledged this would be the album which propelled Metallica to superstar status. Awarding the record three Ks out of five, the reviewer stated, 'Lars's drum sound is really odd. But this album will finally put Metallica into the big league...'

Bizarrely Lars claimed: 'One thing we went for when mixing the album was a very upfront, in-your-face sound. We wanted all the instruments to practically jump out of the speakers and slap you in the face while you're listening to it.' Of course the mere suggestion that the bass would 'jump out of the speakers' in any way when compared to the other instruments, or vocals, was laughable, yet this is what can emerge when a band is promoting an album and doing umpteen interviews a day. Still, Lars made other statements to corroborate this one, asserting that the preceding album was inferior in sound quality to their new opus on numerous occasions. 'What we've created here leaps out in a way that *Master Of Puppets* did not,' he commented.

'I listen to that album now and it's like a wet noodle.'

Yet, several years on, it seemed that the drummer had come to view the release in an entirely different light. Reflecting on some of the band's more questionable musical decisions, Lars admitted, 'It's the only record of ours that I'm not entirely comfortable with; it became about ability and almost athletics, rather than music.' Leave it to James Hetfield to state the bare facts. Speaking in 1991, Hetfield would assert: 'I think the lyrics are really good; I think the production really sucks. We went for something we didn't really achieve. We wanted a really upfront, in-your-face album and it didn't really work out. The drums are fucking awful; there's no depth to it. I don't know what the fuck we were doing, but back then we liked it for some reason.'

It's certainly arguable that the production lets the album down in many ways and you would expect Metallica to have learned an important lesson with this record. Yet, when you compare *...And Justice For All* to later release *St. Anger* in sound quality, for instance, there is no comparison. And ironically the very same people who criticised *...And Justice For All* at the time were ruing the loss of such perfectly constructed metal by the time of *St. Anger*'s emergence in 2003. If the drums sounded 'awful' on *...And Justice For All*, words could not describe their inferiority on the frightful eighth album.

Two overwhelming conclusions can be drawn from Metallica's fourth LP. Firstly, it was their last remotely thrash-orientated album (before 2008's *Death Magnetic*, at least) and, arguably, their heaviest. Yet the band blew their load in many ways, going so over the top that the resulting tour, playing these difficult tracks night after night, was enough to steer them towards more simplistic material next time around. It was a turning point in the band's career.

As usual with Metallica, by the time they had created something original and, in turn, influenced others, they had already moved on to the next groundbreaking stage of their career. When they eventually completed the punishing touring schedule for *...And Justice For All*, Metallica were truly prepared to pare down their style and start again.

But the fallout from the band's most technically accomplished material could still be felt. By the time 1989 rolled in, many bands had sprung up with a sound directly inspired by the technical wizardry of *...And Justice For All*.

Renowned for their death-metal roots, Florida's Atheist were blessed with similar technical nous, which would only increase with each album after their 1989 debut *Piece Of Time*. Also based in Florida, Cynic – commanding a devoted following of worshippers – released a demo in the wake of Metallica's fourth album, and proceeded to hone their tech-death craft with further demos, paving the way for 1993 classic *Focus*. By this time, previously straightforward death-metal bands such as the seminal Death had adapted their original sounds to incorporate complicated riffs and off-kilter time changes as well as gruff, barking vocals. The source of this entire movement, *...And Justice For All* has become a benchmark for virtually any aspiring technical metal band. Its influence continues today with bands such as the Dillinger Escape Plan and the emergence of 'math metal' – a genre which is still as complicated as ever, encompassing such bands as Every Time I Die, Ion Dissonance and Meshuggah. However, despite being the technical musician's choice of worship, ...*And Justice For All* rendered the genre obsolete for Metallica. By the end of their tour in support of the album, the band would be ready to strip their sound down to the bare bones.

CHAPTER 13

DAMAGED GOODS

*'We've always known that there's been a need
or a want for a band like us. We've fought back and broken
through all the bullshit of the business, and now it's great to be able to
say "fuck off" to the whole business and, "We did it our way," and blah
blah blah. We've always had our own way of doing things.'*
Lars Ulrich

With the success of *...And Justice For All*, the tide was turning for Metallica. Though
they'd already established themselves as one of the premier metal acts in the world,
sales of the new release won them a place alongside hard-rock luminaries Bon Jovi and
Van Halen. Suddenly the band found they were matching the sales figures enjoyed
by pop and country singers such as Garth Brooks and even veteran acts like U2. *...
And Justice For All* may have been their darkest, heaviest album to date, but Metallica
found their star rising exponentially. Certain events jumped out as being 'different'
from life as they'd previously known it.

Confronted with the band's newfound fame, Kirk's reaction was incredulous. In
an interview with one guitar magazine, he related, 'We're on commercial flights and
sometimes the stewardess will call you by your first name. It kind of throws you a bit.'
Fred Cotton also remembers the public's altered perception of the band. 'Jason was
about to get married and I had MTV call me up asking me if I could get any pictures
of the wedding,' Cotton says. In many interviews Lars Ulrich was quick to compare
Metallica to rock or pop bands rather than lesser-known metal acts. They may have
been promoting their most monolithic material yet, but Metallica were starting to
rub shoulders with mainstream bands, well outside the elitist metal sphere. As part
of the Damaged Justice tour (in support of the band's fourth album), in just one
week of April 1989, Metallica headlined New Jersey's Meadowlands Arena on three
separate occasions.

Given the fresh impetus of financial success, the band could well have put together
a lavish backdrop for these shows. Yet, they settled on a less pretentious idea inspired
by Pink Floyd, investing in a giant statue of 'Lady Justice' and collapsing her –
symbolically as well as literally – every night of the tour. Other than this, however,
the heavy-metal clichés were kept firmly under control. 'Metallica will never sacrifice
stage bullshit for the venues we wanna play, and we just aren't the type of band that

you sell as a live show,' Lars stated candidly. 'We don't need 50-feet-tall dragons to sell our tickets. A lot of people in America right now are saying that we are doing the same arena-rock clichés that these other bands were doing. It doesn't affect me because · I know what we are doing is something distinctly different.'

The size of the stage may have increased, along with the on-road budget, but this was still the same band from two years before as far as the onstage spectacle was concerned. They whipped, thrashed and flung their sweat-drenched bodies around, all the while holding together the tightest, fastest metal show in existence.

The band began their tour on 11 September 1988, on a trip which would continue for over a year, taking in 222 shows along the way. They started in Europe supported by Danzig, working to promote his immense self-titled debut album. Halfway through the schedule of shows, Danzig were replaced by Queensrÿche, fresh from the release of their progressive metal classic *Operation: Mindcrime*.

The Seattle quintet followed Metallica throughout their US leg of their tour, which – staggeringly enough – took in all 50 states. 'We were sitting in the plane and at the table there's a map of the States,' Lars told one magazine. 'We worked out that we had shows booked in 48 states, but that we'd miss two that pretty much everyone forgets about: Vermont and Delaware. We wanted to book some shows up there, and we were told that there were no arenas really to play. So we said, "Fuck it, let's do it anywhere just to play." We've booked a club date in Delaware and a 2,000-seat venue in Vermont. It's actually quite exciting to have a club date when you've just played 188 arena dates in a row.' Though Metallica would indeed visit Delaware – a state ridiculed in the first *Wayne's World* movie, courtesy of Mike Myers – it would be the only time they did so.

As headliners and, in most cases, arena fillers, Metallica were received by worshipping crowds on every leg of the tour, though it became apparent that the band's earlier material was still better received than their ...*And Justice For All* inclusions. Though the riotous 'Blackened' would often open the set, by the time of the ten-minute epic '...And Justice For All' yawns were being stifled in all corners of the cavernous stadiums. Even the otherwise stupendous 'Harvester Of Sorrow' failed to rouse the crowd, losing much of its power in a live setting. Whereas 'The Frayed Ends Of Sanity' might have made a sure-fire crowd pleaser, the band neglected to perform the song; nor did the expected thrash-fest of 'Dyers Eve' ever materialise.

'I forgot how to play it,' Kirk later admitted. 'We never play it live. Certain members of the band are very adamant about not playing it. I think it's a physical thing. There's some awful fast strums in that song.'

Metallica certainly enjoyed introducing fresh material into their set, but could hardly have failed to notice that few of the new tracks were working; in fact, the convoluted nature of the riffs and structures failed to translate live. Only 'One' could create the electrifying dynamics required for a mass audience. 'Touring for ...*And Justice For All* we realised that the general consensus was that the songs were too fucking long,' Kirk confessed. 'Everyone would have these long faces, and I'd think, "Goddamn, they're not enjoying it as much as we are. If it wasn't for the big bang at the end of the song…" I can remember getting offstage one night after playing "…Justice…" and one of us saying, "Fuck, that's the last time we ever play that fucking song!"'

Such was the struggle in performing the new material, in fact, that Metallica were forced to break out a flurry of cover songs. The now obligatory 'Last Caress' and 'Am I Evil?' were staples of the set, along with an ever-changing array of metal and rock classics. They played Iron Maiden's 'Prowler', Deep Purple's 'Black Night' and 'How Many More Times' by Led Zeppelin amongst several others. There were the needless bass and guitar solo spots and even the Spastik Children-inspired trick of swapping instruments. On various occasions during 'Am I Evil?' Lars would switch to lead vocals with Hetfield on drums (as they'd done for Spastik), Jason on guitar and Kirk on bass.

Behind the scenes, the pressures of live performance provided fresh impetus for the band's constant torment of their new bass player. As well as being subjected to all the usual practical jokes, Newsted found himself routinely ignored by his bandmates. Onstage regular tricks were played with the sound, with the bass completely turned down for certain numbers. On one occasion Jason had all his personal belongings thrown from a hotel window onto the street below.

'We'd just bust into his room in the middle of the night drunk and just attack him,' Hetfield recalled, 'throw all his furniture out into the hallway and then just leave. That was more of the fun stuff.' Yet, as a man who knew what it was to feel isolated and alone, James would also admit, with an air of regret, that 'excluding him from stuff was a little more hurtful'.

'They would cram into a taxi and make me go in a taxi by myself,' Jason said in a 1993 interview. 'They would be uncomfortable in the taxi just so I could ride by myself.' James later confirmed: 'Right from the beginning there was a lot of hazing that just separated him and he was always thought of as "the new guy". I wish that that didn't have to happen. I guess we wanted to toughen him up; we wanted him to be as tough as us. We were brutal with him. And it never ended, really.'

Hetfield also recalled the circumstances which sparked the harsh treatment of their new bassist. 'I remember when we told Jason he was in the band he jumped on the table, and was doing back flips, and it was more of a new kind of youthful fan energy that kind of entered. But I felt that we took a lot of our resentment, a lot of our grief, a lot of our despair around Cliff's death out on Jason. And not to take away from Jason and the process of how we got him and why he was in the band – because he was the right guy – but it was easier to grab somebody because they were there. I didn't think about it too much.'

Jason, however, showed his mettle in response to the treatment, stating that the bullying was 'blown way bigger than it actually was. That's the kind of things people like to talk about and have their fun with. I think that everybody in Metallica at different times had certain feelings towards each other. We knew we had it going really good and we loved each other and counted on each other and relied on each other so deeply, that that stuff was unspoken. But the more surface-y things and the everyday things, after a while rub you wrong. Everybody got rubbed wrong at different times with different things, different people, different opinions.'

In total, Metallica were supported by four different bands on the Damaged Justice tour. In between their American shows, the band played a brief tour of Australia, with a show in New Zealand thrown in for good measure. Here they were supported by Australian thrashers Mortal Sin. Before this however, Metallica parted company with their touring partners for the previous 60 shows – in decadent style. 'The last gig with Queensrÿche was pretty good,' James later explained. 'During one of their songs we hired about four male strippers – real gay-looking guys – and they got up on our back amp line. Everyone could see them – the spotlights were right on them! But the band couldn't really see them, 'cause they were up so high behind them. These fags would be dancing on the amps the whole time! Queensrÿche didn't know what was going on.'

Mortal Sin were at the point of releasing their second album, *Face Of Despair*, a follow-up to the well-received *Mayhemic Destruction*. There were many parallels between the Australian thrash act and Metallica, as singer Mat Maurer explains. 'In August 1988, we were just putting the finishing touches to *Face Of Despair* for Phonogram Records – Polygram in Australia, which basically made us label mates – which was rather good timing as Metallica had just released their ...*And Justice For All* album. Mortal Sin was at that time the biggest name in Australian metal and when news of Metallica's impending tour came through, we were in a good position for the support spot. Polygram Australia contacted us and gave us confirmation.'

The likes of Mortal Sin were often criticised for sounding too much like Metallica, yet in the same breath, these somewhat inconsistent critics also carved them out as being the 'next big thing' in thrash. While this dichotomy still seems to irk most lower-league thrashers, Maurer explains: 'It never really bothered Mortal Sin; I think it actually did us a few favours. I certainly didn't mind being compared to James Hetfield – he is still today one of the most powerful vocalists and I love the way he phrases his words. Back in 1987, when we sent some copies of our debut album to Shades record shop in London, David Thorne of Phonogram Records was in the shop when they were playing it, and asked the staff if it was the new Metallica album (after *Ride The Lightning*), so it's more flattering then anything else – we scored a major record deal from that.'

Naturally Mortal Sin were excited to play with a band of Metallica's calibre. 'The scene in Australia at the time was getting really big, but not many international bands had managed to make their way down under,' Maurer explains. 'In 1987, Anthrax was meant to come out, but the tour never happened. Then in 1988 we were booked to play with Megadeth, but again, it never happened. Fans were getting really frustrated about not being able to see any of the bands they were reading about in *Metal Forces* and *Kerrang!*. So, when the 1989 ...*Justice*... tour was announced and Australia was finally going to get the world's biggest thrash band to our shores, you would have thought Australia had struck gold again! It was probably the biggest thing to ever happen in the Australian heavy-metal scene. People still talk about that tour like it was yesterday, and every gig we play we always get someone saying they saw us with Metallica in 1989. I would almost go as far as saying it was a defining moment in our careers and a perfect launching pad to make us even bigger than we could ever have imagined in Australia, and it was all thanks to Metallica.'

Maurer explains that the association between Mortal Sin and Metallica went far beyond this handful of Australian dates, however. 'We met the guys in 1989, then again in 1990 when we played at the Stone in San Francisco and also again when they returned in 1993 for the Black Album tour, and then I met them again in 2005 when they did the Big Day Out Festivals here for the *St. Anger* album,' Maurer recalls. 'Each time it was quite a different experience. In 1989, James, Lars and Jason were very much the party animals and Kirk was hardly seen. If I remember correctly Lars and Kirk had wives with them on tour. Mortal Sin were just huge fans, so we pretty much acted like fans – I got them to sign almost everything I owned, even an old skateboard! They seemed like they were having the time of their lives and it was very inspiring for us, and basically our first taste of something big. In 1990, Mortal Sin played at the Stone in San Francisco and we were rather surprised to see James and Jason in the crowd showing some support. They came backstage and drank our beer, but it was an absolute honour having such esteemed company! In 1993, we didn't play with Metallica, but my wife and I booked into the same hotel as them when they came to Sydney, so we were able to sit in the bar and share drinks. Jason invited us and some friends back to the hotel after the show for drinks and party time. He came across as very intelligent, warm and friendly and we sang songs with an acoustic, smoked doobies and drank whatever we could get our hands on, on the hotel premises until sunlight. We never saw the other guys again until 2005 at the Sydney Big Day Out Festival, when Kirk seemed to be the party guy, James seemed withdrawn, Lars was nowhere to be seen and new boy Robert was obviously glowing in the limelight. I was working on the show as crew co-ordinator and was wearing a Mortal Sin T-shirt. When I walked past Kirk, he pointed and said, "Wow, Mortal Sin, they were a really cool band," and I whispered in his ear that I was the singer and he laughed saying, "Ha, ha, I knew I knew you."'

Describing the concert dates, Maurer reveals that Mortal Sin were given a much longer set than most support bands can usually expect – just short of an hour. 'We had a really good sound,' the singer says, 'and we met Metallica's sound guy ['Big' Mick Hughes] who we all thought looked like Bill Oddie from the Goodies – he was a great bloke. I think we were only allowed use of a small amount of lights though, which is pretty standard I guess.'

When the bands hit Melbourne, it was like a homecoming gig for Mortal Sin, who had toured there 'heaps of times', according to Maurer. 'Before we went onstage,' he continues, 'our banner went up in the air and the crowd started chanting "Mortal Sin, Mortal Sin!" and 6,000 fists in the air created an atmosphere that was terrifyingly electric. I ran off to the toilet for a nervous leak and two of the touring production guys were also taking a leak and they were saying, "What the fuck is that? Who the fuck are these guys?" We didn't get a sound check, so basically our first song "The Curse" was our sound guy's two minutes to get it right. Lars sat behind drummer Wayne Campbell for the first two songs. Next was Sydney – the last show and our home venue. We were finally comfortable and in party mode, and having a great time. The crowd at the front of the venue was more like an angry mob in a prison. We could hear fists banging on the metal shutter doors and fierce chanting for Metallica. We were onstage setting up our gear when the roller doors opened and we were shocked to see thousands of people running straight for the front of the stage, sort of like a wildebeest stampede! You could feel the tension in the room. We knew these fans were here to thrash their fucking heads off, and thrash they did. We had a blinder of a set that night and felt like we had come of age.'

This was, of course, the height of Metallica's 'Alcoholica'-fuelled excess, and Maurer remembers in particular the perils of Metallica's tipple of choice, Jägermeister. 'We were invited by Metallica to the after-tour party in Sydney,' he recalls. 'Jägermeister all around! That is purely dangerous stuff to the uninitiated, and while Metallica were also the masters of the drink, we tasted it for the first time, not really knowing it's pure evil. Who would have thought that you could drink this stuff all night and not get drunk – until a few hours later? We got smashed and probably made fools of ourselves. I vaguely remember getting into some real trouble with my wife and ended up in the doghouse in the rain at the end of the night, although she denies this. The local Sydney music magazine of the time, *On The Street*, accidentally put Mortal Sin as the main picture of the front cover instead of Metallica, which was pretty cool for us; Metallica got the inset photo that we were supposed to get!'

Evidently, the exposure of these gigs brought Mortal Sin's music to a fresh audience of metal fans and for this, the group remain eternally thankful. 'We were already the biggest name in Australian metal, but somehow we seemed to gain a lot of respect from a lot of different areas – press mostly, but our fanbase definitely grew,' Maurer says, reflecting on the aftermath of the prestigious tour. 'There must have been a lot of ten-year-olds at that show because we seem to get a lot of youngish dudes saying they were there!' Two thousand and nine marks the band's twenty-fourth year as a unit.

Metallica's tour experience was somewhat different, however. For all the high jinks of the Damaged Justice shows, the end of the road brought an important realisation for every member of the band, particularly frontman James Hetfield. 'I look at that tour as a kind of awakening, seeing what we could and couldn't do – especially me,' Hetfield said. 'I found that I couldn't fucking drink like I used to, as far as singing went and being 100 per cent into what the fuck you're doing every night and stuff.'

Kirk explained of the 'Alcoholica' tag: 'It became part of our legend – people would know when we were coming into town to stock their bars and make sure there was always a lot of booze for us to drink. I can't really recall most of the *Kill 'Em All* tour; I only remember the shows during the *Ride The Lightning* tour. But even then, all I remember is driving up to the venues, going in and playing the show; anything that happened after I have no recollection of. I remember a lot more of *Master Of*

Puppets, because by then I was a professional drinker and I knew how to pace myself and I knew not to drink until I blacked out, which was always the norm before. And nowadays I have issues with alcohol because of all that.'

In 1989 Metallica were nominated for a Grammy Award, falling into the category of 'Best Hard Rock/Metal Performance'. Confusingly, prog-rockers Jethro Tull were also in the running, though they had been warned by their manager they had zero chance of winning the award. Acting on his advice, Tull did not even bother attending the event, while Metallica bolstered the otherwise lacklustre ceremony with a monumental performance of 'One'. 'The first TV thing we ever did, which was the Grammys, really turned us off TV,' James later said, still plainly disgusted by the experience. 'You can't do what you wanna do. It's all fucking planned out. They basically told us, "You can't do this; you can't do that." In sound check we were playing the nice little beginning bit to "One", and then we kicked into the double-bass machine-gun fire and they freaked out and said, "Hold it! Stop! There's no way you can do this on TV."'

Lars, however, believed the appearance to have worked in the band's favour, obliterating some of the deluded impressions the establishment still held of heavy-metal bands. 'It is the first time that a lot of people have seen a heavy-metal-type band on a show like this,' Lars reasoned. 'And it showed those who have painted those misconceptions of metal in their minds that they were wrong. I think a lot of people probably thought there'd be satanic cross burning and ritual sacrificing. The ignorant middle-class America who have these weird views saw otherwise.'

Despite censorship occurring behind the scenes, the word was that Metallica had the award in the bag. Yet, despite all expectations to the contrary – rivals Jethro Tull were not remotely heavy metal – the British band won the award. Though the Grammy Award was of little consequence to Metallica's devoted fanbase, the sheer perversity of the judges' decision rankled band members, critics and fans alike. Lars later quipped, 'Jethro Tull is such a weird choice that in weeks to come it will be seen as the time when the judges really had a chance to have their finger on the pulse but, in the end, stuck it up their ass.'

Tull were slated in the press, though it clearly wasn't their fault. They took the ribbing with good grace and released an advert in *Kerrang!* featuring a flute amongst a pile of iron bars, emblazoned with the slogan: 'The flute is a heavy-metal instrument.' In the same magazine, frontman Ian Anderson was asked for his reaction to winning in the heavy-metal category. 'Well, we do sometimes play our mandolins very loudly,' he responded. With obnoxious bitterness, Metallica pressed stickers onto all subsequent pressings of *...And Justice For All,* proudly declaring themselves as 'Grammy Award LOSERS'.

By way of closure on a period which had seen Jason Newsted endure great difficulties while adjusting to his role as 'Newkid', Metallica acknowledged his loyalty and resilience by awarding him a gold disc for *Master Of Puppets.* 'I didn't expect one,' Newsted said. 'That's when it really hit me that I was part of Metallica.'

CHAPTER 14
THE GOD THAT NAILED

'It's not about money anymore. It's about egos. I wanna go out there and be the biggest band in the world and sell more records than anybody else. And I'm not gonna compromise that for anything.'
Lars Ulrich

Before Metallica began recording their fifth album, they kept themselves busy with a variety of activities and hobbies. To celebrate its fortieth anniversary, Elektra Records asked all 38 acts on its roster to contribute a song from one vintage Elektra album for use on a double CD. Metallica went with Queen's 'Stone Cold Crazy', which originally appeared on their 1974 opus *Sheer Heart Attack*. As Ulrich sneered, 'You sit down, look at the song list and go, "Well, maybe someone else should cover 'Hotel California'."'

Metallica's choice was rooted in worship of Brian May, as Hetfield would explain. 'Brian May was the harmony master,' he said of the Queen guitarist. 'He came up with these huge parts that sounded like string sections, flamboyant orchestrations, and he was doing it all on guitar. Along with Thin Lizzy, what he did on those records helped us a lot in using guitar harmonies in our songs.' Compared to the original, Metallica's interpretation is, of course, souped-up to the max – a beefier, accelerated version of the 1974 track. It was also a chance for Hetfield to showcase his vocal prowess, enunciating a string of difficult words, crammed into a few short bars.

The record label also saw fit to release a box set entitled *The Good, The Bad And The Live*. This was an excellent concept in essence, featuring six twelve-inch records packaged in a black-and-white box, complete with a free poster. Included were all the band's singles to date, as well as the *Garage Days Re-Revisited* EP, although the subtitle of *The Six And A Half Year Anniversary* smacked of a cash-in by the label, and Metallica were quick to distance themselves from the release, even encouraging fans to tape the songs from friends.

Meanwhile, Lars was busy working on a compilation of his own. Given his obsession with the NWOBHM, he had been in touch with former *Sounds* editor Geoff Barton discussing his plans for the album, which was to showcase some of the finest bands of the late 1970s. Embracing this chance to create a glorified mix tape,

Lars set about listing the bands and tracks he wanted to see on the compilation. Ulrich was adamant his old buddy Brian Slagel – a bastion of the NWOBHM – should release the record in the US but, as Slagel later explained, the apparently straightforward project was beset with difficulties. 'The project wasn't as easy as Lars expected it to be,' Slagel said. 'He had a lot of problems. I think he felt he would get a band listing together and give it to the people at Phonogram [who released the record overseas], but it wasn't that easy.'

Indeed, despite his metal connections, Lars faced the daunting task of tracking down long-lost, obscure British musicians for permission to use their music on the record. Most of the bands had been out of the music business for a decade or so and, pre-internet, opportunities for networking were few and far between. So Lars let his fingers do the walking and scoured a London phone book to find most of the old musicians. Slagel later described his approach to the search: 'Lars would call all the numbers listed for a certain name and ask, "Are you the guy who used to play in Holocaust?" or, "Were you once the guitarist for Angel Witch?" and so on.'

Yet, even when he did uncover the elusive musicians, some were reluctant to acquiesce to his request. 'Some of the bands had an attitude about being on the record,' Slagel confirmed. 'You would think that you would find this band that existed ten years ago to be very happy to lend their songs, but a lot of these groups had gone through tough periods, or they don't want to remember what they did, or the guys in the band all hated each other – that kind of crap. What began as a fun project became a nightmare.'

Lars persisted, however, and eventually created a painstaking 30-track double album entitled *New Wave Of British Heavy Metal: '79 Revisited* – all of which was no mean feat. Despite the difficulties, Lars succeeded in piecing together a track listing similar to his collection of seven-inch singles, ten years before. Obligatory appearances from Diamond Head ('It's Electric' and 'Helpless') featured in the mix, alongside other giants of the genre, including Iron Maiden ('Sanctuary'), Def Leppard ('Getcha Rocks Off') and Saxon ('Motorcycle Man'). Ultimately the compilation succeeded in bringing once-forgotten bands back into the spotlight, revealing the strengths of a much overlooked genre. For instance, it was refreshing to see the inclusion of Weapon's obscure classic 'Set The Stage Alight', as well as Sledgehammer's self-titled anthem.

There was still one problem to negotiate, however: that of the striking cover image selected by Lars. Featuring Samson's eccentric drummer Thunderstick donning his trademark gimp mask, the picture was a little too risqué for the European label. 'The guy said it looked too much like a rapist who had done a bunch of horrible things in England ten years ago,' Brian Slagel recalled. 'They didn't want that association, so they moved a bunch of other pictures to hide his face. We [Metal Blade] put out the original cover in America, which Lars appreciated.'

It was supposed to have been straightforward, but at the end of the whole compilation debacle, Lars was relieved to return to his day job. Indeed, ever the workaholic, he had been tirelessly researching a different subject. Though the music wasn't to his taste, Lars had been intrigued by the sound of Mötley Crüe's fifth album,

1989's *Dr. Feelgood*. 'It sounded incredible,' Lars enthused. 'It had more low-end and kick drum than we had ever heard before. We had recognised at this point that the *...And Justice for All* album was on the thin side in terms of its lyrics and its sound, so we decided to track down this Bob Rock guy who had made this Mötley Crüe album which really sounds beefy and see what his story is.' Though Lars had contradicted earlier statements (praising Hetfield's lyrics), his frontman was in agreement about one thing. 'The sound needed more muscle,' Hetfield would concede.

And so, the two Metallica mainstays flew to Vancouver to meet with Bob Rock, where, according to Lars, they all clicked straight away. Rock, a native Canadian, had worked on some of the most prestigious hard-rock albums of the 1980s, from Kingdom Come's self-titled debut to the Cult's own breakthrough, *Sonic Temple*. Most notable, however, was Rock's work as engineer and mixer on Bon Jovi's multi-platinum album, *Slippery When Wet*. More than anything, it was this association that had Metallica fans worried, calling into question the direction of the new album. Metallica, of course, had been here before and were not about to let this element of uncertainty cloud their judgement.

Lars, for one, would not be swayed. 'I've heard Bon Jovi this, Bon Jovi that, but the fact is Bob Rock's got an incredible ear for attitude and feeling,' the drummer reasoned. 'We've been very proud of our records in the past but it's gotten so clean and antiseptic that you've got to wear gloves to put the damn thing in the CD player!' James also voiced his support for the choice of Bob Rock. Hetfield pointed out: 'There's people who will always shoot something down before it's even started and they're the close-minded ones. They just look at the track record of what he's done before which is unfair.' However, James did admit that 'if you go back and look at the stuff he's produced, it sounds great, even though the songs were crap and the bands were fucking gay!'.

The band's open admiration for Rock (his real name, incidentally) gave the Canadian license for brutal honesty in the studio. Beating around the bush and telling bands what they wanted to hear had never been Rock's style, and this was precisely what made Metallica warm to him. 'The first thing that he told me was that he felt that we had never made a record that was up to his standards,' Lars recalled. 'That was a bit of a battle cry.' Rock was treading on thin ice with regard to James Hetfield, however. James remembered, 'I came in with my lyrics and he said they weren't good enough. I couldn't believe it; it was the first time my lyrics had ever been questioned. So, I thought, "Well, there's a challenge."'

With Bob Rock in tow, the band once again holed up in One On One Studios in Los Angeles. When they began in October 1990, they didn't realise that – apart from a brief interlude recording in Vancouver – they wouldn't check out until June of 1991.

The sessions were not only lengthy, but found band members at opposite ends of the time schedule. Whereas James Hetfield was eager to work through the day, his drummer preferred not to get out of bed before noon. 'It's always been that way,' Hetfield said of his early-bird tendencies. 'Getting up early was instilled into me from a kid. Dad had a trucking service, and had to be at work at 5:00am. So I'm not very nocturnal at all. It feels like I've wasted a day if I'm not up when the sun's up. The procrastination part of Lars would drive me up the wall. He would get to the studio at 2:00 in the afternoon, eat breakfast, take a nap, start recording at 5:00 maybe. Every night it would be pushing later and later. You'd get home at 6:00 in the morning and I was not digging that at all.'

The band, and indeed Bob Rock, had another element to contend with – the constant presence of filmmaker Adam Dubin. Dubin had been hired to document the recording process for a future film and so, whether they were in the mood for it or not, Metallica were filmed for virtually every moment of their studio time. Dubin says today, 'Bob Rock was very good to me. I always respected him. After all, he didn't sign on for the madness of filming the recording process; it was just sort of dropped on him, like, "Oh, by the way, we are going to be filming this stuff too."'

The bottom line was Metallica had set their sights on recording perfection and it was going to take more time and effort than ever before. With this record – which would become *Metallica* or, as it is better known, the 'Black Album' – the band's methods were completely different, striving for a sound that was more upfront, clean and bold, in keeping with the stripped-down nature of the new material. Rock's first suggestion was for the band to experience recording the album as a unit.

In the past Metallica had mostly recorded their parts separately, giving rise to constant tension and irritability. Suddenly, Rock was encouraging them to approach the recording as if they were in rehearsal. 'Bob was convinced that the four of us playing together has a certain magic or vibe,' Lars explained, 'and that never happens with me doing drums to a click track and James coming in and overdubbing rhythm guitars.' With the Black Album, the drums were recorded with the entire band playing along, which certainly made for some fun. There were occasional temper tantrums, but ultimately a far better, warmer record emerged.

The overwhelming lesson from *...And Justice For All*, and especially the tour, was that Metallica were not suited to playing complex, overlong material for the rest of their career. They had realised, perhaps belatedly, that the songs which worked best live were those which bounced with dynamics – 'For Whom The Bell Tolls', 'Seek And Destroy' and 'One', for example. The idea was to retain the dynamics of this material, but to update it with a new groove and a freshly-defined Metallica vibe. The crude demos Metallica had recorded in their own time on tour were difficult to envisage as titanic heavy-metal cuts, but Hetfield, Ulrich and especially Bob Rock could see the bigger picture. Instantly it became obvious that Metallica had replaced 'speed' with 'groove'. *Rolling Stone* editor David Fricke explains, 'I remember James telling me at the time – "How many times can you be the fastest guy around?" At some point you have to say, why not be a little slower, why not make it heavier. See what else you can do at a different speed.'

There were few high-tempo riffs on the album, and even when these did feature (as with 'Through The Never'), Lars would deliberately offset the beat to half the speed he would normally play. 'I really didn't think about there being no speed songs on the album until people started telling me,' Ulrich explained upon the album's release.

'I just realised that every time I heard a fast guitar riff I wanted it to "swing" a little more. So every time there was a fast guitar riff I put a "half-time" on it. I think it still has the energy, but it also has a little more shit into it. So you can blame it on me.'

Though certain song titles had been around for a while – most notably 'Enter Sandman', 'Sad But True' and 'The Struggle Within' – the album showcased an entirely new-look Metallica. Bob Rock sought to be involved in every aspect of the music-making process, with more time dedicated to vocal recording and the inclusion or exclusion of a bass drum here, a guitar lick there. Initially unwilling to relinquish absolute control over their own output, Metallica soon realised what was needed – for them to put their faith in Bob Rock.

'We had never been challenged before,' Lars admitted, 'and nobody ever really sat down and said, "Well, you can also do it this way and you can also try it in a different key, or why don't you try this kind of drum fill." It was like that. "Why don't you go fuck yourself and stop telling us what to do, just get us that bass sound like the Mötley Crüe album!" But, as the process wore on we very reluctantly realised that maybe this guy had some relevant suggestions and he sort of won us over.'

As a trusted member of the team, it was far easier for Rock to enter the inner world of James Hetfield. The supremely talented, yet still ultra-shy frontman was in need of a mentor, someone with whom he wouldn't feel embarrassed, even whilst pouring out his vocal heart.

'Bob should be given total credit for making James comfortable enough to take that guard down and really sing,' Lars later affirmed. 'We've always thought of ourselves as big, bad Metallica, but Bob taught us a new word none of us had ever heard before – soulful.'

By divulging his true self, Hetfield inadvertently opened his world the rest of the band. Suddenly, the bandmates began to feel closer, functioning as more of a unit than ever. Lars would admit: 'We worked a lot more with the vocals this time, vocal melodies. The vocal thing in the past always remained a mystery to everyone in the band but James because he'd write everything five minutes before he'd sing it in the studio. We're treating the vocals on this record with the same upfront attention as the guitars, bass and drums. We've got all these demo tapes lying around with James going, "Na na na, na na na…"'

Such spontaneity had clearly worked with Metallica's material in the past, but this time around, nothing was left to chance. Bob Rock was a perfectionist and as such, he insisted upon James rehearsing every last line, again and again if necessary. Yet, in his effort to elicit the ultimate Hetfield performance, Rock managed to capture the singer's very soul – an element lacking from much of Metallica's back catalogue. This coaxing from Rock can be witnessed on Dubin's resulting documentary, *A Year And A Half In The Life Of Metallica*. At one point during 'The Unforgiven', James records a line which Bob admits 'sounds pretty good'. He could have left it at that, but instead, the producer persuades Hetfield to sing the line again, reasoning, 'It needs a little more soul and character in there – a little more Hetfield.' The subsequent vocal line produced by the frontman is patently superior.

Hetfield also underwent vocal training. 'We were doing B-sides at the same time, and I blew my voice out singing "So What?" [the band's Anti-Nowhere League cover],' James later recalled. 'That was the first time my voice left the building. The next day it was like, "I'm trying to sing and something's not right here." I gave it a few days, rested it, came back and it was still not right. I got scared, so I went to a throat doctor for the first time. He stuck a little camera down my nose to see my throat – which was a brand-new lovely experience – and said, "You've abused your throat here. You gotta rest it for two weeks." I was like, "No way. I'm indestructible. This can't be happening to me." Watching out for my throat was never important. I'd be medicating it with booze or whatever just to get through the gig.'

Suddenly, James couldn't sing a word of any of the songs; to his despondency, the frontman couldn't even speak. 'Not speaking was a nightmare for me,' he later said. 'I need to communicate with people to feel like I'm really here, and when my voice is in bad way, I'm in a bad mood. So, a vocal coach was suggested. I went to this guy in Los Angeles, and my mind was running wild: "What's he gonna do to me? Am I gonna turn into Pavarotti or something?" He lightened my load by saying, "Even if you wanted to be Pavarotti, you couldn't, man."'

For the first time in his career James was lubricating his throat, preparing it for singing difficult lines without the aid of alcohol. 'I used this tape to warm up, to loosen down,' Hetfield remembered. 'It was a whole new world for me – wow, this is a muscle! You need to stretch it before and after you work it out! The voice got stronger after that and the vocals came out better than I'd ever imagined. I started trying to do new things with my voice: super-low, intense, heavy stuff in "Sad But True", real Chris Isaak-type sensitivity in "Nothing Else Matters". I tried to venture out from the rock bark on the previous records.' Equally, James avoided the banal, elementary vocal patterns Metallica had previously courted. 'We tried things we had never done before,' the frontman explained. 'In the past, I would basically do what Lars was doing with the drums. If a word was wrong, or out of key, we'd punch in that word which was a lot easier.'

Metallica had composed a set of atypically slow, groove-laden numbers, but most conspicuous of all was the proposed inclusion of a song James had written for his own pleasure whilst on the road. He often worked on the tune while locked away, alone in his hotel room after a gig when he couldn't quite wind down enough to sleep. Titled 'Nothing Else Matters', it made 'Fade To Black' sound something like Slayer's 'Raining Blood'. There was little by way of power balladry, the song rolling on the softly lulling acoustic refrain for most of its six and a half minutes.

'The band heard that thing, and said, "Whoa, more of that, dude! From the heart!"' James laughed. He also revealed the intensely personal inspiration behind the track, explaining, 'It stirred up emotions about missing family or my girlfriend at the time.' Lars felt much the same emotional impact. The drummer remembers: 'When I first listened to it I just lost it, it was so huge. When I met up with James again I said, "We've gotta go to work on this one right away." A lot of people are going to be surprised when they hear this song, but to me it just sounded so right and a natural thing to do.'

The recording of 'Nothing Else Matters' pushed Hetfield well beyond his comfort zone and was the most ambitious recording the band had attempted yet. Ultimately, however, it would be worth the effort, and everyone connected with the band felt James might finally receive some recognition for his vocal talent. As Lars said, 'I think James has been a little underestimated as a singer; finally I don't think he will be anymore.'

The most instantaneous track on the album is undoubtedly the opener, 'Enter Sandman', selected as the first single. As natural a choice as this might seem, it was not unanimous but argued by Lars Ulrich, who had to deflect Bob Rock's suggestion that the first single should be 'Holier Than Thou'.

'Enter Sandman' is unique in that it was the first Metallica track to be based around a single riff – and what a riff it was. Penned by Kirk Hammett at three in the morning whilst jamming loudly in his hotel room, the initial riff was slightly different, featuring the tail end of the riff tacked on to each bar rather than at the end of three. The riff sat on a tape full of other guitar pieces, but Ulrich's finely tuned ears were immediately pricked by its catchy, direct sound: there and then, he knew this would be included on the final cut.

Indeed, the sound of this track set the tone for the remainder of the LP. The result was something gargantuan, emitting clean riffs still dowsed in luscious distortion. This rich guitar sound was created by a literal wall of sound (not to be confused with Phil Spector's wholly unrelated, trademark recording style). The studio hands built a wall of foam and U-Haul blankets to envelop the guitar sound in one quiet corner of the studio, and within this environment, the Hetfield crunch was developed.

Also immediately audible on 'Enter Sandman' is the upfront presence of the bass guitar. Gone were the mere background trickles which permeated *…And Justice For All*; instead, the listener was treated to a pounding, high-energy four-string thump. 'Bob Rock came in and explained to me the sound and the tonality of the bass and the part that it plays in the ensemble,' Jason remembered. 'If James is going to be the main songwriter and he puts that stuff up there, then I make it strong, man. I put that muscle behind it. I give it the force it deserves. His guitar is big and huge and his voice is big and huge. He needs a big, thundering bass behind it. That was my job.'

This was certainly achieved and the bass thundered throughout. There was even space for a terrific bass introduction on 'My Friend Of Misery', which Newsted co-wrote with Hetfield and Ulrich. In fact, this would be the only credit Jason received, but his influence is audible on each track of the Black Album. Arguably he plays the bass player's ultimate role – underpinning the overall structure and contributing ideas where necessary.

The slow, colossal rumble that is 'Sad But True' was a triumph of Bob Rock's guidance. Initially, as can be heard on *A Year And A Half In The Life Of Metallica*, the band attempted to play this number at something approaching mid-tempo. Dissatisfied with what he was hearing, Rock suggested they strip it down, almost to the bare bones; build it around the monolithic Hetfield riff with occasional stops to augment the power as the song starts up again. The track's errant heaviness marks

Metallica's first experimentation with lower tuning, dropping the guitars down to D. As with 'The Frayed Ends Of Sanity', the lyrics return to the theme of paranoid schizophrenia and dissociative identity disorder, later usurped by Dave Mustaine for his track 'Sweating Bullets'.

This intimate, personal track was a step ahead of 'The Frayed Ends…' and previous Metallica tracks, carrying a simplistic air of personal identity. Regardless of the lyrics to be found elsewhere on the album, the listener presumed James was singing of his own emotional state. 'Lyrically the album had to go somewhere else,' James commented on his own evolved approach to writing. 'You can't go wrong with raw human emotion: fears, questions, the unknown, authority, childhood issues – all of those things that everyone has. Addressing internal issues instead of just watching the TV was a lot more difficult though.'

Clearly Hetfield's lyrics were to carry as much weight as the music they accompanied. Whereas in times past the music was used to cherry-pick song titles, now the lyrics were an intricate part of the songs' make-up. As Hetfield himself stated, 'Back in the old days, we would start with a riff, then a song title, and try to match them up. It's one of those games. The riffs are on one side, song titles on the other. You try to connect which one belongs with which. Back then I would expand on the lyrics from a title. These days it's a lot different. We'll write songs with lyrics right away, and after we feel it for a while, name the song. It's like giving your friend a nickname or naming the dog – you don't know until you see it.'

This method led to some especially memorable titles, including the likes of 'Sad But True' – the simplicity of which spoke volumes. Administering a heady dose of paranoia and sleepless nights, its lead character tormented by thoughts of a controlling secondary persona, James reveals all with just two words at the end of the song: 'I'm you.' So all-encompassing and pervasive were these captivating lines that lyrics and music became one and, for the first time in Metallica's history, James's heart was beating on the page.

'Holier Than Thou' is an enjoyable track with a terrific riff, but in hindsight, Lars's choice of single was undoubtedly stronger. The most recognisable of all their songs, 'Enter Sandman' has became synonymous with the name of Metallica, drawing a new generation of fans, all of them eager to hear *that* song and most likely disappointed or downright terrified by the rest of the band's back catalogue. Hooking mainstream listeners with 'The Unforgiven' and 'Nothing Else Matters', Metallica's fifth album was prime commercial fodder.

The former found Metallica at their power-ballad best. Beginning with a gorgeous Spanish guitar solo and rolling military drums, this was the most enigmatic and majestic the metallers had ever sounded. 'The bells and horns at the beginning were inspired by Ennio Morricone,' James later revealed. 'I loved the Spaghetti Western music like *Fistful Of Dollars* and *The Good, The Bad And The Ugly*. I wanted to incorporate that into this song somehow to give it some kind of Western regret.'

The gorgeous guitar melody underpinning the verse is worthy of more than a background role, yet it carries the song perfectly, along with Ulrich's deep-rooted toms and Hetfield's crackling, emotive voice. This marks Hetfield's first true performance as a singer on the album, and his growth as a commanding orator is palpable. The lyrics are sheer poetry and the melodies grandiose. Kirk Hammett was memorably filmed being pushed by Bob Rock to go a step further with his solo for the song. Rock insisted he had to 'live and breathe' the solo, working on it again and again until it was perfect. Above all else, he encouraged Hammett to play not the most technical solo, but the most soulful – a goal he magnificently achieved. In fact it rates as one of Hammett's personal favourites and earned him a co-credit for the song. 'It's the type of guitar solo I've been trying to do for the last five or six years,' Hammett admitted when recording was complete, 'and I'm really proud of that.'

Lyrically the track presented another chance for James Hetfield to shine. Drawing upon memories of childhood once again, his lyrics are tainted by the strict Christian upbringing he endured, as well as the harsh necessity of early self-reliance: 'The young man struggles on and on he's known/ A vow unto his own/ That never from this day/ His will they'll take away.'

'It's a showdown with myself,' Hetfield later admitted. '"The Unforgiven" definitely has a major regret theme to it. One of the biggest fears in my life was not living the life that you chose to live. "The Unforgiven" is really blaming other people – "I'll never forgive you for what you've done." But at the end of the day, it's up to me to forgive so I can move on and live the life I need to live. It was one of the first story songs that I'd put together without it sounding really corny.'

'Wherever I May Roam' was a road warrior's song and featured a suitably road-friendly video courtesy of Adam Dubin, editor of the documentary *A Year And A Half In The Life Of Metallica.*

Based around another prime Hetfield riff, this is Metallica's ode to the road, leaving behind a lasting legacy. 'The title was inspired by "Papa Was A Rollin' Stone",' Hetfield later explained. 'There's that line, "Wherever he laid his hat was his home." That was us on the road. Since day one we've been a live band; that's our way of life. At times it's swallowed up relationships and friendships. It's in the lyric – "the road becomes my bride". That's the life we chose.' 'Wherever I May Roam' was also notable as it featured a rather unusual instrument – in heavy-metal circles at least. The introduction is played on sitar, adding one more dimension of sophistication. Though in fact, guided by Bob Rock, Metallica were apt to try many new variants on the guitar sound, from a multitude of different amplifiers, to lovelorn twelve-string acoustic and electric guitars.

Even James's father Virgil, who sat in on some of the recording sessions, was to note that his son's guitar work was now better than ever. 'He's really improved in the guitar playing,' Hetfield senior commented, 'and instead of the power chords, he's getting into some good guitar – I like that.'

The percussive element was equally important to Rock. Or, at least, it was a way to keep Lars Ulrich entertained once his drum tracks had been completed. One day, Ulrich entered the studio to be confronted by a vast array of percussive delights. 'There were tambourines, wood things and shit,' Ulrich confirmed, 'things you shake, things you hit with sticks and iron, things that clap – just any kind of sound you can imagine.' Some of these bizarre effects – including a pump-action shotgun used by James – even made it onto the album ('The God That Failed').

But for all these classic tracks, the record features various others which are not quite so memorable. 'Don't Tread On Me' seemed a feeble excuse for James Hetfield to wax lyrical on his own jingoism; 'My Friend Of Misery' was epic yet slovenly, and album closer 'The Struggle Within' lacked the distinction of a formidable chorus.

Even the lyrically biting 'The God That Failed' failed to hit the mark musically. With this track Metallica attempted to tackle harmonies that were perhaps a little too syrupy – in a rare parallel with Bob Rock's previously renowned work. However, James's lyrics are the song's saving grace. Lamenting his parents' misguided beliefs in lines such as, 'Broken is the promise, betrayal/ The healing hand held back by the deepened nail/ Follow the God that failed,' James is the true saviour of this intensely personal track.

Other tracks, however, revealed the hidden depths of the band as they existed in 1991. Taking in each of their influences past and present, the pairing of 'Through The Never' and 'Of Wolf And Man' featured writing credits for Kirk Hammett, charting the trio's progression as songwriters. Both based around gargantuan riffs, these two songs were simple, yet effective and ultimately memorable. The latter also revealed Hetfield's fascination with the natural world and, more specifically, his newfound obsession with wolves. Indeed, the frontman had even taken to sleeping with a soundtrack of wolf howls in the background, which he maintained, 'helps me relax'.

The wolf was used as a symbol for nature in the song, throughout which there was a palpable sense of the character (James's of course, seeking to revert to nature and 'the meaning of life'. As James would confirm, 'I like the animalistic part of nature. Sometimes I look around and see all the crap that we've accumulated. I mean, what the fuck do we need all this shit for anyway? This song essentially brings things back to the basics, back to the meaning of life. The song illustrates the similarities between wolves and men – and there are similarities.'

Individually, some tracks may not have been the strongest in Metallica's repertoire, but as a whole the Black Album constitutes a solid metal recording. It showed the growing maturity of the band as songwriters and performers and – with a remarkable promotional machine behind them – saw the band move into overdrive in terms of popularity. All this came at a cost, however. The mixing of the album was beset by conflicting opinions and recurring problems. As Ian Christe wrote in his study, *Sound Of The Beast*, 'The gruelling sessions cost the band $1 million and ended three marriages.'

Ultimately however, the lengthy sessions were all about quality control, and the record which emerged was something to be thankful for. 'The recording process went on for so long, much longer than anticipated,' Adam Dubin says, 'and Bob, like everyone else, seemed to be getting burned out. But he never let it diminish the quality of the work. I know that for some people the Black Album is Metallica's best and for other people it is like a sell-out or something but that's just personal taste. Bob

Rock crafted an excellent-sounding record. If you listen to "Enter Sandman", what else sounds like that? It's heavy, but there are amazing subtleties to it at the same time. It's an awesome piece of work for Bob and for Metallica. Bob Rock helped Lars and James along at that time in their process. He came in with detailed notes about each song and worked with each band member to get the best out of them. He was like an older brother who could help show the way.'

The band were thankful to have finished recording and justly proud of their accomplishments. As James Hetfield stated, 'We definitely put 110 per cent into this one, and that's what we got out.' This was a sentiment echoed by Jason Newsted: 'The final product was far and above my expectations from the first time I heard James and Lars's demos,' the bassist declared. 'There was a very big feeling of accomplishment and a good boost for my pride personally.' Newsted had endured and overcome early ribbing from his co-workers, and with the completion of the Black Album, he finally felt he was fitting into place, a critical piece of the band's puzzle.

This togetherness was also acknowledged by Kirk Hammett, who said, 'We all bonded with each other and confided in each other and we realised how much this really means to all of us because this whole Metallica thing will be with us until our dying day.'

Lars Ulrich was exuberant as ever, claiming that the Metallica master plan had finally been set in motion. 'It was like the planets were aligning,' he raved, in typically understated style. 'The right songs, the right producer to take it to the next level. If I looked you in the eye and said we felt it was just another record I would be lying – we knew the Black Album was special.'

CHAPTER 15
BURNT OFFERINGS

'It's too easy to say something like,
"Yeah, we don't care if the album doesn't sell one copy
or 10,000 or 10 million." Anyone who tells you that – deep down,
they're not telling the truth. But at the end of the day, the thing that
matters is that you make a record that's completely yours from beginning
to end, with no sacrifices, no compromises, no corners cut.'
Lars Ulrich

In February 1991, Metallica were awarded a Best Metal Performance Grammy for their rendition of Queen's 'Stone Cold Crazy', the track that appeared on Elektra's compilation album. This time the organisers were savvy enough to nominate *bona fide* metal acts for the category, and so Metallica beat contemporaries Judas Priest, Anthrax and Megadeth to the honour. Nonetheless, Metallica remained sceptical of the judges' decision, especially on the strength of a track which took them all of fifteen minutes to record.

Ever the cynic, Lars Ulrich outlined his own take on the high-profile ceremony. 'If we release anything for the rest of the nineties, every year we'll get a Grammy for it, just because they fucked up that first year,' the drummer spat. 'We go into the studio in January last year and spend the shortest visit we've ever had in the studio and we put down a cover version of a Queen song for an Elektra compilation album, and it's track eleven on side three, right, and it wins a Grammy over fully fledged albums by, like, Judas Priest and Megadeth? Don't you think it's got anything to do with, "Gee, how can we rectify how we fucked up in 1989?"'

The band were far more excited about the premiere of their second ever music video. With the strobe-heavy 'Enter Sandman', it promised to be an epileptic's nightmare on film. Summoning up a child's world of bad dreams in much the same way as the lyrics, the video had a suitably claustrophobic feel. At the time, Kirk Hammett observed, 'The video format is very different now than what we were used to in the early and mid-eighties. All the videos that were being made back then were just plain stupid as far as metal bands were concerned; bands always performing onstage or bimbos running around, and that kinda turned us off to it. We've opened up our minds and our perspectives a bit more now and we've found that we can experiment with the video format and be creative with it.'

There was a definite belief that from now on, Metallica were set to release many more music videos. In fact, the Black Album would contain no less than five tracks for which videos were recorded. Yet 'Enter Sandman' was the most memorable choice for a first single, and it was this track which would be played worldwide to offer a taste of the full album. The song would become one of the biggest metal hits of the time and years later its popularity remains undimmed. The impact of this song as an intriguing introduction to *Metallica* (and the myriad different formats and special editions of the single) ensured swift sales of the LP across the world, making it Metallica's biggest album to date almost instantly. In its first week in stores, the Black Album sold 600,000 copies in the US alone.

In August the band threw an unprecedented listening party for fans in New York, according to a format which would be replicated all over the world. Free tickets were given out to fans allowing them to come for an exclusive first listen of the album in huge auditoriums with colossal speaker systems. For the first groundbreaking airing, fans were invited to Madison Square Garden, a venue usually reserved for giant live concerts as opposed to a mere album playback. But this was not a 'usual' band and – in true Metallica style – there was nothing predictable or customary about this night. In fact, Metallica became the first act to sell out a major venue for a straightforward album session, with 19,000 fans flooding through the doors in anticipation of the release. No doubt, many of them were attracted by the sheer originality of the concept itself. Traditionally, listening sessions were open to jaded journalists only – and rarely would the select few entrants impart any relevant information to eager fans. For the first time ever, swathes of Metallica fans from all over the world were invited to the ordinarily closed sessions.

During these initial playbacks, however, the band appeared uncharacteristically nervous. After all, this was a first indication of how their legions of eager listeners would react to the stripped-down, ambitious material. 'It was weird just walking around the corridors of Madison Square Garden and your album's playing up there and there's thousands of people sitting there. It was really uncomfortable,' Lars said somewhat sheepishly. 'I was more nervous that day than I've ever been for anything else with Metallica.' And Lars was not alone; Kirk Hammett too was anxiously awaiting judgement. 'When the album came out we were a little bit nervous,' he revealed, 'we didn't know how the fans would react to it, because it's a bit *different*.'

Adam Dubin produced an introductory video for the listening sessions. As he explains, 'The intro video was an interesting thing. Here it was that I had shot all this footage of the band from about October 1990 to July 1991 and "Snake Pit" stage for the tour, I got a call to cut together some of the footage into a quick summary of the making of the album and add a quick recap of Metallica's history. So, there I am in an edit studio with all of my footage, which was over 100 hours, and Metallica's archive which includes all the pieces of *Cliff 'Em All*. There was also various home videos from Cliff Burton hanging out, an early Metallica video from the Stone… all kinds of weird and cool stuff.

'So I hammered it together into what became the intro video,' he continues. 'The first place that it was shown was in my hometown of New York City at Madison Square Garden at a listening party for the new album in August 1991. That was a very proud moment. It was great to see my film up on the big screen and 19,000 people watching it. It also proved out the concept that the footage was good and could play as a strong documentary of the band. I'm not sure if this was the exact moment when Metallica decided to use the film as an intro for the Black Album tour, but it certainly showed the way. After that I was editing away on the opening intro film. When my friends would ask me, "Who's opening for Metallica when they hit the road?" I would say, "I am."

'I really love it,' Adam says candidly of the Black Album. 'It still sounds great to me. I was able to come into the Metallica world with fresh ears. I was not a diehard fan. I liked the band but I didn't listen to them regularly. My tastes are a little more towards blues rock. In a way, the Black Album was perfect for me. I remember when Rick Rubin brought back to our dorm *Ride The Lightning* in 1984. He loved it and said, "This is the new shit!" I remember I thought it was good and fast, but I wasn't hooked yet. Rubin was always so progressive. The Black Album was more my speed.'

Dubin envisaged the Black Album as the recording that would truly propel Metallica into the big league. After several months filming with the band in the studio, he explained his firm conviction that what he was hearing was to be a landmark release. 'I think I realised it when I heard "The Unforgiven" coming together,' he says. 'Just the way that song builds is so massive and beautiful. It really got to me. Bob Rock had the band record the drum takes as a band, all in the same room as one can see by watching my film. That was a big step for the band and I think it made a big difference in the sound and the songs; they were all connecting. Sometimes when I am driving and "Enter Sandman" comes on the radio and I crank it, I almost forget that I was there when it was recorded. It sounded great in the demo stage. But once Bob and James built the wall of amps and got the mighty Hetfield sound into it, it was like an unstoppable train barrelling along.'

There were, of course, many who reacted adversely to the new-look Metallica. For all those who believed that the band sold out with 'Fade To Black', 'Nothing Else Matters' seemed especially ambitious. Once again, the band had proved their willingness to jump in the fire, opening themselves to the scrutiny of their fans. And in general, of course, the Black Album was a mid-paced departure from the velocity of old. Ex-fan club chief K.J. Doughton exemplifies a veteran thrasher's reaction to the fifth Metallica LP. 'I think *Kill 'Em All* is my sentimental favourite, just because it so perfectly defines the whole underground metal scene during the early eighties. I think of *Ride The Lightning, Master Of Puppets* and *…And Justice For All* as three pieces of a colossal trilogy. There are structural similarities to each of these albums, including an initial high-speed track, and a more introspective, building song to finish the first side. They can almost act together as a huge concept album. To me, those three records are the band's zenith. I like the Black Album, but didn't think it was the masterwork that everyone else did.'

Critical reaction was paramount, however, and almost universally the Black Album received abundant praise. *Kerrang!* awarded full marks, claiming it was 'their most accessible album since *Ride The Lightning*. Musically it leaves …*And Justice For All* on the scrap heap.' *Spin* suggested that 'this record's diamond-tipped tuneage strips the band's melancholy guitar excess down to melodic, radio-ready bullets and ballads', while *Rolling Stone* (who also gave their highest rating) intimated, 'Several songs seem destined to become hard-rock classics. They effectively bridge the gap between commercial metal and the much harder thrash of Slayer, Anthrax and Megadeth.' Writing for the *Washington Post*, Richard Harrington echoed the virtually unanimous critical opinion. He wrote: 'Metallica is the only heavy metal band that adults could listen to without feeling their IQ diminishing.'

Indeed, though metal magazines were predictably bowled over by the album, the reaction of the more commercial music press was the real indicator of how far Metallica had crossed into the mainstream. The indie press too were enthusiastic, with *Melody Maker* touting the album as one of the best of 1991. Their reviewer affirmed: 'In a committed move away from their thrash roots, the Black Album was slower, less complicated, and probably twice as heavy as anything they've done before.' *Q* magazine later stated the Black Album had 'transformed Metallica from cult metal heroes into global superstars, bringing a little refinement to their undoubted power'. Even *Entertainment Weekly* offered the album a grading of B+. However, there was some indication that publications such as this one, with scant knowledge of the metal genre, were ill-qualified to judge – as demonstrated by *Entertainment Weekly*'s cringe-inducing misunderstanding of pace. 'Rock's pre-eminent speed-metal cyclone... Metallica may have invented a new genre: progressive thrash,' raved one misguided writer.

The clearest evidence of Metallica's mainstream prowess was to be found in the American charts. Metallica went straight in at Number One on the *Billboard* chart and remained there for a month. This news met with a strangely subdued reaction from the band, however. As Lars Ulrich indicated, 'You think one day some fucker's gonna tell you, "You have a Number One record in America," and the whole world will ejaculate. I stood there in my hotel room and there was this fax that says, "You're Number One." And it was like, "Well, okay." It was just another fucking fax from the office. It's really difficult to get excited about it. We never tried to be Number One, but now we're Number One, and it's like, okay.' Ultimately the Black Album would reach sales of over fourteen million, becoming the twenty-fifth best-selling album of all time in America alone.

The release of 'Nothing Else Matters' would also show just how far Metallica had progressed – from thrashing purveyors of mayhem to housewives' choice. The song hit Number Six on the UK singles chart, while in America it reached Number 11. Though the song's orchestral undertones are still audible, Rock's original version was more string-heavy by far. Composer Michael Kamen was brought in to collaborate with the band on the track, but his inclusion of a 70-piece orchestra went far beyond Metallica's humble expectations. Thus, the instrumentation was somewhat toned

Onstage with new recruit Jason Newsted (far left) back in 1988, James and Kirk show why Castle Donington's Download Festival was once known as 'Monsters of Rock'.

Opposite: Jason 'Newkid' (second from right) flipping all the right fingers on a shoot with the band in Chicago, 8 June 1989.
Above: *Lars and James take a moment to appreciate the soft furnishings and chilled beer backstage at Oakland Coliseum, 24 September 1992.*
Left: *James Hetfield, the ultimate lead singer – unique, commanding, mesmeric in November 1992.*

Left: Jason Newsted and Kirk Hammett in 1998. According to Jason, 'Metallica is going to be one of those bands that in the future people will still listen to the way I still listen to Zeppelin and Sabbath albums.'
Below: Stepping into the spotlight, Metallica's fourth bassist Robert Trujillo (far right) takes his place alongside James and Kirk in 2009.
Opposite: In search of a new direction? Metallica navigate the city streets, April 2003.

Above: *'I'm not trying to be Jason [...] I just try to give everything I've got.' Rob Trujillo lets his fingers do the talking at Glasgow's SECC, 26 March 2009.*
Opposite: *Once burned... years on from his disastrous experience on tour with Guns N' Roses, James indulges in further pyrotechnic action.*

'Here's to the metal purveyors and long may they reign.' Rob, Lars, James and Kirk take a bow at the end of their show at Earls Court, London, 19 December 2003.

down for the album and single version of 'Nothing Else Matters' (though the full orchestra can be heard in the 'Elevator' version of the song, which appears as a B-side for the 'Sad But True' single and features no electric guitars whatsoever). 'Nothing Else Matters' would also become renowned for its video, pieced together from a series of amusing clips from Dubin's documentary. Adam Dubin explains: 'After I got the intro film going, Lars asked me to take a crack at editing together the documentary footage for the "Nothing Else Matters" music video. He specifically wanted to see if the footage would take the viewer away from the idea that it is essentially a love song.'

Dubin is also of the opinion that '"Nothing Else Matters" presented the band in a way that viewers could relate to them – basically as people doing normal things. It's different than something like "Enter Sandman" or "The Unforgiven". In "Nothing Else Matters" they are more unguarded. That's what I wanted to show. It seems to have worked because people reacted well to it.'

Dubin believes the video was only possible with the privileged access he was granted to the band – from which one especially memorable shot emerged. 'I was around the band at certain times,' Dubin says. 'I was in the studio when significant events happened in the recording and only on about half of the dozen songs on the album. My shooting day would be as long as they were there, usually from the afternoon to late at night. I did a shoot day with Jason at his home in San Francisco. He was very kind and it gave me some insight into his life. I used some of that footage in the film and the video for "Nothing Else Matters", such as when he attempts a basketball shot.'

If the recording of the Black Album had been stressful and long winded, the resultant tour would show just how many new fans Metallica had suddenly inherited. They would essentially be on the road for two years promoting the album. To keep the show interesting, the band and their management designed a new stage set-up. Metallica would play on a diamond-shaped stage with a special area called the 'Snake Pit' in the centre. Housing 120 fans as close to the band as possible, this was arguably the best way to experience a Metallica gig. 'The pit is elevated up just a little bit so that your head and arms are at stage level,' Jason Newsted explained. 'So we're just milling around you and spitting, sweating, and whatever – wiping boogers on you the whole time. It is the eye of the hurricane. We're around you constantly.' James Hetfield was quoted as saying the band did not like to 'separate ourselves from our audience'.

The typical live show was shunned by Metallica in favour of the same video piece they had used for the listening sessions. Adam Dubin's video would be beamed as the 'opening act' at every date on the Wherever We May Roam tour. To compensate for the lack of any support band – reasoning that they'd have been allocated a 30-minute set at the very least – Metallica would routinely play extended shows, between two and a half and three hours long. These would include extended solos on guitar and bass, plenty of new material, and a selection of expected classics, from 'Seek And Destroy' to 'One'. These solos gave James Hetfield and Lars Ulrich much-needed breathing space, though the affair was a little less rock'n'roll than one might think. As Kirk would say, 'I have a little table with a reading light, and those guys have made it quite cosy too. I'm not to the point where I take newspapers down there yet, but

I have seen certain band members reading scuba magazines while other guys solo.' He was referring to Lars Ulrich who, during the tour for the Black Album, started studying for a scuba-diving license.

Far more embarrassing for the drummer was the time when, during a show in Madison, Wisconsin, his drum kit fell through a hole in the stage that should have been there to make the drum kit rise. A red-faced Ulrich cringed at the memory of the mishap, which occurred in full view of 20,000 people. 'They couldn't get me back up,' he told *Rolling Stone*. 'I ended up playing two or three songs under the stage.'

Though the band played a multitude of dates throughout the States and Europe, two gigs in particular rank among the most special in Metallica's career. On 28 September 1991 the band joined AC/DC, the Black Crowes and Pantera, playing for an estimated million-strong audience. A free concert in a city which rarely witnessed rock or metal shows, the event drew an unprecedented crowd to the Tushino Airfield in Moscow, Russia. It was even rumoured that Mikhail Gorbachev, Russia's then Prime Minister, personally invited the band to play the concert. For a country which, at the time, was unused to high-profile gigs, the security was an overwrought, draconian affair.

During Pantera's performance, which was filmed and released on the band's *Vulgar Video* set, several fans can be seen in altercations with the military police patrolling the front of the crowd; many of them were hit with batons and kicked maliciously. The official records list 53 injuries that day, but it seems likely many more were attacked by some of the thousand-strong militia men present. Metallica's set was magnificent as usual, but charged with extra energy given the crowd were so fired up, appreciative of the rarity of this event. 'I was walking into the lobby, some kid had snuck in, and he just stood there in front of me, crying, "You don't know what it means to me for you to come here,"' Lars later said in an interview on the *Cunning Stunts* DVD. 'I stood there, watching him break down in front of me. I don't even know how to express how it made me feel. These kids were so appreciative of the fact that we were coming there, and it was very heavy to think that maybe our music gave them a little something to grasp on to.'

Metallica then appeared at the fabled Freddy Mercury Tribute Concert. Mercury, Queen's beloved singer, had died just six months earlier at the age of 45 from HIV-related complications. He was honoured by a phenomenally strong bill of musicians which included Robert Plant, David Bowie, Guns N' Roses, Elton John and Tony Iommi. James Hetfield also played a riotous 'Stone Cold Crazy' with the remaining members of Queen. Metallica played a three-song set which featured 'Enter Sandman', 'Sad But True' and a poignant 'Nothing Else Matters'. The Freddie Mercury Tribute Concert for AIDS Awareness was held at Wembley Stadium on Easter Monday, 20 April 1992. All 72,000 tickets were sold off within hours of going on sale, even though the acts had not been announced at the time. The concert was televised live worldwide to an estimated audience of one billion viewers. All proceeds from the gig were donated to Freddie Mercury's AIDS fund.

'That gig was really cool, but actually the rehearsal was even cooler,' James later revealed. 'I thought it was going to be a little rehearsal room, but it was a little bigger. There were a *few* more people there than I expected. And I was already nervous as shit. But as soon as I talked with the guys, they were really cool, really mellow – they made me relaxed right away.'

Adam Dubin, of course, filmed the whole build up and finally, the gig itself for the *A Year And A Half In The Life Of Metallica* documentary. He says today, 'One of my favourite segments is the whole Freddie Mercury Tribute footage. It was a great time, especially the rehearsal with Tony Iommi. I had to work hard to get the clearances to get Spinal Tap in there, but I am very proud that they are there. Once I saw that they were in the next dressing room over from Metallica, I knew that it would make a great segment. The minute everyone was in the same room I turned on my camera and they were off and running. It was very funny.'

On 25 February 1992 Metallica were awarded a Grammy for Best Metal Performance for the Black Album. This time, the band attended the ceremony and graciously accepted the award, though Lars could not resist a last dig at the organisers. 'I think the first thing we've gotta do is thank Jethro Tull for not putting out an album this year!' Lars joked. 'I wanna thank all the radio stations and MTV, without whom all of this was possible anyway! Just kidding…'

In a move they would later come to regret, Metallica were then to co-headline a series of stadium dates with Guns N' Roses throughout America from July to October 1992. The idea had long been mooted and in May of 1992 Metallica's Lars Ulrich, along with GN'R guitarist Slash, spoke at a press conference to officially announce the tour – touted as one of the biggest of all time.

Despite the glaring stylistic differences between the two bands and, to a certain degree, their fanbases, they were, at the time, the two most influential acts in the world of rock. The news that they were joining forces for this unprecedented event was thrilling for fans of either band, leaving every promoter hungry for a piece of the action. Lars Ulrich was, by his own admission, the one 'closest to some of those guys' and he spoke of 'late night drinking babbles where we would speak about actually going out and playing some gigs together'.

Despite Lars's friendship with the members of Guns N' Roses, even he would be forced to admit the sheer scale of the union was daunting. 'I don't think any of us realised when we sat down and had our drunken talks about doing this tour together, how tough it would be to get the three months of this happening,' the drummer admitted. 'It's down to the persistence of the band members that this is happening, because if it was left to the managers, agents and accountants, this would have never got off the ground.'

The principal difficulties of the two bands touring together centred round GN'R frontman Axl Rose, who had by this time begun to seize control of his band's business affairs. The quintet had reached the very height of their popularity, having toured for almost as long as Metallica in support of their *Use Your Illusion* double-album set. Rose was a notoriously awkward individual, prone to storming offstage early or, in some cases, not showing up at all. Metallica expected this unprofessional attitude to change for a double-bill tour, but they underestimated the GN'R vocalist's excess. In 1993, James Hetfield spoke about sharing a stage with the temperamental singer. 'It was different,' Hetfield laughed. 'It was a good idea. We really had no idea what was going to come with it. We were out to show people that there was something a little more progressive and hardcore out there than Guns N' Roses – and to go about it our way. But it was hard going on, dealing with Axl and his attitude. It's not something we'd want to do again.'

Indeed, where the rest of Metallica seemed to accept Rose's often bizarre, egomaniacal behaviour, James was notoriously outspoken and honest on the subject. In a segment included in Adam Dubin's documentary, James is filmed making fun of Axl and his rider requirements for each date of the tour.

Hetfield snorts, 'Horrible truths: the piddly wants and needs of certain folks on the road. Axl "*Pose*" dressing room requirements.' Sneering, Hetfield reads from the list: 'Absolutely *no* substitutions. One cup of "cubed" ham, it's got to be cubed so he can get it down his little neck... one rib-eye steak dinner – I didn't know the guy ate meat, looks like a fucking vegetarian... pepperoni pizza, fresh – I think that's just for throwing around – one can of assorted Pringles chips – that's the greasy shit so he can grease his hair back.' Amidst sniggers from the rest of the Metallica camp at Hetfield's obvious distaste, the vocalist continues, 'Honey – that makes him SING LIKE THIS! One bottle of Dom Pérignon – hey, that's where the money's at, right there.' Having recited every item, he exclaims, 'It's just fucking crap,' and stamps on the paper, all the while being filmed.

A further bone of contention was the sarcastic note put up by Metallica in their dressing room, entitled 'The Six Phases Of Any Stadium Tour'. It listed the following quip:

Enthusiasm,
Disillusionment,
Panic,
Search for the guilty,
Punishment of the innocent,
Praise and honours for the non-participants.

A seventh scrawled point read, 'Killing the prima [which was crossed out] lead singer.' Tensions between the two bands were pushed to breaking point at a show in Montreal, Canada, on 8 August 1992. There was confusion over where James Hetfield should stand during a part in 'Fade To Black' where a twelve-foot flame shot out from beneath the stage. Unfortunately Hetfield positioned himself right in the middle of the flame and suffered second and third-degree burns to his face, arms, hands and legs. 'His skin was bubbling like on *The Toxic Avenger*,' Jason later said. James's left hand and wrist were so badly blistered he could barely use his hand, much less play guitar.

Pandemonium ensued. The depleted Metallica trio bravely announced to the miffed crowd that James had been taken to hospital and they could not finish their set, promising to return to play for the fans. Though the disappointment was palpable, the audience seemed to accept what they were hearing. Events had spiralled out of the band's control, and they were simply concerned for James's health.

Given the bedlam behind the scenes, Guns N' Roses took to the stage an hour late and were apparently suffering sound problems, with certain musicians unable to hear particular instruments. Axl Rose later claimed his throat was sore. Whatever the reason, the singer went storming off the stage before the end of the night. It soon became apparent he wasn't to return and the crowd – by now furious with the night's events – turned into a riotous mob. Spilling out into the surrounding area, frustrated fans proceeded to overturn cars, smash windows, loot local stores and even set a number of fires in protest. It took several hours for local authorities to contain the mayhem, by which time the true culprits of the night – namely, Guns N' Roses and Axl Rose – had inadvertently caused thousands of dollars worth of damage. A disgusted James later said, 'That's how they get attention. Their set's kinda boring so they have to do something like that. Rose had to top what I did. "I know, I'll start a riot and steal the press away from this burning thing!"' GN'R were heavily fined and it was later revealed by guitarist Slash in his autobiography that the band made very little money from the tour given their regular fines for late appearances or damage to property, as well as Axl Rose's lavish backstage parties, thrown by the vocalist every night.

For Metallica, however, the most serious obstacle was James's injured hand, though as Kirk Hammett would explain in a TV interview, it would take more than a few burns to stop the Metallica frontman. 'James was very motivated to heal himself as quickly as possible,' said Hammett. 'And James is the kind of guy who doesn't like letting people down.'

James himself seemed similarly keen to downplay his injury, describing it as being 'like a rug burn for a while. The hand is pretty sensitive. I can still make a fist and shit, but I can barely bump it.' His scars took six months to heal, during which time the guitarist had to wear special gauntlets to stop the skin cracking and blistering. Just seventeen days later, however, Metallica were back in action, with James in tow, appearing merely as a vocalist. Once again, loyal friend John Marshall stepped in to assist the band.

'Being a frontman was weird,' James said of singing without a guitar in hand. 'It reminded me how much I really loved fucking playing rhythm guitar. Especially during some of the older songs, where there's a lot of guitar work or instrumental shit. It's like, "What the fuck do I do?" I'd just leave. Go backstage and have a beer.'

There were another eighteen shows for Metallica to endure with perennial rebels GN'R but, despite a reluctance to play with such a volatile band, Hetfield and company fulfilled their contract, playing each date on time and with renewed gusto. Overall, on paper at least, the tour was a success; Metallica had ensnared a new group of fans and made a good deal of money in the process. James's hand had now healed and they were ready to break for Christmas before returning for the final leg of their mammoth tour.

The third stage of their travelling live show proved beyond doubt just how far Metallica had come since their early days. Nineteen ninety-three saw the band travel to Mexico, Indonesia, Thailand, Brazil, Chile, Israel and Slovakia amongst a string of other countries they had never visited.

Their series of dates in Southeast Asia were unprecedented for a major heavy-metal band and provided some much needed amusement for band and crew. It may have seemed a great proposition to travel to exotic, hitherto unexplored lands, but there were many logistical issues to be addressed – not least band members' conduct on the hallowed stages of the distinctly polite, well-behaved Southeast Asian people. Metallica's production manager Jake Berr took the brave step of posing most crucial questions of etiquette in preparation for the band's show in Singapore. The response, as printed in Metallica's *Live Sh*t* photo book (from the *Live Sh*t: Binge & Purge* box set), made for hilarious reading.

For Attention:

Mr. Jake Berr
Production Manager
Metallica

Date: 22 March 1993

Dear Jake,
To reiterate our conversation of yesterday and in reply to your fax, I submit the following answers to your questions:

Q: Can the band spit onstage?

A: Emphatically no. Spitting is an offence in Singapore and is a punishable one at that. If it is a situation that has become a degree habitual, then all I can say is to please exercise some constraint and if they absolutely must, exit the stage right or left, get rid of the offending problem and return to the performance.

Q: Can the band use swear words e.g. fuck?

A: Please no. Not if they can possibly help it. In particular I must put the emphasis on the ever popular phrase of 'mother-fucker'. At all costs endeavour to avoid this. Any reference to the word 'mother' in this society must be with the utmost reverence.

What they say and do in the privacy of their hotel rooms, dressing rooms, catering rooms, etc is entirely their business, however when they are up there onstage and have at least 7,500 adoring fans hanging on every word and the press in attendance, it would be appreciated if the more colourful adjectives were given a rest for the evening and replaced with something a little less crass.

Returning to Europe for the final stretch, Metallica ended their longest tour ever, in Werchter, Belgium. They had played a remarkable 250 dates all over the world and – despite their success – the band's rootless existence was beginning to take its toll. 'It was more than my body could take,' James affirmed in a 1999 interview. 'You're there and your head tells you that you have to go on, but your body is close to giving out. Five to six days a week, I was onstage for about two and a half hours every night. Doing that for over two years, my larynx didn't feel great; it felt like my vocal chords were just falling apart.' Once the tour had finally come to an end, the band found they no longer knew quite what to do with themselves. James admitted, 'It is strange because it does just feel like a break in the tour. After the last show I had a couple of bottles of wine to myself and ended up throwing up before my flight.'

The band's incessant touring, combined with the sheer volume of people who'd come to hear Metallica's music, solidified their position as the world's premier heavy-metal band during the early 1990s – at a time when few established bands were managing to stay afloat with any degree of success at all. With the onset of the unstoppable establishment of grunge, fans were drifting further from once beloved metal bands. The only type of metal still thriving was the thrash crossover style pioneered by Pantera (with their classic *Vulgar Display Of Power*) and the reinforced death-metal crossover of Sepultura's *Chaos A.D.* Elsewhere the previously loyal metal press seemed besotted by the likes of Alice In Chains, Nirvana, Pearl Jam and Soundgarden.

Interestingly, Metallica never distanced themselves from more varied forms of alt rock, taking Faith No More, featuring James's good friend Jim Martin, on the road with them for the Guns N' Roses tour, in a support slot they'd originally offered to grunge behemoths Nirvana (who turned it down).

Most metal bands were steadfastly clinging to their image as metal titans, in the misguided belief that heavy metal had to remain as it was back in the 1980s if it was to retain any degree of legitimacy. They blamed the likes of Nirvana for the destruction of their scene. Metallica, by contrast, had long been advocates of *their* own style. For them, boundaries of genre had never mattered, and consequently they transcended the normally frosty borders separating metal from the masses. Thus, even as metal was dying a commercial death, Metallica, the hardcore 'thrash' band, succeeded in selling fourteen million records.

CHAPTER 16
BINGE AND PURGE

'Yes, we do sell out, every single time, everywhere we play.'
Lars Ulrich

On 17 November 1992, the much anticipated home video *A Year And A Half In The Life Of Metallica, Part 1 & 2* was released. The documentaries focused on the lengthy recording process of Metallica's Black Album, as well as the tour that followed. Director Adam Dubin explains how he became involved with the project, gaining him unprecedented access to the band's most clandestine studio sessions. 'I got the job because my manager at the time, Juliana Roberts, knew Metallica's manager Peter Mensch, and they got to thinking that someone should document Metallica as they entered the studio to make what everybody knew would be their next great album,' Dubin says today. 'The question was who could do this job. I guess I was the sacrificial lamb as it were. I went in and luckily they didn't kill me! Remember, at that time, Metallica was famous as the band that didn't make music videos or cater to MTV. I am glad that Lars and James and then Kirk and Jason were able to allow me into their process of creation. It was touch and go at first, but I think I was able to show the band that I could film their process without affecting their creativity. My job was to be a fly on the wall; not to be noticed.'

Ironically, Dubin revealed the secret of the film's success – an all-inclusive air which appealed to fans outside of Metallica's world. 'I approached it as a documentary film about a process,' the director explains. 'I knew that if I just made a film that sucked up to Metallica fans then only Metallica fans would buy it. I realised as I was filming that there was a chance to gain the interest of a much wider audience; people who would never listen to Metallica but would watch Metallica as they created their new music. People are fascinated by process, hence all the cooking shows and building shows on TV. It's the same thing with Metallica. People wanted to see Metallica going through the recording process. I made the film with that in mind. If the film could sustain the interest of non-Metallica fans then surely the fans would love it. It seems to have worked.'

It is perhaps surprising to learn that Metallica were permissive and accepting of a camera being in their faces almost 24-7. Since then, of course, they have opened themselves to an even greater extent for the documentary *Some Kind Of Monster*, but in 1991-92 at least, Metallica were renowned as an intensely private band. Their frontman in particular was a shy, retiring personality who shunned excessive attention unless it was absolutely on his own terms. Yet while James displayed an ability to ignore the camera (or at least so it seems on film), Lars was often the moodiest band member to come under the scrutiny of Big Brother's gaze. Despite some reluctance from the drummer, it was understood that, for the video to work, the acquiescence of each musician was required. As Dubin makes clear, 'The one part that I as a director can't beg, borrow or steal is the cooperation of the band. Each member of Metallica – James, Lars, Jason, Kirk – was incredibly generous and let me into an aspect of their life and that allowed me to make the film that I made. Without that, it would just be a very cold process, like watching paint dry. The kudos goes to Metallica for having the balls to allow a documentary filmmaker into their world and not setting up a bunch of rules and regulations. Lars always said to me, "Just film everything." He was as good as his word. The band would never redo or repeat anything because that would be fake – nor would I ask them.'

Old habits die hard, however, and on the matter of the final product Metallica were as stubborn as ever. The documentaries have subsequently been released on DVD, but at the time they were shot video was the only choice, causing the manufacturers one insurmountable problem. '*Part 2* was two hours and twelve minutes long,' Dubin explains. 'Once you go over two hours on a VHS tape it requires a special tape to be made, so Warner Bros. was begging Metallica to cut some stuff out so they could use a standard tape, but Metallica stuck to their guns and said, "This is the way we want it, so too bad." That's the way it was with Metallica – the music came first.'

Dubin remembers some defining moments from the second documentary and describes how filming started: 'After I finished the "Nothing Else Matters" music video, but before it premiered on MTV, I got a call that Metallica wanted me to come out on the road with them and document the tour. I went to the Grammys on the night they won for the Black Album. That was a great night and an amazing party afterwards thrown by Warner Bros. Records: a real rock star "who's who" event. I shipped out with Metallica the next day. They had to get back on the road. I shot a quick segment with Kirk at a monster memorabilia shop in New Jersey. Everyone knows Kirk loves and collects that stuff. Then we went to the airport to board the Metalliplane. There are some shots in the videos of Lars getting out of a van with shades on. Then James gets out and gives the finger to the camera. That was from that day at the airport. After that, everything got crazy. It was fun being on the road at this level. I travelled with the band, so it was good living. One time the plane was going through turbulence. Lars was nervous. To cut the tension, James starts singing Lynyrd Skynyrd songs and everyone laughed. Things were different then. The band would hang out together a lot, go out drinking after shows. I'm not saying it was better; it's just that's what they did during that period. But make no mistake, the music always came first.'

Dubin also offers an explanation of the tensions made clearly visible to the armchair voyeur. 'When people see members of Metallica squabbling in *A Year And A Half In the Life...* or even later in *Some Kind Of Monster*, it is important to understand that these folks are extremely dedicated to what they are doing. If they weren't artists with strong creative drives, they wouldn't have gotten where they are. And it's not just Lars and James. When you have very strongly creative people in a room there is natural tension. When it works out well, some really creative and powerful things come out of it. It can also lead to difficulty. I think it is to Metallica's credit that they have overcome their differences and that's because the music always comes first. It would be so much easier to disband as so many other great bands have done, but they have persevered and I think it shows. I am very proud and happy to have been there to document this pivotal period in the band's life. I am also privileged to have a continuing relationship with the band wherein I can film them every once in a while as the years go by.'

Most memorably, as with their other innovations, Metallica (and Dubin) established a genre that is now *de rigueur*. 'I remember that before I did that film there really wasn't much like it before,' Dubin confirms. 'Now, because of the advent of inexpensive video cameras, any band almost can have a recording or tour documentary, but back then there was almost nothing. Aerosmith had put out a video of themselves recording *Pump*, but it wasn't very good – more like a series of shots than a complete storyline. I wanted to tell a story. I had to go back and look at two classic pieces of filmmaking for my inspiration. One was the Beatles' *Let It Be*, which is a document of them recording and basically breaking up in front of the cameras. The other was the great tour documentary of Bob Dylan, *Don't Look Back*. I had seen them before, but when I started to shoot the Metallica documentary, I watched them again. I know that *A Year And A Half In The Life...* is viewed by many up-and-coming bands because almost every band and musician that I have talked to knows the film. Some musicians know it inside out.'

The second part of the documentary reveals the ever intensifying worship of the fans. Dubin's intimate portraits depict a band coming to terms with their own increasing fame and all the obligations associated with this, from the established 'meet and greets' and merchandise signings, to jamming with a devoted fan in the studio. The fan in question, John Smith, was terminally ill from cancer and, thanks to the Make-A-Wish Foundation, he was able to accomplish his dream of playing with Metallica. He was filmed for posterity, playing 'The Four Horsemen' with his idols.

Whilst accommodating and polite, the notoriously private Hetfield was clearly finding life in the spotlight difficult to deal with. Even with side project Spastik Children, he had always shunned recognition for his part in Metallica's success; with the band experiencing fame on such a vast scale, he was feeling more uncomfortable than ever. 'You try to evaluate it as best you can – it's a fucking lot more difficult,' James said of commercial success. 'Everybody's trying to get at you, and there's a lot more shit to do, a lot more people to please. I've never really liked people much anyway. Overall, it's harder to keep in contact with the folks who are coming to your show, and hear what they have to say about it.'

This was the beginning of Hetfield's love affair with country music, as one thing he found was that country music lovers didn't know who he was, and even if they did, they didn't care. 'I don't get mobbed there,' Hetfield said of country-music bars. 'I can shoot pool and no fucker bugs me at all. A lot of times I wish I could turn the clock back a couple of years. Sometimes I think, "Goddamn! Why do all these people want my fucking autograph?" or, "Why are so many people wearing Metallica shirts?" I don't really know if I want them to wear them.'

This attitude was certainly unusual. Most bands, or performers of any kind for that matter, are largely driven by an internal desire to have people look at them and pay attention to their every move. This narcissistic mechanism rarely switches on and off, but instead is perpetually engaged with the need for celebrity. This crude yearning for self-gratification often creates an unusual power, whereby the celebrity feels untouchable.

James Hetfield, however, was perfectly satisfied with his two or three hours onstage in the limelight. Beyond that, he yearned for something resembling a normal existence. And the one thing that truly exasperated him was the mistaken belief of certain fans that they truly knew their idols. 'Fans don't know what we're like,' Hetfield vented. 'I think the music is, to the fans, real personal, and they think they know us just because of the lyrics or seeing pictures. Of course they don't know you and probably never will.'

The band would maintain that, despite their increasingly demanding schedule and growing staff roster, they were still in the same headspace as before. 'I look at the itinerary and there's two more pages of crew than there were last year; there's more people wandering around the hallways with laminates on that you don't know the names of,' Lars said bluntly. 'There'll always be isolated incidents, but I don't think that much has really changed within the close confined spaces that we operate in.'

Still, it was difficult to argue that things were anywhere approaching 'normal'. As *Kerrang!* reported at one stage of the Black Album tour, 'Deep in the belly of the stadium, the true scale of the backstage set-up becomes apparent; there are rooms full of computers and telephones, and 128 people keep this band on the road. To an outsider, some aspects of the day-to-day touring routine seem hilarious – the ride from the band's hotel to the gig, for example, with an escort of wailing sirens and police motorcycle outriders.'

Yet Lars Ulrich was adamant that being famous shouldn't mean the band had changed; they simply had more opportunities and freedom than before. 'Of course it's different from ten years ago,' he acknowledged. 'Metallica is a big business. We employ 75 people on the road; we're responsible for scores of people in offices around the world. But, we also had those companies back in 1984; the difference is now we're making enough money to pay 'em. Many people worked for free back then because they believed in what we were doing. We have remained inside of what's going on. It's like a spectacle to us. We're watching all this activity around the band; it just doesn't seem to touch us.'

Ulrich was always savvy enough to admit his desire for fame and fortune. In contrast with the take-it-or-leave-it attitude to success displayed by other bands, claiming to play for themselves alone, without a care for record sales, Lars Ulrich's ambition was never in question: he wanted to make his band the biggest in the world. Thus Metallica sought to reach more people than ever before.

As Ulrich jibed, 'Apart from that guy in Nirvana who'll lie to you and say that, "Uh, we don't want anybody to buy our records," 99.9 per cent of people in bands would like people to hear their music and get into their band. That's a fucking fact.'

By way of closure and to mark the end of their colossal touring schedule, Metallica released their first ever live album, and in the grand tradition of their musical career, they did it bigger and better than most. Not content with releasing a straightforward double live CD, which would no doubt have flown off the racks in any case, Metallica put together a stunning box set which featured three live CDs, three live home video cassettes, a stencil, and a Snake Pit pass and book. Entitled *Live Shit: Binge & Purge*, the box set was packaged as a mini road case, in homage to their non-stop touring lifestyle. 'I think it's turned into a great way of getting the last three and a half years out of our systems,' Lars confessed. 'We wrote the album, made the album, toured the album and here's the documentation of the album's music on the road. Now we can start with a clean slate. Everything about this tour is gone.'

The set – taken from various performances in Mexico City – was a well-considered trawl through great tracks from all eras of Metallica history, featuring a cleverly tailored medley of segments of the lengthy songs from …*And Justice For All* combined to save time as well as attention spans.

Without doubt, the years of incessant touring had been a resounding success, establishing Metallica as the world's premier heavy-metal band. Intriguingly, this would be the last time, up until 2008's *Death Magnetic*, that the band would feature their original logo on any new release. This small visual change represented the fact that the band were about to diversify in a manner that even their most open-minded fans were apt to question. It was time for Metallica themselves to go 'stone cold crazy'.

CHAPTER 17
ROCKED AND LOADED

'To me the most boring thing in the world is safe, mainstream heavy metal... I'd rather listen to Madonna.'
Lars Ulrich

Before recording their sixth album, Metallica would have fun with a string of intriguing concerts. Firstly, they wrapped up warm for a trip to the Arctic Circle, where they were billed to play the Molson Ice Beach Party. An unprecedented event by any standard, this was the largest gig ever staged so far north. Along with a bizarre selection of support bands, including US alternative acts Veruca Salt and Hole, Metallica headed to the minute town of Tuktoyaktuk, in Northern Canada. The place was so small and remote that the only way in or out was via charter flight. Huge heating units were set up to keep instruments and amplifiers in working order despite the sub-zero temperatures. James would later concede it was the 'weirdest' gig Metallica ever played. 'It was the show where 500 contest winners got flown to this little Eskimo village,' he later said, 'and we played this tent in an area that was the last camp before the North Pole. We played for a bunch of contest winners and Eskimos who were huffing gasoline.'

It was a fun, if freezing, event for Metallica to play, but behind-the-scenes preparation went far beyond that required for any conventional gig, and the band's team had no intention of revisiting the venue anytime in the near future. Writing for the Metallica fan-club magazine, tour manager Tony Smith revealed: 'The logistics of doing a show in the Arctic Circle were immense. You then have to think that you're inside the Arctic Circle in the late summer and that when the snow moves in they are snowed in for eight months. So I was bringing in 700 people to an infrastructure that could only support 40 per cent of that amount. So you bring in extra food and water; nobody knows you're doing it of course. I planned for being snowed in.'

Luckily the band escaped the frozen wastes, swapping them for LA's Sunset Strip just a few months later. In celebration of the birthday of Motörhead frontman Lemmy Kilmister, the band played a low-key gig at the Whisky A Go-Go. Motörhead had, of course, been a longstanding influence on the band. Along with Metallica, Lemmy and his band are still considered originators of the speed-metal style. Indeed, Lars would later reveal: 'In 1981 I ended up running some of the Motörhead appreciation stuff and also following them around on tour. A few years later when they were in LA, I went down to the hotel room to see Lemmy. I started drinking and ended up passed out in his room having thrown up over myself. He took a picture of that and put it on one of Motörhead's records.'

Billed as 'the Lemmys', Metallica took to the stage, each member resplendent in the Motörhead leader's trademark attire – black shirt, bullet belt, oversized shades after dark and a mane of flowing black hair. Their set featured several of their own numbers as well as seven Motörhead covers. Lars, who had by now cropped his own hair to shoulder length (along with several other Metallica members), explained, 'After some initial hesitation, I don the wig and shades – try playing Motörhead songs when you have a three-foot black wig on and can't see shit! – and as we walk towards the Whisky stage, for the first time since supporting Saxon in 1982, the fucking look on people's faces... classic. I start "Overkill", immediately swallow half the wig – but, who gives a fuck? – and off we go!'

Lemmy, who is a resident of Los Angeles and a permanent fixture in the clubs and bars of Sunset Strip, was flattered by the Metallica tribute. He said, 'They all dressed up as me, and I thought that was great. They all had long black wigs on and pencilled-in moustaches, and a tattoo drawn on one arm, with a black marker. They got their tattoos on the wrong arm, too, every one of them.'

Metallica would work on their sixth studio album over the course of 1995 and the first few months of 1996. Songs were written between live shows and in the comfort of band members' homes. Recording was soon underway at the Plant Studios in Sausalito, California, but compared to previous sessions it was a decidedly relaxed affair. Band members came and went as they pleased and only played together in the studio when absolutely necessary – which was surely a sign of the problems to come. In the aftermath of the best-selling album of their career, and, indeed, one of the best-selling metal albums of all time, Metallica's reaction was to reconvene, relax and wait for inspiration take hold. It was simply impossible to follow the Black Album in any artificial, contrived manner – and the band were well aware of this fact.

For the sessions, which would produce two albums worth of songs, Metallica honed their new influences, creating a rather intriguing hybrid of metal, indie, rock and country. This, of course, would have been unheard of in camp Metallica just a few years before, but times were changing; the metal scene had all but died a commercial death, and Metallica instinctively realised a change was needed. Just how far they could push their inherent desire for rebellion and experimentation was the only question. Lars had been spouting praise for a most unlikely group: Manchester's indie-rock kings Oasis, whose albums *Definitely Maybe* and *(What's The Story) Morning Glory?* he had on permanent rotation. Ulrich's devotion and passion for new music was as strong as when he was collecting NWOBHM records, but by the mid-1990s the tune was decidedly different. 'This album and what we're doing with it – that, to me, is what Metallica are all about: exploring different things,' Lars rationalised. 'The minute you stop exploring, then just sit down and fucking die.'

As for James Hetfield, he had fully embraced his country-rock roots (his father had been a devoted listener), shunning the stigma attached to any 'metalhead' with such a penchant for country. In fact, in many ways James felt far more comfortable in a country bar than a rock club. The frontman was quoted as saying, 'Five years ago I would never have listened to Waylon Jennings,' but by 1995 the influence was all-pervasive, lending a distinct country edge to Metallica's latest compositions. There was no room for the speed metal of old, with new material stripped down even further than the radical content of the Black Album. The resulting sound was cleaner by far, with a rumbling bass that did not come to the fore in quite the same way as it had done on the preceding LP. The four-string influence had in fact been pushed below the radar once again, with not a single writing credit for Jason Newsted.

Even without Newsted's contribution, however, the band had penned so many new tracks that they initially considered releasing two albums or a double album on the same day. This was vetoed in favour of releasing the albums singularly, a year apart. 'Those songs were written pretty much at the same time,' James Hetfield later explained. 'It was crazy; it was like an artist having too many colours to paint with. That seemed to be the era of the double record. Guns N' Roses had done it and a few other bands had, but it was kind of like, "Why are we doing this?" So that's when we decided to split it into two records.'

The albums were entitled *Load* and *Reload* and, in true Metallica fashion, the band went with releasing the more experimental album first. As James outlined, 'Our attitude was, "We don't give a fuck what people think. So, why should we start now?"' *Load* was an epic, twisting listen, difficult in parts and sounding more like an extended jamming session than a coherent set of song structures. 'Ain't My Bitch' and 'Hero Of The Day' were decent rock songs, while 'Wasting My Hate' and 'King Nothing' were the standout cuts and the nearest Metallica ever got to pure metal on the album. Elsewhere the songs were overlong and short on ideas – the principle offenders being 'Ronnie', 'The Outlaw Torn' and 'Poor Twisted Me' – mingled with moments of emotional catharsis, in the shape of both 'Until It Sleeps' (the lead single) and 'Mama Said'.

These two songs are charged with the album's strongest lyrical theme, centring on James's relationship with his mother, Cynthia. 'Until It Sleeps' evokes her losing battle with cancer, while 'Mama Said' is Hetfield's own sombre elegy, captured on record and cuttingly direct. Essentially a heavy-hearted, country-tinged strum, this number is carried through to its gorgeous conclusion by the sheer force of Hetfield's emotion. Featuring the most incandescent vocal performance on the album, the lyrics fill the listener with tearful empathy. 'I need your arms to welcome me,' Hetfield pleads, 'but a cold stone's all I see/ Let your son grow/ Mama, let my heart go.'

A poignant goodbye to James's buried grief, the song dragged to light the emotions he'd worked so hard to hide for the past decade and more. Frighteningly raw and perhaps even out of keeping with rest of Metallica's output, the track is nonetheless one of the band's greatest triumphs. Credit must be given once again to Bob Rock for leading James down the path to lyrical freedom and the point where he no longer felt embarrassed to bring a country-inspired song to the table. Hetfield himself would confirm, 'Nowadays it's a little easier to figure out where some of the feelings are coming from. But still, it's mass confusion.' Typically, the frontman downplayed his gift for self-expression. 'I look at it and go, "Wow, I might be really messed up, but I sound pretty good. I sound like I know what I'm talking about,"' he said.

James named 'Bleeding Me' as another of the hardest listens for him on the album, stirring some of the frontman's most 'intensely personal' memories. He explained, 'I was going through therapy at the time and I was so unwilling… it was like the therapist had put leeches on me just to get it all out. There was a lot of secret pain, so that song came from me experiencing therapy for the first time.'

During the sessions for *Load*, James also had to contend with the death of his father Virgil, who passed away at the end of a two-year battle with cancer (Lars also lost his mother Lone to cancer in early 1998). 'I kind of went back to when Cliff died,' Hetfield later confided. 'We got back to work and got some of the feelings out through the music. And keeping busy, talking to family a lot helps. I'm not the most talkative person in the world, but you do have to talk about shit like this.' James also revealed the deeper source that inspired certain lyrics on *Load*, saying, 'I went through the religion thing again, my phases of feeling total disbelief in a lot of things. It really got to me.'

Yet Jason Newsted observed Hetfield's unbreakable will kept him going through the painful loss of his dad. 'He still smiled, he cracked silly jokes,' Newsted said of the Metallica frontman. 'He doesn't wear anything on his sleeve. He wants your respect. He wants you to show his father respect. But as far as any sign of pity – fuck that. Don't even think about it.'

Though the musical direction of Metallica circa 1996 was questioned by many fans, their response to *Load* was nothing compared to the sheer outrage and confusion provoked by the band's new image. Not only had Metallica's logo been replaced by a bland, shortened version of the old font, but each band member now resembled a Mafioso pimp, complete with short cropped hair, white vests, and braces. Smoking cigars and apparently ready to attend a cocktail party, the sight of every band member (bar James Hetfield) with made-up faces was more than many fans could bear. Hetfield later admitted, 'Right around *Load* and *Reload* we felt like we were very sophisticated. We'd sit in the large dining area at Kirk's house with pitchers, smoking cigars and drinking martinis. It was a piss-take at first, but then it became something else. Martinis were definitely free flowing and we all got very good at making them.'

'Doing things the way you see it, going by your own heart and soul, that is pure artistic integrity,' Lars Ulrich proffered. 'Whether the hair is six or 60 inches long, the eyes have make-up or not, the riffs are in E or F sharp, the amps are Marshall or not; all those things don't matter if you are doing it for the right reason, which to me means doing it for yourself.'

Metallica were certainly doing that, just as they had always done. If nothing else, long-established fans and observers could give them the kudos for sticking to their guns and branching out regardless of critical opinion. At a time when many successful metal bands were playing embarrassingly safe (the Iron Maiden line-up of the time being a case in point), Metallica dared to try something different, rallying against the perceived boundaries of the metal genre. Could they still be termed a metal band? Essentially yes, but with a whole host of elements most bands were either incapable or frightened of portraying. *Kerrang!* later mused, however, that *Load* was the album that 'stripped the metal from Metallica'.

Generally, though, critical reaction was positive. Both *Q* and *Rolling Stone* awarded the album four stars out of five. The former observed astutely that 'these boys set up their tents in the darkest place of all, in the naked horror of their own heads'. *Kerrang!* also awarded four out of five Ks. Editor Phil Alexander wrote, 'Metallica have opened up their Pandora's Box of influences and let their individual talents breathe. For the most part *Load* hits the mark, illustrating that Metallica still tower over the competition with audacity and power.'

Indeed, the general consensus was that this album was above average, if not of quite the same standard as the band's previous offerings. *Melody Maker* turned in a mixed review, striking the right balance between gushing approval and sheer confusion. They suggested that 'a Metallica album is traditionally an exhausting event. It should rock you to exhaustion, leave you brutalised and drained. This one is no exception. It is, however, the first Metallica album to make me wonder at any point, "What the fuck was that?" It's as if the jackboot grinding the human face were to take occasional breaks for a pedicure.'

Regardless of the change in image, the altered, dissipated sound and the unbridled experimentation, *Load* went on to sell over five million copies – and with a front cover displaying semen and blood. Artist Andres Serrano created this unique work by mixing the bodily fluids between two glass slides. For the follow up album Metallica would use another of Serrano's notorious pieces, featuring a potent mixture of urine and blood.

Just over a year later Metallica would release *Reload*, finally providing fans with a new look that was more acceptable. *Reload* was heavier than its predecessor and arguably features stronger songs. However, the band's penchant for experimentation meant *Reload* too had its highs, lows and complete underground moments; times when the rambling, convoluted material had listeners scratching their heads even upon the tenth listen. Perhaps as a consequence of the mild disappointment of *Load*, the follow-up album sold less copies overall.

'As far as I'm concerned, you can take any of these songs and interchange them on the two albums,' Lars explained when describing *Reload*. Indeed, this may have been the best way to experience Metallica's two sets of compositions. Had they extracted the strongest tracks from each album, they could have compiled an instant classic. Instead, their desire to include the maximum amount – seemingly for the sake of it – diluted the immediacy and longevity of the material. In both cases, there was simply too much to digest and too little inspiration behind many tracks.

Despite the novelty of melodies played on violin and hurdy-gurdy, 'Low Man's Lyric' remains an unmemorable, lacklustre effort. Recruiting English songstress Marianne Faithfull to provide the hoarse, haunting backing vocals for 'The Memory Remains' was a bold move which generated much controversy. Yet her talent could not detract from the simple truth that the lead single was a poor composition with an especially weak chorus. Conversely, Metallica were at their best on the likes of opener 'Fuel', the inspired follow-up to an old favourite in 'The Unforgiven II', and the closing 'Fixxxer', endowed with a fantastic lead riff.

Other tracks were saved by virtue of Hetfield's unmistakable vocals and typically immense guitar playing, but missing something more besides – indeed, it seemed Metallica had added elements of experimentation into the mix to disguise their lack of inspiration. 'If people think we've lost our minds, I think we're doing the right thing,' Kirk Hammett said somewhat unconvincingly. 'These songs have definitely landed in a place we've never been to before, and that's great. I think it's good for people to expect the unexpected from us. At least you're provoking them and challenging them to think.'

'Fuel' is a riotous beginning to an album which promises much. The frontman's ode to driving extremely fast, Hetfield admits this song never fails to get him 'pumped up' for a live performance. 'Gimme fuel/ Gimme fire/ Gimme that which I desire,' is the song's hypnotic grind of a refrain, led by the obligatory Hetfield crunch. Yet the woeful 'The Memory Remains' retains credence simply for seeing Metallica at their head-scratching best. Here, Metallica combined nothing more than a passable riff with an overdrawn chorus and the ill-fitting, eerie tones of Marianne Faithfull. 'It is the most seasoned voice I've ever heard,' Lars said, explaining the presence of the veteran performer. 'It has so many emotions, and they're all there – dramatic, sad, beautiful, sincere. That voice has lived – you can hear that. She's a very, very elegant and pleasant woman, very "been there, done that". You could learn a lot from that.'

Unfortunately the proof was in the listening, and despite Faithfull's colourful past (tainted by personal tragedy and drug addiction), the simple fact remained: her voice did not fit the song – or any Metallica track for that matter. Suffering perhaps from its affiliation with the overrated *Load*, *Reload* received average marks across the board, with the normally reliable *Kerrang!* grudgingly awarding three Ks out of five. Most major music publications followed suit, emphasising the group's focus on blues rock and rhythm as principal criticisms. Others, however, seemed to miss the point entirely. *Musician* puzzlingly claimed that *Reload* 'captures one of rock's greatest bands at its peak'.

Regardless of critical opinion, James Hetfield did at least prefer it to the more experimental *Load*, reasoning, 'I tend to like *Reload* more. I suppose you could say I prefer the look of urine and blood rather than jizz and blood!'

Despite critical indifference to both albums, Metallica remained a sure-fire favourite amongst music fans of every persuasion – as exemplified by their appearance at the alt-rock festival Lollapalooza in the summer of 1996, alongside such acts as Soundgarden and Rancid. In the face of predictable criticism for playing a non-metal festival, James Hetfield showed a typically defiant front. 'We did Lollapalooza 'cause we wanted to and it was cool,' he said matter-of-factly. 'It was as simple as that. We got to see a few great bands and make some new friends. We played in front of some people who came to see us and some people who wouldn't normally listen to us. That's what it's all about for us – writing songs, getting it together then playing in front of people and watching their faces.'

In 1996 Metallica provided the soundtrack for a harrowing documentary produced by filmmakers Joe Berlinger and Bruce Sinofsky. *Paradise Lost: The Child Murders At Robin Hood Hills* was a disturbing picture focused on the murder of three young boys in a remote area of West Memphis, Arkansas. Three teenagers were accused and tried for the murder. Jason Baldwin and Jessie Misskelley Jr. were both sentenced to life imprisonment, while purported ringleader Damien Echols was sentenced to death. The three murdered children had been sexually mutilated and the prosecution alleged that this was a ritual killing, in line with supposed satanic beliefs. They built their case around the fact all three 'killers' were fans of heavy-metal music, specifically bands such as Metallica. This was used as 'evidence' of their satanic beliefs.

The case against the teenagers, who became known as the 'West Memphis Three', was flimsy at best, with reams of contradictory information and many unresolved lines of enquiry. The Berlinger-Sinofsky documentary brilliantly exposed the farcical nature of the small-town trial, raising serious questions as to the legitimacy of the US legal system. Essentially it portrayed the startled youngsters as innocent of the crime and covered the remarkable efforts undertaken to free them. As of 2009, however, they are still incarcerated.

Berlinger approached Metallica in the hope of using their music in the film. He later outlined his reason for approaching the band. 'Damien Echols listened to Metallica music and because Metallica lyrics were actually introduced into this absurd trial as evidence that he must be a killer, we felt that Metallica music, when we were editing the film, would have to be in the film.'

As he also revealed in his book, *Metallica: This Monster Lives* (which detailed the making of the documentary he and Sinofsky would eventually shoot on the band), the two directors were expecting either a negative response, or none at all. To his delight and surprise, Metallica manager Cliff Burnstein called the filmmaker personally to express how much he and the band had enjoyed some of his previous work and to give permission for 'Orion', 'Welcome Home (Sanitarium)' and 'The Call Of Ktulu' to be used for the documentary. Berlinger later explained, 'Metallica had yet to give any music to a film. We reached out to them and they really responded to the story and gave us all the music in both *Paradise Lost* movies (the second was entitled *Paradise Lost 2: Revelations*) for free, which was really great, and that established a friendship with the band and that friendship led to the Metallica movie. I was not a heavy-metal fan, but I was making a movie about this bizarre murder case where somebody's musical tastes were actually part of the evidence the prosecutor had.'

Some may argue Metallica could have done more for the West Memphis Three.

They may have agreed to donate some of their music, but, after all, this took little effort. With three seemingly innocent young men rotting in jail, Metallica could perhaps have shown the same solidarity they did in standing against Napster. Their considerable weight within the music business would surely have helped. Many other artists – from Pearl Jam frontman Eddie Vedder to Henry Rollins – donated much time and effort to the cause, spreading the word about the case and campaign for a retrial in a court outside Arkansas. Yet Metallica have said comparatively little on this subject since the documentary was first aired.

Though the mid-1990s were a strange time for Metallica, they never lost their place in the pantheon of metal giants. However, as the end of the decade neared, things were about to get a whole lot weirder.

CHAPTER 18

MORE MONEY, MORE PROBLEMS

'I see things about the internet being something that people take for granted… they're becoming so comfortable with it that they feel they have a right to any piece of information… the internet is changing our perception about a lot of things; almost everything around us in society.'
Lars Ulrich

After the dates they played in support of *Reload* Metallica had just one day off before deciding to reconvene for rehearsals in Kirk Hammett's basement for a special project of cover songs. The plan was to include each of their previous cover efforts, plus eleven new tracks, on a double CD set. 'We spent a few days choosing and arranging the tracks, then went into the Plant and started rockin' just like the old days,' Jason told the Metallica fan-club magazine.

Most of the band's choices for fresh tracks to cover were rooted in familiarity – be it the Diamond Head cut 'It's Electric' or the medley of Mercyful Fate numbers, simply titled 'Mercyful Fate'. However, few Metallica fans would have heard the name of Bob Seger before, or been particularly familiar with Nick Cave's back catalogue. Nonetheless, tracks from both these artists were to feature, the wild cards in a pack of established favourites. Diverse as the track listing turned out to be, there was the potential for it to be even more so, as Lars himself hinted. 'Cover songs are a part of our history,' the drummer said. 'It wasn't like, "You pick one, then I'll pick one." I mean, I can't hold a gun to James's head and make him sing a George Michael song or "Wonderwall" by Oasis just because I like them. They are all songs we agreed we could handle and collectively do justice to. It has less to do with artists than it does with songs. We weren't dying to cover Seger. No disrespect to Bob, but we chose "Turn The Page" because it's an amazing song.'

The band laboured through a number of potential album titles. Some of the best included 'In Garage We Trust', 'Garage Up Your Ass', 'Dark Side Of The Garage', 'Use Your Garage I & II' (surely they should have gone with this?) and 'Gives Good Garage'. Eventually they went with a take based on their old song 'Damage, Inc.' and named the double set *Garage Inc.*

Revisiting Black Sabbath's legacy may have seemed a natural choice for the album. After all, almost any heavy-metal band able to cite the originators of the genre as an influence would win themselves instant kudos, but Metallica were altogether more honest about their reasons for selecting Sabbath's 'Sabbra Cadabra'. 'Black Sabbath were not a direct influence on our music,' Lars would claim. 'They had been going for too long. But they were a big influence on the four of us as we were growing up.' 'Sabbra Cadabra' was a song Metallica had long favoured due to the main riff, which Lars would dub 'the fucking riff from hell'. It was a track Metallica had deliberately played when on tour with original Sabbath singer Ozzy Osbourne in 1986. Lars lamented, 'We were doing it, hoping he'd be backstage in his dressing room, hear us and come out and jam.' Ozzy never joined them.

Most of Metallica's choices featured gorgeous guitar interplay, woven with double harmonies which made for catchy renditions of classic rock staples. Though these songs were long established for good reason, the 1970s production left much to be desired in many cases. On Thin Lizzy's 'Whiskey In The Jar', for instance, Metallica's upfront guitars lead the song with a modern groove which could not possibly have existed in the original 1972 version, while the slovenly sludge of the original Sabbath track was dragged screaming into a dynamic new era. Even when covering comparatively modern acts such as the Misfits, Metallica improved tremendously on the sound and execution of the original. 'Die, Die My Darling' was a track from 1984 that carried little of the direct punch of Metallica's version. Precisely how they extracted such a venomous, memorable romp from a regrettably drab recording is anybody's guess.

Some songs were arguably best suited to the original artists. Despite an admirable attempt to cover a Nick Cave track, the overlong, overwrought 'Loverman' was perhaps a poor choice, proving one step too far for Metallica's ambitious project. Few other bands could have done justice to the unique, personalised sound of Nick Cave And The Bad Seeds, and it seems safe to say that they could hardly have been counted amongst the metal fraternity – though this isn't to suggest that Metallica were not capable of tackling other genres of music. They successfully turned the Bob Seger track into a Metallica power ballad of sorts, and happily nailed Hetfield's longstanding favourite, 'Tuesday's Gone' by Lynyrd Skynyrd. 'I always loved that one,' James later said. 'It's a moving on song – you're splitting, you're leaving your woman at home. You're off doing your own thing, it really fits the road.' A hick-friendly homage, the song showed Metallica had lost none of their sense of humour. The eleven-minute track ends on a tongue-in-cheek tribute to the Waltons, with James giving thanks to everyone in the studio.

The track also invoked the memory of Cliff Burton (as did the cover of his beloved Misfits number). Kirk recalled, 'I remember him really loving the way Ed King of Lynyrd Skynyrd played guitar. He'd always ask me to show him Skynyrd licks, and then he'd end up saying, "Man that's tricky, that's really tricky."'

In many ways *Garage Inc.* was a chance for Metallica to rediscover their collective passion for playing old-school heavy metal and speedy punk. Disc one of the album delivered at least seven heavy tracks, while disc two gave the band a chance to revisit their formidable collection of archive cover versions – all of which were metal or punk-orientated. Mostly, the album served as a timely reminder of the band's comfort zone – showing they'd always be able to draw upon richly varied musical history and proving that Metallica were not too proud to display their roots, paying homage to musical masters. 'The songs we write are dissected and analysed,' Ulrich observed. 'We sit with them for months. With someone else's song, you only have to capture the moment. And there will always be a real need for us to have that outlet, as long as there is a Metallica. I really believe that.'

In November of 1998 Metallica set a precedent for the near future, with the filing of a lawsuit against Outlaw Records, Dutch East India Trading, Music Boulevard and others who had marketed and distributed a bootleg album called *Bay Area Thrashers: The Early Days*. The bootleg status of the offending release was never an issue; after all, hundreds of bootleg LPs had surfaced in Metallica's years together. The problem lay in distributors' claims that the album had been approved by the band and compiled from supposed live recordings. In truth, these were not live tracks, but incomplete demos dating from 1982 onwards, with added crowd noise and onstage banter from James strategically edited in to suggest authentic live recordings. Metallica easily won the suit and the record was removed from the public domain – a clear warning the band would not tolerate the use of their name in any way that they had not previously approved. With time, the case would prove entirely prophetic.

Before long, Metallica were working to further another longstanding ambition, appearing with a full orchestra for a special two-show live performance. The band had been ruminating on the possibility of a symphonic collaboration ever since their work with Michael Kamen on 'Nothing Else Matters'. Several years on, Metallica had become successful and wealthy enough to indulge in creative experimentation. Thus, with Kamen ready to take the conductor's baton, they announced their next unique musical event: a concert featuring familiar Metallica tracks, played with backing from a hundred-strong symphony orchestra.

Before the day of the gig, however, on a trip to London for the purpose of promoting *Garage Inc.*, Kirk Hammett was taken to hospital, experiencing severe stomach pain. He was diagnosed with acute appendicitis and rushed into surgery for an emergency appendectomy. Fortunately, Kirk made a quick recovery and was soon back on the road, with minimal disruption to the touring schedule.

On 21 and 22 April 1999 Metallica took centre stage at Berkeley Community Theatre, backed by the Kamen-led orchestra. James Hetfield was in a buoyant mood and suggested, given his past experience with pyrotechnics, that the band may introduce a 'flaming violinist', with the orchestra pit becoming a mosh pit. Kamen, (who sadly passed away in 2003 after suffering a heart attack), was adamant that the presence of the full orchestra should not interfere with the band's performance style in any way. 'I say let Metallica be Metallica and let the symphony be the symphony,' he stated frankly. 'The two have more in common than not. But Metallica will need to go full-tilt to be heard over a hundred-piece orchestra!'

For Metallica, the dilemma lay in deciding which of their songs would benefit from and be truly complemented by the rich layers of instrumentation. Critics and fans alike had been drawn to the symphonic edge of much of Metallica's music, especially the products of Cliff Burton's overactive, classically-obsessed imagination. But Kamen and Metallica were aiming for a seamless integration of instruments – violins, cellos, flutes and guitar – and how these classical undertones would translate on the stage was anyone's guess. 'Nobody really could imagine what would work and what would not,' James admitted. 'We were tossing ideas and songs around. For example, we wanted to leave out "Enter Sandman" because we thought our fans wouldn't like it in a classical arrangement, but Michael had such a great arrangement that we had to give in: we just didn't have any other choice. Then we thought we'd give "The Unforgiven" a try, but it just didn't work. Even Michael couldn't do anything with it.'

Truthfully, there was very little in the ambitious project which did work. Often the orchestra would purposely not follow the band – or at least many separate sections did not – and consequently, the performance took on the haphazard air of an orchestra conducting a sound check in a room unfortunately placed next door to a Metallica gig. Lars, as usual, was adamant that this was the right move, speaking in vehement defence of the project, though he seemed to be stretching the bounds of plausibility, he suggested, 'We made a record that isn't a fucking Metallica live album with a bunch of symphony bits scattered around in the background. It truly is a combination of Metallica and the orchestra, equally represented.'

Certain songs seemed tailor-made for such a collaboration, particularly 'The Call Of Ktulu' and 'The Thing That Should Not Be' (unsurprisingly Burton-era tracks), but elsewhere the more straightforward rock and metal direction of the chosen tracks simply did not suit the orchestral backing.

Yet, unusual as the collaboration might seem, Metallica's ties with the classical world were not to be severed at the end of the last performance with Kamen, but continued with Finland's Apocalyptica. The quartet made a name for themselves with the release of their debut – an album of Metallica tracks played on cello only. *Plays Metallica By Four Cellos* was based around an innovative concept that worked surprisingly well, with the Finns belting out classics by the bucket-load. Intricate tracks such as 'Master Of Puppets' and 'Harvester Of Sorrow' were covered faithfully and there was even a place for epic groove 'Wherever I May Roam' alongside the obligatory 'Enter Sandman'. On the strength of this initial success, Apocalyptica not only released further cover tracks, but – most strikingly – recorded a host of original material which continues to blur the genre divide. A band of classically trained musicians, they possess the ability to create heavy-metal sounds on orchestral instruments. Metallica are known to approve of their idiosyncratic cello covers.

Despite the ambiguity of Metallica's orchestral set, they released the concerts in record format as well as on live DVD. Both releases were titled *S&M*. In 1998 Metallica also released *Cunning Stunts*, another video comprising a live show and a multitude of extras filmed by Adam Dubin. 'I think Metallica was comfortable with me and so it was easy to have me along,' Dubin explains. 'Kirk always says to me, "I love seeing old faces." The requirements for *Cunning Stunts* and *S&M* were different. My job was to create DVD extras so that's what I did. For *Cunning Stunts* I was showing how the tour comes together from behind the scenes. I really like that one because it allowed me to showcase Metallica's crackerjack touring crew. I had known those folks for years and now I could make them the stars. For *S&M*, it was such a cool idea to have Metallica with the symphony that it was fun to just show how it all came together. One day maybe they will let me put a whole long film together. It will be quite something.'

Metallica were apparently moving along at their own pace, with little to trouble them, but this was all about to change. In the process of recording a song for the *Mission: Impossible II* soundtrack, the band made a shocking discovery: a demo version of the track was already being aired on radio stations around the States. Given that the song was still unfinished, Metallica rightly questioned precisely how the superb 'I Disappear' had found its way into the public domain. The answer presented itself in the form of a peer-to-peer file sharing service called Napster. This enabled computer users to share particular files on their own personal computers, swapping material with others anywhere in the world. Once one person had shared the demo, it was potentially available to millions of registered users. When Metallica discovered the source of the leaked demo, they were astonished to see that their entire back catalogue – including some genuinely rare tracks and bootlegs – was equally readily available. After consulting with their lawyers, Metallica took Napster to court for breaking three different laws of fair use, specifically copyright infringement.

Of course, many computer users – typically counted amongst the band's younger fans – had been downloading tracks in this way for at least the previous year and the file-sharing process was quickly becoming a problem for major record companies, watching further cuts of their exorbitant profits slip away with every track ripped from the internet for free. As soon as fans and the media heard of Metallica's involvement in such a case they were aghast. The common consensus was incredulous. Why ever would Metallica – a band who had sold close to 60 million albums – care whether people paid more money for their music or not? And in any case, as would be argued by many a Napster member, true fans would more often than not pay for a hard-copy album, provided they liked the track(s) they had heard for free. Lars Ulrich took on the role of chief party pooper and held his ground, despite vehement attacks from all comers. Speaking in fierce defence of the cause, he explained, 'I don't care if people don't like me. Do we need money? No, we're fine. Thank you for asking about my financial situation, but I'm taken care of for ten fucking lifetimes. Is it just possible this could be about something else?'

Armed with a huge dossier containing the names of 335,435 Napster users who had downloaded Metallica tracks, Ulrich made sure the blacklisted fans were banned from the site. Rapper Dr. Dre then joined the assault, prompting Napster to ban a further 230,142 users. Yet they weren't finished there: backed by Dre, Metallica began pushing to see Napster shut down altogether.

In his written statement to the court, Ulrich reasoned, 'We take our craft – whether it be the music, the lyrics, or the photos and artwork – very seriously, as do most artists. It is therefore sickening to know that our art is being traded like a commodity rather than the art that it is. From a business standpoint, this is about piracy – a.k.a. taking something that doesn't belong to you – and that is morally and legally wrong. The trading of such information – whether it's music, videos, photos, or whatever – is, in effect, trafficking in stolen goods.'

It was a far cry from their standpoint on such matters just twelve years before. In 1988 the band briefly allowed fans to come and record their shows. Lars had said, 'That's an idea Cliff Burnstein came up with. Basically, where we can work it out with the promoter, we set up this platform behind the soundboard and sell, like, 200 or so tickets specifically for people who wanna come along with their walkman and tape the show. Of course, they're gonna end up on vinyl, but who gives a shit?' Intriguingly, when pushed as to whether this would affect Metallica sales at the time, the drummer responded admirably. 'I really don't think it affects anyone,' he suggested. 'No one's gonna tell me that the people who collect bootlegs are not gonna buy the new Metallica album when it comes out on the proper label. These are people who are die-hard fanatics who collect all this shit and, if anything, I think it makes the whole situation better.'

Had the band's principles changed so radically, or was this merely a case of Napster taking things one step too far? Would Metallica have taken action if it was just their back catalogue being downloaded? Perhaps the leaking of an unfinished single pushed them to take the matter to the courts? Addressing the issue of the lawsuit in an internet chat with fans, Lars explained: 'Metallica is suing Napster because we felt that someone had to address this important artistic issue, and we have always been known for taking a leadership role in the fight for artists' rights. We were the first band to sue our record company, Time Warner, for the right to control our future. Rather than allowing the record company or any other corporation to own our recordings and compositions, we chose to fight for (and eventually win) control of our music. This issue is no different. Why is it all of a sudden okay to get music for free? Why should music be free, when it costs artists money to record and produce it?'

Eventually the attempt to shut Napster down was successful and the service would only return later once the company had agreed to charge people per album or per track, paying bands their share of the royalties (a policy many companies and services have since followed).

'I think we've resolved this in a way that works for fans, recording artists and songwriters alike,' Ulrich said persuasively. 'Our beef hasn't been with the concept of sharing music; everyone knows that we've never objected to our fans trading tapes of our live concert performances. The problem we had with Napster was that they never asked us or other artists if we wanted to participate in their business. We believe that this settlement will create the kind of enhanced protection for artists that we've been seeking from Napster. We await Napster's implementation of a new model, which will allow artists to choose how their creative efforts are distributed. It's good that they're going legit.'

Unfortunately for Metallica, they came to be seen as a (particularly vocal) mouthpiece for the 'industry viewpoint'. Scapegoats in a tangled debate of art, commerce and ethics, Lars and his bandmates have been portrayed as the big, bad wolves of the case, greedy for a cut of the profits. While other lower profile peer-to-peer file sharing services continue to operate unabated and music can still be found for free, Metallica lost the respect of fans and outsiders alike. Realistically, file sharing is not something that can ever be completely controlled. Still, Lars's argument that no band should be expected to make music for nothing is a powerful one – even when applied to the case of multi-million-selling stars of rock.

'I Disappear' was one of Metallica's most memorable efforts in quite some time and would have been worthy of a place on any album. Written directly for the movie, it still shines on an otherwise lacklustre soundtrack. 'This is the first time we've ever written a song with a movie in mind,' James explained. 'They came to us and said they wanted a brand new song, and we basically said, "Okay, we'll write the song and if you don't like it, tough shit!" What did we have to lose? Nothing!'

However, Metallica were about to lose something much more tangible than James could have known. Preparing to play one of the strangest venues of their career, to an audience of 200 fans in a car park outside that year's VH1 Music Awards, little did they realise that this gig would be Jason Newsted's last ever.

CHAPTER 19

STONE COLD CRAZY

'I work in the mental health field, and I know that psychoanalys is can be a painful, personal experience. I don't understand why the band would want to commercialise it for public consumption.'
K.J. Doughton

In 2000 Jason Newsted formed a side project named Echobrain along with friends Dylan and Adam Donkin, Andrew Gomez and Brian Sagrafena. Stifled by the lack of creative freedom within Metallica, Newsted sought to write more of his own material, shaking off some of the stringent restrictions he felt as the band's replacement bassist. The problem was that James Hetfield did not approve. In a revealing set of interviews conducted for *Playboy* magazine, tensions between Hetfield and Newsted were dragged to light. It was becoming clear that the latter could not tolerate his state of frustrated creativity for much longer. 'I have made some incredibly wonderful music with other musicians,' Newsted said. 'It would just floor people – it has floored people. But I just can't release it. I would like James to see that this music is truly a part of me, like his child is a part of him.' Jason added bitterly, 'I can't play my shit, but he can go play with other people.'

Hetfield had indeed made the odd guest appearance, on Corrosion Of Conformity's (better known as COC) album *Wiseblood* in 1996 (he contributed backing vocals to 'Man Or Ash'), and he had also contributed vocals to 'Hell Is Good', a track which features on the movie *South Park: Bigger, Longer And Uncut*, though admittedly the song never made the soundtrack album.

Hetfield responded, 'My name isn't on those records. And I'm not out trying to sell them.' This was not strictly true, however. In fact, he was credited for the COC track and initial pressings of the *Wiseblood* album featured a sticker boasting of Hetfield's contribution.

Despite his own extra-curricular activities, Hetfield felt convinced that Newsted's project would detract from his commitment to Metallica. 'Where would it end?' the frontman pondered. 'Does he start touring with it? Does he sell T-shirts? Is it his band? That's the part I don't like. It's like cheating on your wife in a way. Married to each other.' It seemed it was Hetfield particularly, rather than Metallica *per se*, who took exception to Newsted's other band. Comments made by Lars and Kirk in the same interview show them to be indifferent to Jason's side project. As far as they were concerned, Jason could play bass for Girls Aloud – so long as his contribution to Metallica was not affected. 'Jason eats, sleeps and breathes music,' Kirk observed. 'I think it's morally wrong to keep someone away from what keeps him happy. I just hope we can survive this in one piece without tearing each other's fucking throats out.' From Ulrich, there was a resigned shrug, the drummer insisting, 'I just can't get caught up in these meltdowns. I've got some issues in my family life with my wife that are a little more weighty than, like, whatever James Hetfield and Jason Newsted are bickering over.'

Directly or otherwise, the *Playboy* interview signalled the end of Newsted's nearly fifteen-year tenure with the band. This was one outcome James Hetfield had clearly never anticipated, and the frontman was less than pleased by Newsted's 'selfishness', as he saw it. Ever the diplomat, Newsted suggested his departure was due to other factors. 'Due to private and personal reasons, and the physical damage that I have done to myself over the years while playing the music that I love, I must step away from the band,' his official statement read. Newsted admitted that he had taken 'the most difficult decision of my life, made in the best interest of my family, myself, and the continued growth of Metallica. I extend my love, thanks, and best wishes to my brothers: James, Lars, and Kirk and the rest of the Metallica family, friends, and fans whom have made these years so unforgettable.'

Director Adam Dubin spent much time in Newsted's company whilst filming Metallica and his words confirm the bassist's reputation as a genuine, hard-working, loyal member of the band. It seems a shame, therefore, that his lengthy association with the group had to end as it did. 'I always have the utmost respect for him as a person and a musician,' Dubin says. 'He was like a Metallica fan who got to be in Metallica. He did not have a lot of input on recordings but playing live he was incredible. He gave 100 per cent all the time and he would meet and greet every last fan that he could. On a personal level he welcomed me into the band's environment and was always a gentleman. I had to work a little harder as a filmmaker to make sure that Jason got enough face time. It's not easy in a band dominated by Lars and James. And Kirk naturally shines with his fluid guitar solos. So I always had to make sure to show Jason and he always made time for me. He is a stand-up guy: a team player. Any band could count itself lucky to have someone like him.'

Yet, Metallica's world was about to be rocked further still. In the aftermath of Newsted's resignation, with their frontman preparing to check into rehab, already frayed relations within the band were put under the added strain of perpetual filming by Bruce Sinofsky and Joe Berlinger.

In early 2001, the band had hired Phil Towle, a self-proclaimed 'Performance Enhancement Coach' at the cost of a mere £20,000 a month. His mission was to restore a semblance of togetherness in camp Metallica, but ultimately, the presence of an outsider was just another contributory factor to the departure of Jason Newsted. 'I told them, "I think this is really fucking lame and weak,"' Newsted said of Towle's involvement, 'that we cannot get together – us – the biggest heavy-metal band in the world. The things that we've done and the decisions we've made about squillions of dollars and squillions of people – and this, we can't get over this?'

Metallica had palpably lost their spark, though even they did not realise to what extent. Lacking a riff, a lyric or even the most provisional segment of a song, they installed themselves within a former military barracks called the Presidio in San Francisco to begin recording their eighth studio album. They chose a portable, makeshift studio described by producer Bob Rock as being 'deliberately uncomfortable', the idea being this would extract extra bile, anger and passion from the band. 'The idea should sound like a band getting together in the garage for the first time,' Rock reasoned, 'only the band is Metallica.'

In the absence of a permanent bassist, Bob Rock personally assumed all four-string duties, helping the band out as they began to construct the new songs. Unfortunately nothing recorded at El Presidio would be used on the album. By July 2001, James Hetfield decided he should enter a rehabilitation centre, citing alcoholism amongst other 'unnamed' addictions. Realisation came for James on one vodka-fuelled hunting trip. While he'd been away, he'd missed his son's birthday. Immediately all work on the album was halted.

Publicly the band gave full support for James's decision, issuing an official statement to this effect, but behind closed doors, Lars Ulrich's reaction to this latest complication was somewhat different. The documentary *Some Kind Of Monster* reveals the full extent of Ulrich's bitterness towards his friend and co-writer, underlining just one more contradiction in the world of Metallica. 'James is working hard toward recovery and, needless to say, he has our full support,' the band's statement read on www.metallica.com. Yet, on camera, Lars admitted to feeling 'disrespected' by James and the manner in which he had taken it upon himself to enter rehab. Worryingly the drummer would add, 'If he walked away from Metallica I'm not sure it would surprise me.'

Kirk later said, 'After James announced he was going into rehab it was just Lars and I, and that was a very, very scary thing. We went from four to two in the course of six months. And it freaked me out, it freaked Lars out, it freaked everyone out. The most difficult thing was trying to maintain some sense of normality in the wake of all this. You know, Lars and I tried to hold it together as best we could along with Bob Rock, who really kind of helped us stay together too.'

For all Bob Rock's support, there comes a sad moment in the documentary when Kirk reveals, after a phone conversation with James in the rehabilitation centre, that the Metallica frontman associates Rock with the business side of the band only and not as an integral part of their friendship. Rock's disappointment is palpable. 'It's taken its toll on myself; I'm very worried about him,' Kirk would say of Hetfield. 'Whenever you check yourself into rehab, they don't just focus on alcohol, they go much deeper, they go *way* deep, they cut you open and examine all the things right there on the table. I've spoken to him a few times and I know he's having a rough trip. But no matter how bad it gets, eventually things seem to sort themselves out, sooner or later, whether it's good or bad, they sort themselves out.'

At this point, the future was the most uncertain it had ever been for Metallica. James would leave rehab shortly before Christmas 2001, but six months away from the band meant that the creative partnership between him and Lars was more volatile than ever. James insisted, 'I really learned some things about myself in there. I was able to reframe my life and not look at everything with a negative connotation. That's how I was raised. It was like a survival technique for me.' In coming to terms with his personal feelings, James felt better equipped than ever to open up to his bandmates. 'There's a lot of machismo in this world, but I suppose the most manly thing you can do is face up to your weaknesses and expose them,' James affirmed. 'And you are showing your strength by exposing your weaknesses to people. And that opens up a dialogue; it opens up friendship, which is definitely what it has done for me.' Yet Lars still felt aggrieved and betrayed by James, and the relationship between the two was at its most strained.

The most difficult transition concerned James's new working hours. He had been advised to work from noon until 4:00pm only each day during the week – a new routine which took its toll on a unit who had been used to recording as and when they pleased. Lars Ulrich took the rigid regime to heart, and Hetfield's insistence there should be no work on the album – or even any playbacks of recorded material – when he wasn't there to contribute only intensified the drummer's resentment.

In one memorable scene in the documentary, Lars is filmed screaming 'fuck' in Hetfield's face. This follows a tirade in which Ulrich unleashes twenty years of pent-up animosity. 'I just think you're so fucking self-absorbed,' he screams at Hetfield in front of Hammett, Rock and Phil Towle. 'What makes it worse is you always talk about me and use the words "control" and "manipulation" a lot. I think you control on purpose, I think you control inadvertently, I think you control with the rules you always set, I think you control with how you always judge people, I think you control all this even when you're not here.'

The crux of Ulrich's speech, and indeed the movie, is the realisation that, despite years on the road together, the bandmates have essentially failed to connect. 'I don't understand who you are,' Ulrich candidly admits. 'I realise now that I barely knew you before. All these rules and all this shit – this is a fucking rock'n'roll band. I don't want fucking rules. I understand and respect you need to leave at four o'clock, but don't tell me I can't listen to something with Bob at 4:15 if I want to.' Tellingly, Lars intimates, 'I don't want to end up like Jason; I don't want to be pushed away. Let's do it and let's do it full on, or let's not do it at all.'

Crucially, this fractured relationship began to spill into the practice room and, at one stage in the documentary, James is shown telling Lars, 'I'm just not enjoying being in a room with you playing.' During this period – a time when Phil Towle's expertise was needed more than ever – it is hard to see exactly how his advice benefits the band in the slightest. In fact his three clients, along with Bob Rock, are openly frustrated by some of Towle's techniques. In one particularly ambiguous scene, Hetfield refers to Towle as 'the father figure' he never had, insisting that 'he has been like an angel to me', but that the band did not want 'their hand held'. As tensions in the studio somehow begin to ease, it becomes clear that, on one issue at least, the band members are in agreement: Towle should leave them to it.

Towle, who lived in Kansas, was reportedly intending to move 1,500 miles to set up a base in Metallica's home city. 'I'm just afraid that he thinks he's in the band,' says Hetfield in one of the most revealing quotes of the entire movie. When Towle refuses to cut back on his time with the band, or withdraw his services entirely, his frankly childish response leads the viewer to conclude that he is more concerned with his own financial prospects and career than what is best for the band. The dispute pretty much signals the end of Towle's relationship with Metallica.

Perhaps one of the most intriguing aspects of the documentary is the sharp contrast between Metallica circa 1991-92 and the band's present incarnation. Kirk openly reveals he has cut back on drugs and drink in favour of surfing and spending time riding horses on his San Franciscan ranch; James is witnessed attending his daughter's ballet class and draped with children while trying to record vocals for the album. But nowhere is the change more apparent than in several minutes' footage of Ulrich auctioning off a significant portion of his art collection. In a scene which renders Lars's campaign for compensation from Napster more trivial than righteous, the viewer is treated to the sight of the drummer selling some of his most sought-after pieces, including an original Jean-Michel Basquiat, which fetched the sum of five million dollars.

The reunion between Lars Ulrich and long-lost Metallica member Dave Mustaine is one of the central scenes of the movie, yet perhaps its importance has been exaggerated by the two editors. After all, Mustaine has had a successful career with Megadeth, and his resentment of Metallica's greater success seems like a case of sour grapes rather than anything more serious. Still bitter over his sacking twenty years before, Mustaine cuts a depressive, rather pathetic figure.

Commendably, Ulrich lets Mustaine speak, allowing his former bandmate to criticise his behaviour on camera. Reacting in typically contradictory fashion, Mustaine was ultimately unhappy with his portrayal on film and objected to its inclusion in the movie, despite the fact he had been made fully aware the conversation was being filmed at the time. Lars's father Torben Ulrich spoke to a Russian website about the *Some Kind Of Monster* documentary, commenting on the infamous scene with Mustaine. 'With regard to the scene with Dave and Lars in the movie, I thought it was quite moving,' Torben said, 'and if Dave Mustaine now feels that maybe it was not quite right or quite fair, then I would say that you always take that kind of risk when you appear before a camera or a computer, and so if you agree to participate, then that's more or less what you can risk, and things can always either take a turn that you did not anticipate or, worse, they can be distorted to a degree that you never imagined.'

For all the outside distractions portrayed in *Some Kind Of Monster*, there was the small matter of an album to be written and recorded. In truth, the early Presidio demos produced by the band were approaching dreadful and sounded nothing like the Metallica of old. Musically, things began to improve after James's return from rehab, though there was still the uneasy feeling that the album was being produced simply to fulfil critical expectation, rather than it being the right time for everyone involved.

Some Kind Of Monster leaves the viewer in no doubt: years away from the recording studio had altered Metallica's sound considerably. For one, Hetfield and Ulrich were no longer in favour of guitar solos on the album. Kirk Hammett was understandably reticent to leave the solos off entirely, suggesting they be included intermittently, rather than not at all. Ulrich contested that such extended passages of shredding were an 'outdated' concept. In a rare moment of authority, Hammett insisted it was 'bullshit' to cut the solos and that in doing so, the band would date the album to 2003, bringing it in line with the current 'trend' for dispensing with them. Predictably, Hammett lost this particular battle: ultimately the album that would be titled *St. Anger* was not to feature a single moment of indulgent fretboard action.

Once the band have produced a draft album, they are filmed playing the tracks for Cliff Burnstein's approval. Their manager looks suitably unimpressed. His opinion – eventually to be shared by a multitude of fans – was that the first four songs ('Frantic', 'St. Anger', 'Some Kind Of Monster' and 'Dirty Window') were decent enough, but the rest were 'watered down somewhat'.

As the final days of recording approached, Metallica focused on finding Jason Newsted's replacement. 'It's very important that our personalities vibe and that this person is going to be around for a long time,' James said. 'We are excited about jamming with these people and getting a vibe with them. The vibe is the most important. We know the people we have on our list can play, and we don't like the revolving-door syndrome.'

There were auditions for Scott Reeder (of Kyuss fame), ex-Marilyn Manson four-stringer Twiggy Ramirez and even Hetfield's good friend Pepper Keenan of Corrosion Of Conformity. Keenan was guitarist and frontman for the band better known as COC and found Metallica's notoriously strained politics difficult to contend with. As the frontman stated in no uncertain terms, the prospect of dropping to a background role did not appeal to him in the slightest. 'They asked me to play bass and I was into it,' Keenan says today, 'but I think we all realised it was between me and Trujillo, and if I had got the gig I don't think I would have been happy no matter how much fucking money they threw at me. They know that I'm not a "yes" man. I write songs. I think I'd have been going crazy because they'd have been saying, "Dude, do it like this," and I'm not going to put up with that shit.' Keenan's rival was one Robert Trujillo. Short-listed along with a select few contenders, the veteran bassist had most notably performed with Suicidal Tendencies and Ozzy Osbourne.

Pepper remembers the audition experience clearly. 'The deal was to play one of the songs on *St. Anger*, and they were going to try and stump me with some weird song I'd never fucking heard before. But basically it was a drop-tuned song that sounded like a Down [Keenan's side project with ex-Pantera singer Phil Anselmo] riff. It was too much, it just destroyed it. It didn't sound like a Metallica song anymore.' Keenan was filmed – like everything and everyone connected with the band at this time – though his footage almost didn't make it to the final cut. 'I told them I didn't even want to be filmed,' he laughs. 'I said, "I'm very happy in my other two bands. You don't need to film me; nobody knows I'm here if I don't get the gig." I didn't even tell anybody I was trying out. At the end James asked me to sign a release paper because he thought it was important for me to be a part of it, so I did.'

According to Bob Rock, Metallica had, since the death of Cliff Burton, been about the three surviving members. He insisted they would 'never, ever find a permanent bass player'. Of course, the band would hire a replacement for Newsted – of this there was never any doubt in Rock's mind. Rather he was suggesting that, as with Jason, even after well over a decade together, the union could not last. His insinuation was simply that no one would, or ever could, replace Cliff Burton.

Eventually, Metallica opted for Robert Trujillo, impressed with his versatile playing and relaxed persona. All three Metallica members were filmed in the crucial stages of decision making and, above all else, it was clear they had been floored by Trujillo's musicianship. 'He was the only guy who didn't look like he was struggling,' Lars enthused. 'The way he played with his fingers like that,' Kirk observed (Trujillo did not use a pick), 'it hadn't been that way since Cliff.'

Crucially, after offering Trujillo a place in the band, James explained the principal reason he was selected for the job. 'You make the band play better,' he told the new bassist. 'When Rob came to San Francisco the first time and jammed with us, we all felt this incredible magic between the four of us,' Lars later said. 'It was just something that we could not describe – we all just knew it. To welcome Rob into Metallica in 2003, after all the growth and soul-searching we've been through for the last two years, feels so fucking awesome. Being at full strength again is at this moment indescribable.'

'I have the utmost respect for Jason and Cliff,' Trujillo later explained, 'and what I love about Cliff is where he was coming from as a bass player in this genre of music, metal, he had a real voice and he was speaking with his instrument. Very melodic, this wonderful stage presence. He was just a very unique individual and very talented obviously. Jason offered a more meat-and-potatoes kind of vibe to the band. None of us – me or Jason – are trying to be Cliff. I'm not trying to be Jason. We're our own entities. I just try to give everything I've got.'

Trujillo was offered a million-dollar advance as a sign the band were 'serious' about their latest addition to the line-up – a gesture which met with a sincerely shocked response from the easygoing musician. Though Trujillo had had his first taste of mainstream success playing with Ozzy Osbourne, for much of his impressive career he had never quite received the respect and fortune his talent warranted.

Robert Trujillo was born Roberto Agustín Miguel Santiago Samuel Trujillo Veracruz on 23 October 1964 in Santa Monica, California, but grew up in Culver City, in the Golden State. Trujillo told one magazine of his gang-infested upbringing. 'It was interesting,' the bassist said, with some understatement. 'A lot of my cousins were in gangs. Some of them were in gangs in Culver City, and some of them were in gangs in Venice. If you're from California you'll know that those two cities don't get along. It made family get-togethers interesting. You couldn't always have the same people there, let's put it that way.'

For Trujillo, music was a means of escape and he grew up listening to some of the best bass players of all time (much like Jason Newsted), with the remarkable sound of Motown. His mother, a native of Durango, Mexico, was a colourful influence on young Robert's musical palette. 'It was all about the music at home,' Trujillo would say. 'My mother was a huge fan of people like Marvin Gaye, James Brown and Sly And The Family Stone. She was really young so her and her girlfriends would be dancing and there was this chest of drawers I'd climb up on and play air guitar or air saxophone – air anything. Then I'd go hang out with my Dad who lived in Venice, and he'd play anything from the Rolling Stones to Led Zeppelin to Beethoven. But then my cousins were listening to Black Sabbath, or on the R&B side they were listening to Parliament.'

As Trujillo entered his teens, he began to be influenced by the burgeoning skateboard scene. Through this he developed a love of heavy music and, by his own admission, was soon playing in 'a lot of backyard party bands. I played a lot of Sabbath, a lot of Ozzy, Rush, but challenging Rush, Zeppelin, it goes on. I went to jazz school when I was nineteen. I really wanted to be a studio musician but I was still passionate about rock and metal.'

It didn't take long for Trujillo to discover that he had a natural flair for the bass guitar and, with his technical expertise improving all the time, he was able to combine his immense enthusiasm and innate gifts with first-rate tutelage. He found his first big break with skate aficionados (and rumoured Crip gang members) Suicidal Tendencies in 1989. Trujillo would spend six years with the band, contributing some of the finest material of their formidable 30-year career.

Released in 1990, *Lights...Camera...Revolution!* should have been the album which broke Suicidal to mass success, especially with backing from the Epic label. A flawless take on the metal-hardcore crossover style, the album notably included some of ST's most feral, focused material to date – be it the frantic, poetic 'You Can't Bring Me Down' or the evangelist attack 'Send Me Your Money'.

Though there were hints at the raw emotion of frontman Mike Muir on this album, the follow-up, *The Art Of Rebellion*, took the passion to a whole new level. Trujillo's bass playing was some of his most soulful and accomplished yet, underpinning Muir's breathless vocals with expressive empathy. 'Nobody Hears' and 'Can't Stop', for instance, remain some of the most heartfelt rock songs of all time, featuring Muir's unsettling audible breakdown. When touring for *Lights...Camera...Revolution!*, Suicidal were lucky enough to play on the same bill as Metallica. On that tour, Robert met the band for the first time. 'What I remember most about that tour was Metallica giving all of us in Suicidal Tendencies $1,000 each as a bonus after the first leg of the tour was done,' Trujillo later explained. 'It was a gift from Metallica and that was the most money we had ever made. We'd actually have to steal their leftover food each night after they'd leave the venue because we were so broke that we couldn't always afford food of our own.'

Trujillo was also privy to Metallica's prankster-ism, typical of the time. He would reveal: 'We had plenty of crazy, drunken moments with the guys. On one night in particular I was doing shots with Lars and James, or rather I *thought* I was. It turns out that they were just feeding me shots without taking any for themselves. I suppose their hazing began on that tour.'

Trujillo made two more albums with Suicidal: the underrated, but certainly less accomplished *Suicidal For Life*, and the feral reworking of old Suicidal material that was *Still Cyco After All These Years*. He also took part in an entertaining side project with Mike Muir, the funk-rock crossover Infectious Grooves, for which his bass playing took on a different attack altogether, rooted in slap bass and riotous fret exploration. Infectious Grooves released four albums, all of which featured Trujillo. The best of these was arguably the diverse *Groove Family Cyco*, which received little media attention. However, it was the band's first album which garnered most notoriety within the metal fraternity. *The Plague That Makes Your Booty Move...It's The Infectious Grooves* was the band's debut, released in 1991 by way of an introduction to their sound.

Ozzy Osbourne, who was recording in the same studio as Infectious Grooves at the time, was invited to appear on the excellent 'Therapy' track, and because of this Trujillo forged a connection with the former Black Sabbath singer. He then became a live bassist for Osbourne's band before eventually appearing on the singer's *Down To Earth* album and re-recording bass tracks for the reissued *Blizzard Of Ozz* and *Diary Of A Madman* albums. Colourful as Trujillo's career had been so far, no amount of musical experience could have prepared him for life as a member of metal's most prestigious band. However, he did adjust to the experience commendably well and, perhaps more importantly, displayed greatest respect for his new bandmates' privacy. Trujillo felt that when he first joined Metallica, 'It seemed like James was walking a tightrope, on thin ice, he seemed very guarded and he had a lot of things going on in his personal life. Everything was according to a schedule. Now it just seems like he's got his juju back. He's sober of course, but he's got that Hetfield attitude that's confident and powerful and creative, but he's also very inspired by ideas that I have.'

Though Trujillo was a seasoned musician, at heart he was as excited by the experience as Newsted had been. The bassist revealed he was a 'huge fan of *Ride The Lightning* and *Master Of Puppets* back in the day. What was so special about Metallica was the creative energy that seemed to flow out of their songs. They took a genre of music and filled it with a lot of non-pedestrian elements, particularly when it came to what Cliff Burton was doing on the bass.'

One of the initial duties of Trujillo's new role was filming the video for 'St. Anger', the title track and first single from the new album. In a typically unprecedented move, Metallica shot this footage at San Quentin State Prison, with an audience of genuine prisoners. As a 'thank you' for their participation in the making of the video, Metallica returned the following day to play a groundbreaking live show for the inmates, leaving concerns for their own safety at the prison gates. It was a dangerous show that could well have ended badly for the band – as the correctional officer who welcomed them to the prison was quick to illustrate. 'San Quentin has a "no hostage policy",' he casually explained, 'which means if someone gets taken hostage, there will be no negotiating: you are on your own, buddy.'

However, after James Hetfield addressed the assembled throng of prisoners with a heartfelt statement – admitting at one stage, 'If I hadn't had music in my life, it's quite possible I could be in here, or be dead. I'd much rather be alive' – the inmates seemed to warm to the band, especially in light of Metallica's obvious enthusiasm for their new material.

On 5 June 2003 Metallica released *St. Anger* as a two-disc set: the album plus a special DVD featuring rehearsal footage. The overwhelming shock for most fans was the sound of the drums. If people had balked at the tone of Ulrich's snare on *...And Justice For All*, then they were physically jolted by the high-pitched echoing snap that marred each and every song on *St. Anger*. Arguably, the snare sound detracted from the band's innate power, affecting a set of otherwise credible songs. Oftentimes the drums sounded as if they were tracked to a different song. Quite what possessed the band to release an album with such a muffled, tinny, percussive sound after their belated criticism of *...And Justice For All* remains inexplicable, but one thing is clear: *St. Anger* is a painful listen in many respects, yet this seems a fitting reflection of the angst which accompanied its making.

More than two years of painstaking editing were required to produce a recording the band were anywhere near happy with. Along the way they lost their bassist, saw their singer suffer physical and mental meltdown, underwent band therapy – all before eventually engaging the services of a new bassist to begin the recording process all over again. That the resultant album is unfocused at times, lacking any clear direction, seems particularly unsurprising. The sonic equivalent of *Some Kind Of Monster*, *St. Anger* showcases the sound of a band carrying too much baggage, and the ensuing chaos when they are finally forced to confront it.

The release is further beset by Metallica's misguided belief that they did not need guitar solos, that they could produce a sound of inferior quality to most bands' demos, distinctly lacking in harmonies and melodies, and still get away with it. Certainly upon first listen, *St. Anger* was a bitter pill for longstanding Metallica fans to swallow. In hindsight, however, perhaps there was an element of radicalism, producing something truly unique and exorcising their collective demons with a stripped-down, raw, challenging set. It was Metallica, but as fans had never heard them, and perhaps the negative reaction was inevitable after the experience of recording the album.

Naturally enough, bands will champion fresh material with predictable claims that this is their 'best set of songs ever'. Yet Metallica had always avoided such grandiose claims of perfection, duly waiting for fan and media reactions before commenting on their own work. In the past, of course, the band had been convinced of the quality of their output – arguably unmatchable by 99 per cent of their contemporaries. It is intriguing to note, therefore, that for their weakest set of songs to date, Metallica went on a verbal binge to underline exactly how vital and amazing *St. Anger* truly was.

'This material is very strong and very representative of where we are now musically, personally, emotionally and mentally,' Kirk would rave. 'It's the most complete band statement that we've ever made.' On one hand perhaps, he wasn't far from the truth. This was the first time each and every member of the band had contributed song lyrics – be it a single line or a full set of words – and, musically, the most balanced compilation the band had put together yet. And this is exactly why it didn't work. Metallica were a band who thrived on the individual components working in tandem, but without one element ever overstepping another. James wrote the lyrics; he and Kirk wrote the riffs; Kirk penned the solos more often than not, and Lars always contributed with arrangements and the perennial back beat. As soon as this formula was altered, it changed the very make-up of the band – the unique construction that made Metallica the beast it was.

'We are so in love with this new album it is sickening,' James gushed unabashed. 'We can't stop playing it. It is pumping through us. We can't wait to get out and play this stuff live.' However, once the band took to playing the material in a live setting – in much the same way as realisation dawned after attempting to recreate the technical flashes of ...And Justice For All onstage – it became apparent that these songs no longer worked. Furthermore, they were simply not to the tastes of most fans. Only 'Frantic' and 'St. Anger' could truly be considered worthy additions to the Metallica archives, and this was magnified in a live setting. For the other tracks, there was too much experimentation, too little focus on clear, definable song structures and, most transparently, a reluctance to acknowledge when something just didn't quite work.

The upfront nature of the album, with its down-tuned aggressiveness, did at least mark the band out as risk-takers and a group who could compete with the current craze for overtly aggressive, string-rattling heaviosity. As Lars would say, 'One of the things I'm proudest of with this new record, we've proven not only to ourselves, but to the immediate, second tier around us. A lot of people didn't think it was possible to make a really aggressive, angry, dynamic, brutal, fucked-up record if everybody in the band got along really well, and if there was a good sense of communication, camaraderie, respect, love, all this type of stuff with the guys in the band.'

The final curtain to be drawn on a remarkable few years in the history of the band was the release of the Berlinger-Sinofsky movie Some Kind Of Monster. The final documentary was a superb piece of filmmaking, condensing a staggering 1,200 hours of footage into just 135 minutes. The DVD sold well and even won the Independent Spirit Award for Best Documentary Feature. 'They do let it all hang out for us,' Bruce Sinofsky revealed, promising, 'the film will show sides to Metallica that not only the fans don't know, but also the band themselves didn't know. It is incredibly honest and revealing.'

Joe Berlinger went a step further, musing on the essential fascination of the film for many viewers. 'On the surface it's about the making of St. Anger, but it's much more a film about human relationships and the creative process,' the editor suggested. 'It asks how you manage the multiple issues of being big rock stars while approaching middle age, being fathers and not wanting to party the way you used to party. And most importantly, how do you stay vital musically when you're incredibly successful?'

Kirk himself would reveal, 'I feel that this film shows a part of Metallica that is just really intimate and honest [...] a part of the band that you don't really see a lot with other public bands. This is a window into our private life and how we interact, and it's all just very natural and honest. What the people will see when they see this film is basically how we really, really are offstage, out of the studio, in the studio, whatever. It shows a real human side to Metallica that is not really brought to light.'

Ultimately however, the overwhelming impression made by *Some Kind Of Monster* is that we, as voyeurs, should respect Metallica's willingness to be filmed and their absolute honesty – for better or worse – for as long as the cameras were rolling. As Adam Dubin says, 'I thought *Some Kind Of Monster* was a good film. I know the filmmakers Joe and Bruce and they are first-class documentary guys. I think at that point Metallica just wanted someone else for that portion of their journey. I respect their decision and it's not something that I am jealous of. In fact, they used some of my footage in their film. It is hard for me to watch because I know the guys and it is painful for me to watch what they are going through. I respect the band for allowing themselves to be seen like that. It's a very hard thing to do.'

Metallica once again played the Donington Festival in 2004, but it was no longer known as Monsters Of Rock. In 2003 the organisers had cheekily changed the name to 'Download' in the wake of the new phenomenon of MP3 and personal digital music players. The move met with resistance from long-time Donington attendees, but times were irrefutably changing. Before Metallica's set at the 2004 festival – featuring a vast array of metal acts, from Slayer to Korn – it was announced that the band had travelled without their drummer, who had been hospitalised in Zurich after the previous night's show. The reasons for this were unclear, but Ulrich soon returned to the fold, acting as if nothing had happened. Rumours were rife; after all, this was the first gig Lars had ever missed. His replies to press questions did little to silence the increasingly outlandish suggestions as to why he was hospitalised.

According to some accounts, the drummer had suffered a panic attack after attending a particularly exhausting party the night before, but perhaps best of all was the rumour Lars had been discovered by his wife in bed with two women. He had then apparently gone on a cocaine-fuelled rampage that had left him unable to perform. 'I should be so lucky as to even be caught with one groupie at my age,' Lars said in response to the hearsay. 'For the record, my wife did not catch me with two groupies. None of that is true. I absolutely deny the charges.'

Yet, when pushed to offer a truer version of events, Lars remained puzzlingly ambiguous. 'My hangnail was hurting,' he said unconvincingly. 'I had to lie down as they say. I had a little episode and I thought it best to get it checked out. This is the first Metallica gig I've ever missed, but sometimes you just gotta do what you gotta do.'

'Unfortunately our drummer, Lars, is in the hospital,' James announced from the Donington stage. 'We don't know what's wrong, but we wish him all the best. Some friends of ours are gonna help us out, so we're going to make rock history tonight!' Enlisting the services of Slipknot's Joey Jordison, as well as drumming monolith Dave

Lombardo of Slayer, this was a claim the band made good. Lars's drum tech Flemming Larsen also turned in a sterling performance on 'Fade To Black'.

For Metallica, much of the following year (2005), was spent resting and recuperating, aside from two shows supporting the Rolling Stones at hometown venue AT&T Park. Devoting time to personal hobbies and their families, the band essentially went into hiding. No doubt this period was necessary for them to recover from the colossal pressure of filming *Some Kind Of Monster*, and the difficult reception to *St. Anger*. Following their withdrawal from the public gaze, the band members were determined: their new ideas were not to be influenced by anything outside of their own hearts and minds.

Nonetheless, Metallica opted to pay tribute to composer Ennio Morricone, along with several other high-profile artists, on a compilation album called *We All Love Ennio Morricone*. They recorded their familiar introduction 'The Ecstasy Of Gold', with added guitars for a much fuller sound. The group also released a DVD containing all of their music videos to date, unimaginatively titled *The Videos 1989-2004*. Aptly enough, this collection of videos marks the end of another era for Metallica. With the events surrounding *St. Anger* – be it James Hetfield's stint in rehab, Lars's brush with Napster or the controversy of the music itself – it was going to be very difficult for Metallica to reinvent themselves with a positive slant. But this was exactly what they were about to do.

CHAPTER 20
LIFE IN THE OLD GODS

'St. Anger was the low point of the roller coaster
but we're back at the top now.'
James Hetfield

As a band and as individuals, Metallica had been through the mill and, though *St. Anger* and *Some Kind Of Monster* seemed to somehow survive the criticism, doubts still lingered in the minds of many fans: perhaps this was the end for the band. The documentary closes with footage of the group triumphantly taking to the stage, complete with their new bass player, putting an emphatic end to the awkward focus on squabbling band members, with suggestions of a bright future for Metallica. Yet, could the band ever leave behind the pain of the past? Had they truly healed as individuals and bonded as a unit? 'The temptation to drink is with me forever,' James Hetfield has confessed. 'When you've done something a certain way for so long, doing it a different way is difficult. You start to doubt yourself. I'll never be cured. It's one of those things that I'll have to deal with all my life.'

While Hetfield's point of view was refreshingly realistic, it certainly begged the questions: could he stay clean? Was touring for years on end the best method for dealing with the threat of alcoholism? Had Hetfield and Ulrich's relationship truly been repaired, or did they merely agree to persevere in the interests of Metallica? Was Robert Trujillo the right choice for bass player? All these questions, and many more besides, arose from the aftermath of *Some Kind Of Monster*. That is to say nothing of *St. Anger*'s musical failure, and the most blindingly simple query of all: were Metallica still a viable musical force?

'Through the movie we saw what we really looked like,' Lars said of *Some Kind Of Monster*. 'It was a great mirror to see yourself acting like a twelve-year-old. We were frigging egomaniacs. We all had different character defects and it was good to see them on screen. I think it was more educational for us than for our fans. It was very therapeutic for us to put that out there.' In a 2008 interview Ulrich revealed that the members of Metallica had matured as individuals and, if nothing else, *Some Kind Of Monster* helped the band realise the serious need for them to do so. 'I'm 44 years old.

I argue enough with my kids about finishing their vegetables,' the drummer said. 'I don't like to argue about which guitar solo should be on song nine. These days I have nothing to complain about. If you hear me complain then you've got permission to smack me.'

Several years after the dust from *St. Anger* had settled, Ulrich would admit that it was 'a difficult record', but that 'it was the right thing to have done in 2003'. In order to move forward to their ninth studio album, Metallica felt that the staff behind them had to change. First and foremost, it was agreed that Bob Rock should leave the comfortable confines of camp Metallica. Rock's presence was almost habitual and a new producer was required to shake up their environment. 'We'd been making records together for almost twenty years,' Lars explained. 'That's as creative a relationship as you can come up with in music, film – just about anything. But it had got to a point where we would both finish each other's sentences. We needed to look somewhere else for our own sanity, survival and fulfilment.'

Crossover maestro Rick Rubin was suggested and soon became the band's first choice. Rubin had become an important player in the music world and, in truth, had developed a reputation for more than just his production skills. He was listed in *Time* magazine's '100 Most Influential People In The World' in 2007 – a far cry from the humble record company he set up in the 1980s. Rubin brought hip-hop label Def Jam to the public and, along with it, the first fusion of metal and rap, with Aerosmith and Run DMC's collaboration 'Walk This Way'. Unleashing the Beastie Boys onto television screens in the 1980s, he had besieged the snobbish masses and, crucially, co-produced the thrash-metal classic *Reign In Blood*, by Slayer.

Rubin was also known for his role in the Red Hot Chili Peppers' breakthrough to mainstream success, having overseen their landmark album, *Blood Sugar Sex Magik*. The New Yorker has also been credited with reviving Johnny Cash's music career from 1994 onwards, with the release of Cash's *American Recordings* and four further albums – all of which garnered critical acclaim. MTV named him as 'the most important producer of the last twenty years'.

However, Metallica's own requisites for the job were simple enough. According to Lars Ulrich, 'We needed someone to be a pain in the ass. If there is one area where we probably have been at our worst, it's been self-editing. In the 1990s we fell into a trap that everything we wrote was great because we're so cool. We wrote a lot of songs: 30 songs and ten made it on this record.'

Despite the fireworks so visible throughout the making of *St. Anger,* the band felt that they needed to argue more this time around, on musical matters at least. 'It was time to get a fresh set of ears,' James Hetfield said with reference to Rick Rubin. 'Bob Rock has done amazing stuff with us. It got a little comfortable. Maybe the fire wasn't there as much, in our viewpoint. Bob is a great person, a great friend. I feel extremely safe and comfortable with him, and maybe that wasn't what we needed to feel on this. We needed to argue a bit. We needed to get shaken up a little bit. That's what the mission was.'

Hardcore metal fans had long been screaming for Metallica to return to their 'roots'. These roots had of course been contested by the band themselves; even in the 1980s they were averse to the 'thrash' tag. Yet the simple fact remained Metallica would be left with very little new ground to tread if they were still to be known as a metal band in *any* sense. They had accomplished most things in their career and attempted virtually every style even vaguely associated with the heavy-metal tag. *St. Anger* itself was a large-scale experiment that hadn't worked out; perhaps now was the time to combine 25 years or more of Metallica history in one convenient package. Their ninth album, titled *Death Magnetic*, would feature elements of all their previous recordings, with an exciting new slant that would once again invite criticism from many quarters.

Metallica were no longer a thrash band and not about to attempt to recreate that style for any length of time; odd moments would feature in songs, scattered here and there, but nothing beyond that. Yet Metallica's status as a metal band had not changed, and so *Death Magnetic* would scream heavy metal from the rooftops. Groove was back on the agenda, but not at the expense of intricate guitar work, or indeed Kirk's beloved solos. Guided by Rick Rubin, Metallica realised the need to embrace their past – learning from successes and failures alike – while pressing on regardless, recognising their strengths and charged with fresh purpose. Many heralded *Death Magnetic* as a deliberate return to Metallica's 'glory years', but this was simply not the case. It was very much a modern album, with an abundance of fresh input – be it Rubin's involvement, Robert Trujillo's first touches on bass, or the elegant piano addition to 'The Unforgiven' trilogy. For Metallica to avoid their own legacy was an impossibility; they would always feature Hetfield's instantly identifiable vocals, Ulrich's atypical drumming style and Kirk Hammett's oft-frenetic, yet soulful axe work.

'We just wanted to make the best record possible,' Lars would say. 'We had a weird taboo relationship with our early records that we felt scared to revisit because we'd be in some way cheapening them. Rick made us feel pretty good about doing that: going back and not copying, but trying to put ourselves in the same headspace as much as possible. Rick wanted us to play together, lock in with each other, and play with energy in a really connected way instead of overdubbing and being all perfect.'

The latter statement may echo the old rhetoric of *St. Anger* and, indeed, the Black Album, but *Death Magnetic* was very much about combining those two distinctly different eras with the spirit and verve of early Metallica. In many ways, it would become their ultimate album. One practice Rick Rubin instilled was for the band to learn new songs off by heart, lending natural spontaneity to the way these numbers were performed in the studio. As Lars explained, 'Rick's big thing is to kind of have all these songs completely embedded in our bodies and basically just go in and execute them. So you leave the creative element of the process out of the recording, so you go in and basically just record a bunch of songs that you know inside out and upside down, and you don't have to spend too much of your energy in the recording studio creating and thinking and analysing and doing all that stuff. His whole analogy is, the recording process becomes more like a gig – just going in and playing and leaving all the thinking at the door.'

In embracing their full heritage, Metallica quickly found that they still rather enjoyed complex song structures, despite their later penchant for melody and the interplay of clean and distorted guitar sounds. To their ears, their old approach to the material could easily be made fresh again, under the ever-present influence of Rick Rubin. 'He said that he wanted to make the ultimate Metallica album,' Kirk Hammett said of Rubin. 'In his mind, the ultimate Metallica album would be more along the lines of what we did back in the 1980s.'

Indeed, there was one specific album upon which Rubin felt the band should be basing their modern approach – the same release which took Metallica from being chief thrashers to global stars, *Master Of Puppets*. 'The direction is embracing our past in the now,' James Hetfield stated frankly. 'We know what we know. It's hard to erase that. But to strip it down again and get back to why we're doing this? Why did we write songs that way? The template was *Master Of Puppets* and the strength of that record. How can we do that now?'

Everything about the record screamed of Metallica's enduring desire for control, along with a mature acceptance they had learned along the way, and a willingness to listen when it mattered. Hetfield and Ulrich's approach to songwriting was fiercely original as ever, but now they would take onboard suggestions from a handful of trusted collaborators and, as James Hetfield himself acknowledged, 'It was better. I was very willing to look at it and try it. If Rubin was suggesting it, there's a reason behind it.'

Death Magnetic was the first album on which every band member was credited with writing music for each and every song – a far cry from the former dominance of the Hetfield-Ulrich partnership. In a particularly welcome return to past practice, all lyrics were penned by Hetfield, but musically everyone was given the chance to contribute to each track on the album. Finally, the controlling, stubborn coupling of Hetfield and Ulrich had relinquished their stranglehold on Metallica's output and the results were all the better for it. Quite simply, 2008 was the year Metallica introduced democracy. As was quickly becoming apparent, the move was perfectly timed.

James Hetfield was particularly lavish in his praise for Metallica's new bassist. Insisting he meant no disrespect to Jason Newsted, he praised Trujillo's way of playing with his fingers (instead of a pick), enabling him to create a fuller sound. Most revealingly, Hetfield said, 'Rob has already written more on this album than Jason had in his whole fourteen years. A lot of that had to do with us not being willing, and I totally understand that, but just his material seemed to gel better. It feels as though we've known him forever, basically, is what it feels like. And there's still times when I see him in pictures with us, and I go, "Oh, yeah! He's in our band. Dude, we kick ass even more now." It's a good feeling.'

Certainly Trujillo's early funk influences, combined with a solid set of heavy credentials – honed playing genres from classic metal through to full-on punk and thrash – enabled him to incorporate a multitude of styles, hinting at a wide variety of material, in his own bass playing.

Death Magnetic begins with a beating heart, setting the pace for the rejuvenated pulse of Metallica. As soon as the heavy guitar kicks in for opener 'That Was Just Your Life', it becomes immediately apparent that the band have rediscovered a cleaner distortion on guitar, more in line with Hetfield's classic style. The more considered snare-drum sound is another source of instant gratification for many fans – gone is the tinny snap of the *St. Anger* era. Hetfield's vocals are clear, concise and considered. The opening track features a raft of breathy vocalisms, with a series of difficult lyrics strung effortlessly together. This is one of the hardest songs Hetfield has ever attempted to carry off and the result is sheer metal poetry. As *Death Magnetic* progresses it's clear the band's renewed vigour is not about to let up. Whereas later Metallica albums deliver adrenaline-fuelled openers, only to slow in pace and direction with subsequent tracks, *Death Magnetic* loses none of its ferocious energy, keeping the listener captive for the duration. It is Rubin's trademark style to segue directly from the end of one song into the beginning of the next with barely a millisecond between. For *Death Magnetic*, however, he smartly dispensed with this gimmick, giving the listener a few seconds' pause in which to digest between cuts.

It isn't until track four (and lead single) 'The Day That Never Comes' that the pace slows and the relentless groove is interrupted, but for a song this powerful, a small respite is more than welcome. 'The Day That Never Comes' sees James Hetfield at his vocal best, tunefully carrying the verse before erupting into the famed Hetfield snarl with a stunning chorus. Here Robert Trujillo proves his ability as a soulful bass player, capable of carrying the rhythm slowly and purposefully with the distinctive backing of Ulrich's inimitable drums. In truth, the breakdown and subsequent climax to the song is a little histrionic and doesn't quite fit with the verse and chorus, yet still serves as a grandiose announcement of Metallica's return. The video that accompanied the song featured war scenes which inspired some comparison with the controversial footage used for 'One'. But, once again, the so-called political statement was not one Metallica ever intended to make.

As James Hetfield explained, 'That's the beauty, I think, of writing vague, but powerful lyrics. The one thing that I wasn't keen on here was Metallica plugging into a modern war or a current event that might be construed as some sort of political statement on our part. There are so many celebrities that soapbox their opinions, and people believe it's more valid because they're popular. We are hopefully putting the human element in what is an unfortunate part of life. There are people over there dealing with situations like this, and we're showing the human part of being there.'

A far more typical subject for Metallica was the H.P. Lovecraft-inspired 'All Nightmare Long', referencing *The Hounds Of Tindalos* and described by James Hetfield as 'another crazy mind-fuck about these wolves that hunt through their nightmares and the only way you can get away from them is to stay with angels. You can't even escape through sleep.' 'All Nightmare Long' is Metallica at their contemporary best, featuring a dark, low-slung riff and a groove-laden chorus played at heart-stopping pace.

The second half of the album is less immediate and, in parts, almost throwaway. The near ten-minute instrumental 'Suicide & Redemption' is an exercise in patience rather than enjoyment, sounding more like a few abandoned riffs from stoner rock trio Karma To Burn than anything musically similar to such classics as 'To Live Is To Die'.

'The Judas Kiss' stands out as a song with a lengthy guitar solo and Kirk Hammett's opportunity to redress the balance so lacking on *St. Anger*. The six-stringer raved, 'I fucking love "The Judas Kiss" and the minute-and-a-half guitar solo in the middle is a high point for me. After *St. Anger* you could definitely say that I overcompensated on that one.'

'The Unforgiven III' is perhaps the standout track of the second half of the record. The song represents another important exorcism of James Hetfield's personal demons – much like the two previous instalments in this trilogy. 'How can I be lost/ If I've got nowhere to go?' the frontman muses in a set of cryptic lyrics centred around redemption and forgiveness, tugging on the heartstrings with a series of dazzling backing guitar parts. The heart of the song is the lyrical lament mingled with the luscious rhythm track. 'It takes me to another level,' James admits. 'If there was any song that I could listen to a hundred times in a row that would be it.'

Robert Trujillo echoed the frontman's sentiments when he revealed, 'It was really a labour of love for James. He felt very connected to this song; it's very special to him. It's important for this album as it really balances it out. The lyrics can be taken in many ways because it's very clever. There's a certain thread that channels through this album and that's death. To me "The Unforgiven III" is not as dark and gloomy – there's a little light in the song.'

Yet Trujillo explained the song almost didn't make the album. Initially Ulrich and company were simply not convinced it was worthy of inclusion. The fact that they eventually changed their opinion is testament to the sheer force of Hetfield's – as well as Rubin's – own conviction. 'There probably won't be an "Unforgiven IV",' the bass player announced, 'because there almost wasn't a "...III". We had to sit down as a band and there was a split for it. James said, "I'm going to war; I'm fighting for this song!"'

'My Apocalypse', the closing track, is rooted in *...And Justice For All*-esque riffage and finally sees Metallica completing an album in the right manner, with a fast song – an event which hadn't occurred since 'Dyers Eve' closed their 1988 opus. 'My Apocalypse' also referenced the album title with an ominous phrase suggested by Kirk Hammett – 'Death magnetic, pulling closer still.' In homage to the late Alice In Chains vocalist Layne Staley (who passed away in 2002 from an overdose of cocaine and heroin), Hammett brought a photo of the singer to the studio while Metallica were recording *Death Magnetic*. 'I think it pervaded James's psyche,' Hammett later affirmed.

'*Death Magnetic*, at least the title, to me started out as kind of a tribute to people that have fallen in our business, like Layne Staley and a lot of the people that have died – basically, rock'n'roll martyrs of sorts,' Hetfield confirmed. 'And then it kind of grew from there, thinking about death. Some people are drawn towards it, and just like a magnet, and other people are afraid of it and push away. And the concept that we're all gonna die sometimes is over-talked about and then a lot of times never talked about. No one wants to bring it up; it's the big white elephant in the living room.

But we all have to deal with it at some point.' As part of this obsession with death and suicide, Metallica almost named the album, 'Songs Of Suicide And Forgiveness'.

Death Magnetic saw worldwide release on 12 September 2008 and, contrary to other popular bands whose material has leaked onto the internet months before the official release date, Metallica escaped relatively unscathed, with the album leaked just ten days early. Though the album was distributed via the usual vilified peer-to-peer sites, prompting Vertigo Records to make the official release two days ahead of schedule, Lars Ulrich was surprisingly happy with the outcome. 'By 2008 standards, that's a victory,' he said realistically. 'If you'd told me six months ago that our record wouldn't leak until ten days out, I would have signed up for that.'

It was also revealed, some months after the release of the album, that Lars had actually done the unthinkable and, a few days after it leaked, downloaded *Death Magnetic* for himself. 'I sat there myself and downloaded *Death Magnetic* from the internet just to try it,' Lars explained, also admitting he did not pay for the download. 'I was like, "Wow, this is how it works." I figured if there is anybody that has a right to download *Death Magnetic* for free, it's me. I was like, "You know what? I've gotta try this." So I sat there, and 30 minutes later, I had *Death Magnetic* in my computer. It was kind of bizarre.'

In keeping with Metallica's habit of releasing special editions with lavish packaging, one version of *Death Magnetic* came packed in a coffin-shaped box, though the price reflected how quickly the production company expected it to sell, coming in at over £100. The box set featured the CD album, a CD of demos, a behind-the-scenes DVD, an exclusive T-shirt, a flag, a collection of guitar picks, codes for special live downloads and a poster.

Death Magnetic sold almost half a million copies in the United States alone in the first week of release and went on to stay at Number One on the *Billboard* 200 Album Chart for three consecutive weeks. It topped the charts in many other countries around the world. Though it was by now considered a virtual requisite for any new Metallica release, with the band themselves having lost count of the number they'd amassed since 1989, Metallica were awarded two further Grammy Awards for *Death Magnetic*: 'Best Metal Performance' and 'Best Recording Package'. For the second time in his career, Rick Rubin received the accolade of 'Producer Of The Year, Non-Classical' for his work on *Death Magnetic*, as well as albums by Weezer and Neil Diamond.

The media response to *Death Magnetic* was crucial in re-establishing Metallica's seemingly withered credibility, and in general, the reviews were positive. *Rock Sound* rightly pointed out, 'There's a part of *Death Magnetic* that gives you a sense of déjà vu as you listen – it's like listening to *Ride The Lightning* and *Master Of Puppets* melted together and recreated twenty years later.' *Kerrang!* stated that this was an album 'packed with moments of exhilarating brilliance, of original thinking, of technical dexterity exercised not in the name of indulgence, but of songs. Metallica's latest release may not be suitable for mainstream radio, but neither is it a return to the music the group made before they became one of the world's biggest draws.'

Of course, despite having released a glorified heavy-metal album, Metallica's status meant that they were courted by the mainstream regardless. The American establishment has a particularly good relationship with Metallica. Few metal bands can lay claim to their music being used on such prime-time television shows as ESPN's *Monday Night Football*. In 2008 the network often played 'The Day That Never Comes' between games.

This flirtation with the mainstream is not without its dangers, however; most notably that mainstream television researchers usually have little knowledge of heavy metal. On 10 September 2008, Sky News reported *Death Magnetic*'s impressive return to form, making numerous ill-informed statements. Referring to *Master Of Puppets* as Metallica's 'acclaimed first album', the newsreader's commentary was wincingly far off the mark, stating that 'their 2003 work *St. Anger* disappointed fans for being too soft and full of solos'.

One undeniable element of *Death Magnetic* is the curious sound levels employed. Over the preceding few years, CDs in general had become progressively louder. By and large this can be explained as the industry's own reaction to the advent of digital music. Fans of official releases, as opposed to digital MP3s, argued that CD sound was vastly superior to downloads, though this is still a point of some debate. Therefore, in order to exemplify the supposed superior quality of their recordings, record companies endeavoured to make them louder, the inference being that 'louder' meant 'better'.

In accordance with this misguided judgement, the mixing of *Death Magnetic* was hopelessly ruined, with distorted drums and an overall volume that's 10 per cent higher than is acceptable to the average human ear. Despite their musical return to form, Metallica's comeback was marred by this one frustrating element. For the hardcore fans who'd waited patiently for the band to deliver, the disappointment was too much to tolerate. Thousands signed their names to an online petition urging the band to re-mix the album and release it again. Yet, for chief Metallica spokesman Lars Ulrich, along with co-manager Cliff Burnstein, there was little to address. As Burnstein protested vainly, 'The complainers are a tiny minority. Ninety-eight per cent of listeners are overwhelmingly positive. There's something exciting about the sound of this record that people are responding to.'

Even Ted Jensen, industry veteran and the album's mastering engineer, sympathised with the growing viewpoint of the fans. 'Believe me, I'm not proud to be associated with this one,' he admitted. Lars Ulrich, however, remained indignant, commenting, 'A Metallica record is too loud for people? That's a statement in itself – the irony of that! Welcome to the world of digital recordings, compression overload, MP3s. People are moving in a different direction and things are becoming more linear, less dynamic. We can't put out records for every niche in our fan base. We attract such a diverse group of people, we can't please everybody. Metallica has made a career out of doing what we need to do for ourselves.' In a statement that was dangerously close to the justification given for *St. Anger*'s sound at the time, Ulrich insisted, 'I love the way the album sounds. Rick pushed it as far as he needs to go. Did he push it too far, farther than some people wanted? Absolutely. In a world of compression, maybe it's too hot for some people. But there is some perverse beauty in knowing that a Metallica record is considered too loud.'

A video, titled 'Mastered By Muppets', incorporated many fans' frustrations and essentially placed the blame for the sound of the album on Rick Rubin, who incidentally produced the spectacularly loud (yet undistorted) Red Hot Chili Peppers album *Californication*.

'Mastered By Muppets' was created by a band known as Clipping Death. The song takes the form of a clever parody of 'Master Of Puppets,' replacing the original lyrics with pertinent references to the sound of *Death Magnetic*. The lyrics, written by Dan Weapon, are reproduced here by kind permission:

End of session day, Rubin works away:
I'm your source of song-destruction
Tunes that hurt you ear, poor sound engineer
Leaving spikes on my instruction
Trust me you will see
Volume's all you need
Dedicated to
How I'll limit you

Compressing faster
Limit your Master
Your albums sell faster
With a loud Master
Master

Mastered by muppets, brickwalling your dreams
Clipping, distorting and smashing extremes
Ruined by me, you can't hear a thing…
Just spiking snares, and auto-tuned screams
Mastered
Mastered
Rubin's my name, and I'll hear you scream
Bastard
Bastard

Need to mix this way, never you dismay
Loud makes *Death Magnetic* clearer
Gain monopoly, ritual Waves L3
Squash your tracks 'til it's severe
Gate and you will see
More and more dB
Dedicated to

How I'm killing you

Compressing faster
Limit your Master
Your albums sell faster
With a loud Master
Master

Mastered by muppets, brickwalling your dreams
Clipping, distorting and smashing extremes
Ruined by me, you can't hear a thing…
Just spiking snares, and auto-tuned screams
Mastered
Mastered
Rubin's my name, and I'll hear you scream
Bastard
Bastard

Master, Master, where's the version I've been after?
Bearded, Bastard, you promised only lies
Blaster, Blaster, recorded on a ghetto blaster?
Laughter, laughter, laughing at those highs
Spike to me!

Lars ain't worth all that – 'natural' kick and hats
Kirk adds wah without a reason
Never ending phrase, Jaymz goes on for days
Rob, your shirt is out of season…
I'll record 'til five (then)
I will help you buy
Sandals that suit you
Now you look cool too.

Despite these reservations, however, Metallica had undeniably reinvented themselves with *Death Magnetic* and gone a long way in redressing the balance after the poorly received *St. Anger*. They created a set of blistering songs – still swaying with barely controlled emotion – silencing all doubters in the aftermath of *St. Anger* and thus re-establishing their credibility as the world's premier heavy-metal band. After all they have been through – and survived – few would begrudge the band their continuing success and ever-growing list of accolades.

Metallica's live shows for the World Magnetic Tour met with a positive response from fans and critics alike. Metallica had visited different destinations throughout the world, but this tour seemed extra special. Not only did the band believe their new material to be superior to that of *St. Anger*, but fans whipped up just as much enthusiasm for *Death Magnetic* tracks as the old classics.

James Hetfield's ex-girlfriend Leah Storkson says today, 'I hadn't seen Metallica play live since about 1992, exploring many other genres of heavy music. But a decade later, I found myself quite intrigued and interested in hearing their new album due to come out in late 2008. I'd heard rumours it was fuelled by fire of the old aggressiveness, passion, and absolute power we had come to love about Metallica. They had a new killer and experienced bass player, as close to Cliff as they'd ever had, and had apparently gone back to their roots, so to speak.

'With the release of the new album, I listened with great anticipation,' Storkson continues. 'I was not disappointed by any means and when their Bay Area show was announced for December 2008, I decided it was time to go back in time and see Metallica live once again. As I watched them play in the round, I was amazed at how I was actually able to forget I was standing in a coliseum with 50,000 or so people, Instead, the music, both new and old, brought me back to seeing them play at the Old Waldorf, or the Kabuki, with all the prowess, speed, passion, and power of the past. The only difference was, it is a different era now, we have all changed from our many experiences… how can one not?'

As Storkson observes, the mass audiences of the World Magnetic shows were a far cry from those in attendance at small, sweaty shows of the band's early days. 'Obviously, Metallica has influenced a lot of different types of fans,' she says. 'People who don't even like metal now like Metallica. And I think that is so great! Alongside the twenty-year-olds are the 40-year-olds from the "old days". You will also notice the 50-year-old grey-haired men in power suits with their ten- and twelve-year-old kids attending their shows.'

It is a sign of just how far Metallica have come that, in 2009, they were awarded their own video game. The band were invited to create a customised version of the immensely popular *Guitar Hero* series, whereby the gamer can play guitar via a console, following onscreen prompts to press certain buttons which would otherwise be frets. Metallica were only the second band (after Aerosmith) to be offered their own game and altogether they licensed 28 of their own songs for the purpose. It may have been an easy way to make more money – as of March 2009 the *Guitar Hero* series has generated over $1.6 billion in retail profits – but the band were nonplussed by the idea of such a game. Kirk Hammett expressed surprise that people would rather hit a piece of plastic corresponding to a screen shot than play an actual guitar, but the very proposition shows Metallica's radical changing fortune since their inception in 1981.

Another indication of the changing times is the realisation that, as of November 2008, Metallica are effectively without a record label, having reached the end of their deal with Warner Bros. Despite the turning tide in the music industry over the last few years, with CD sales dwindling rapidly, major labels are fully aware that one band who will still sell consistently are Metallica. Therefore it seems likely that the group will be offered a ridiculous amount of money to sign with another of the major players in the industry, though Lars Ulrich has intimated that the band may take control of their own affairs, using the internet to their distinct advantage. 'We're free of our record contract,' Lars explained. 'We have that element of complete freedom with the next record, so we can do whatever we want. We could do an internet thing.'

If there were any doubts as to Metallica's viability as they hit middle age, then *Death Magnetic* dispelled them swiftly and almost effortlessly. The background has changed, as have the reasons for the band's continuing existence, but the result remains the same: Metallica are still one of the best bands in the world. The fact that each band member has a wife and young children is almost impossible to believe. 'That's brought a different balance to the band,' Lars said of the impact of family life. 'Metallica is no longer the most important thing for all of us. Finding the right balance with our families and each other is. Metallica is probably more a place of refuge, a place to have fun. It's made the band more of a frigging picnic.' This is some progression from a band whose frontman once said, 'I am married to Metallica and Metallica comes first.'

Yet the past is now exactly where it belongs, and Lars cannot help but smile as he recalls, 'The old days were crazy, chaotic and involved strip clubs and talking to strangers in bathrooms just to nick their blow. Now it's more about family, museums and kids. I'm proud that after everything we've been through over the years I can still speak in coherent sentences and have fathered three healthy children.'

On 4 April 2009 Metallica were inducted into the Rock And Roll Hall Of Fame (along with Run DMC, Bobby Womack and Jeff Beck) – a supreme achievement for any heavy-metal act. In fact, Metallica were only the second metal band, after Black Sabbath, to receive the honour. They joined such rock greats as the Beatles, the Doors, AC/DC and Aerosmith. Tellingly, all three bass players were listed as inductees. Jason Newsted even rejoined the band on the night to play with them for the first time in over a decade. On 'Master Of Puppets' and 'Enter Sandman' he and Robert Trujillo played together with the band. Lars Ulrich spoke of his pride at Metallica's accolade. 'Sometimes, especially with younger people, one has a tendency to say, "Well, that doesn't mean that much. Try me again in ten years, darling,"' the drummer jibed. 'But I'm 45. I'd much rather be inducted into the Rock And Roll Hall Of Fame while I'm still conscious enough to experience it and enjoy it and certainly more interested than being 65 years from now or whenever when it would be a different thing. So I'm proud, I'm psyched.'

Jason Newsted, who seemed to take it all in his stride, said, 'We have a lot of roots going very deep that will be in the room with us on the moment, and that gives us strength that's really indescribable.' Dave Mustaine was invited to the ceremony – but not as a member of Metallica. As such, he would not actually have been inducted into the Hall Of Fame. Lars Ulrich explained his reasoning. 'You've got to kind of cap it somewhere,' he said. 'Dave Mustaine never played on any Metallica records. No disrespect to him, but there were half a dozen other people that were in the line-up in the early days. We thought the fair thing to do would be to include anybody that played on a Metallica record.'

Mustaine was complimentary of the band, but ultimately believed he should (and would one day) be inducted personally. 'I think Lars and James handled it very well, and I'm glad I was invited,' Mustaine said. 'But I turned it down – partly because I'm on tour and partly because if I'm going to be there, I would like to be inducted along with them. I don't want to go there just as an invited guest. You know, anyone can be invited to these things. I'll be in the Hall Of Fame one way or the other. I know that.'

Many associates from Metallica's past were gracious enough to accept their invitation, however. Here was a crucial difference between this band and many other big names within the music world: Metallica remembered those who had helped them become the band they are today and acknowledged the help of musicians who barely contributed to their musical legacy – guitarist Lloyd Grant was invited, for instance. Also present were the likes of Johnny and Marsha Zazula, K.J. Doughton, John Marshall, Adam Dubin and even Cliff Burton's father Ray, who made a speech.

The band were inducted courtesy of Red Hot Chili Peppers bassist Flea, who made an impassioned speech in Metallica's honour. The event was shown live on pay-per-view television in the United States. After almost 30 years in the business, with many trials and tribulations as well as a wealth of classic material behind them, Metallica had ultimately reached the place they belonged – the halls of the all-time greats.

EPILOGUE

'Say or think what you want, but for me Metallica is the best band ever!'
Willy Lange, Lääz Rockit

Without question, Metallica's story is one of endurance and perseverance against the odds. The trauma they have endured as a band – from Cliff Burton's death to their most public disintegration – would have floored any lesser group, and it is a testament to their collective spirit and guts that they are still alive and making music, much less flaunting it on such a globally popular scale. *Death Magnetic* was their best album for many years and, far from underlining the question mark hanging over the band's future, it has opened up the possibility of many more years in the spotlight.

Perhaps they will be unable to go on for more than a decade at the frantic pace they've set in recent years, but Metallica will be savvy enough to recognise when it is time to call it quits, rather than milking their past success to the bitter end, as other big-name bands have done before them.

Throughout their career, Metallica have influenced countless bands – and not just within the metal genre. Their legacy encompasses everything from a trend-setting image (when Kirk Hammett opted for a labret piercing, thousands of nu-metal devotees followed) and a plagiarised logo (permeating your local high street in overpriced *faux* fashion lines as you read this), to their enduring back catalogue of music – still an important source of inspiration for new and older bands alike, even as Metallica approach 30 years in the business.

Indeed, Metallica are one of a select few bands who possess the appeal to straddle a variety of genres. Despite their own resistance to the tag, much of their material – especially the earlier works – can be placed in the thrash-metal category, and the band continue to earn the respect of speed-metal addicts for the potency of their *Kill 'Em All* to *...And Justice For All* period. Yet, still more impressive is their ability to draw fans of all tastes to their material, experimenting with styles other so-called thrash bands would be afraid to attempt.

Other influential thrash acts, be they Slayer or Testament, have focused almost entirely on this genre, but even before they hit the mainstream airwaves, Metallica have never cared for conventionality or for the opinions of others, refusing to submit to the stereotypes placed upon them. Above all else, this penchant for risk-taking has been the root of their success. They have been experimental, but always kept their metal base, and their enduring attitude of – let's face it – stubbornness has stood them in good stead from day one. Even in the garage, Hetfield and Ulrich shared a single vision from which they were unwilling to deviate – it was simply their way, or nothing at all.

Because of this more than any other reason, Metallica have endured and grown beyond all expectation. The strength of their back catalogue, renowned within the metal genre, is remarkable, particularly for a band formed more than ten years after Black Sabbath – the gods of heavy metal. 'Creeping Death', 'One' and 'The Unforgiven' stand out as shining examples of the genre, yet Metallica have created songs as strong as these at every stage of their illustrious career. They are simply untouchable and have been since the very first spin of *Kill 'Em All*.

As Leah Storkson says today, 'It is uncanny to think that a band starting out as they did made it what they wanted it to be, and made it as big as they are today, despite all obstacles [...] Much respect has been earned. Cliff would be very proud.'

Here's to the metal purveyors and long may they reign.

ACKNOWLEDGEMENTS

Fred Cotton, Mat Maurer, Henrik Jespersen, Terry Lauderdale, Adam Dubin, Andy Battye, Bob Nalbandian, Brian Slagel, Brian Tatler, Buffo Schnadelbach, Chris Caffery, Corinne Lynn, Craig Locicero, Dave Donato, Dave Marrs, David Fricke, Dimitris Sirinakis, Flemming Rasmussen, Gary Holt and Exodus, Gem Howard, Harald O, Heather Hayward, Jason Brown, Jim Martin, John Kornarens, K.J. Doughton, Keith Burton, Ken Anthony, Ken Jacobsen, Lauren Collins, Lloyd Grant, Martin Hooker, Matt Mahurin, Megan Callaghan, Michael Alago, Mike Meals, Nick Bollettieri, Paul Owen, Paul Speckmann, Pepper Keenan, Ray Del Rio Jr, Rich and Ron Veloz, Ron McGovney, Ron Quintana, Rosemary Cotton, Ross Erkers, Steve Kachinsky, Tomasz 'Titus' Pukacki, Torben Ulrich, Troy Gregory, Willy Lange

The author wishes to express very special thanks to Leah Storkson for her help in putting this book together – for her words, her skills and her friendship.

Many thanks also to Sakis Fragos for interview assistance and for kind permission for the *Rock Hard Greece* interviews. (www.myspace.com/rockhardgreece).

Photographs in plate section pages 1-24 by kind permission of:
Buffo Schnädelbach: pages 4, 7 (2 photographs), 9, 10 (2 photographs), 11, 12 (2 photographs), 13, 14. Henrik Jesperson: page 1. World Entertainment News Network Ltd: page 1 (3 photographs). Frank White: pages 2, 3, 15, 20 (2 photographs), 23. Frank White Agency/ Kevin Hodapp: pages 5, 6, 11. Frank White Agency/ Stuart Taylor: pages 4, 8, 14.Frank White Agency/ Debra Trebitz: page 16. Getty Images/ Redferns/ Fin Costello: page 15. Getty Images/ Redferns/ Pete Cronin: page 9. Getty Images/ Redferns/ Giambalvo & Napolitano: page 19. Getty Images/ Redferns/ Ross Gilmore: page 22. Getty Images/ Redferns/ Mick Hutson: pages 21 and 24. Getty Images/ Michael Ochs Archive: page 17. Getty Images/ WireImage/ Paul Natkin: page 18. Getty Images/ Time & Life Pictures/ John Storey: page 19.

SOURCES

Websites

www.metallica.com, www.metontour.com, www.metclub.com,
www.metsanitarium.com, www.myspace.com/metallica, www.encycmet.com,
www.imdb.com, www.bbc.co.uk, www.orionturk.com, www.youtube.com,
www.wikipedia.org, www.entertainmentwise.com, www.metallica.ru, www.mtv.com,
www.metallicaworld.co.uk, www.jameshetfield.com, www.missionmetallica.com,
www.usweekly.com, www.metalremains.com, www.news.sky.com,
www.downeyca.org, www.spastikchildren.com, www.christianscience.com,
www.atlanticrecords.com/metallica, www.warnerbrosrecords.com/artists/metallica,
www.allmetallica.com, www.metallica.lt, www.webmetallica.tk,
www.intersandman.com, www.songfacts.com, www.4horsemensite.com,
www.roadrunnerrecords.com/blabbermouth.net,
www.roadrunnerrecords.com/artists/ShockwavesSkullSessions,
www.metal-archives.com, www.bnrmetal.com, www.jasonnewsted.chez.com,
www.artistwd.com/joyzine/zoe/zoe9.php, www.myspace.com/fredcotton,
www.mortalsin.com.au, www.myspace.com/kolonihaven, www.terrylauderdale.com.

Newspapers

The *Sun*, the *Washington Post*, the *New York Daily News*, the *Los Angeles Times*, the *New York Times*.

Magazines

Alternative Press, Brave Words & Bloody Knuckles, Circus, Classic Rock, DRUM!, Entertainment Weekly, Guitar Sound, Guitar World, Guitarist, Hard N' Heavy, Hit Parader, Kerrang!, Maximum Guitar, Melody Maker, Metal Attack, Metal Forces, Metal Hammer, Metal Mania, Metal Maniac, Metal Maniacs, Metal Rules, Musician, NME, Playboy, Player, Powerplay, Q, RAW, Record Collector, Revolver, RIP, Rock Hard, Rock Sound, Rolling Stone, So What!, Sounds, Spin, Terrorizer, Thrasher, Total Guitar, Transworld Skateboarding.

Books

So What!: The Good, The Mad, And The Ugly by Metallica and Steffan Chirazi, *Metallica: The Inside Story Of The Hit Film Metallica – Some Kind Of Monster* by Joe Berlinger and Greg Milner, *Metallica: The Frayed Ends Of Metal* by Chris Crocker, *Metallica: In Their Own Words* by Mark Putterford, *Unbound* by K.J. Doughton, *Metallica: The Stories Behind The Biggest Songs (Stories Behind Every Song)* by Chris Ingham, *Encyclopaedia Metallica* by Brian Harrigan and Malcolm Dome, *Metallica And Philosophy: A Crash Course In Brain Surgery* by William Irwin, *Damage Incorporated: Metallica And The Production Of Musical Identity* by Glenn Pillsbury, *Metallica* by John Hotten, *Sound Of The Beast* by Ian Christe, *The Collector's Guide To Heavy Metal* by Martin Popoff, *Heavy Metal (20th Century Rock N' Roll)* by Martin Popoff, *The New Wave Of British Heavy Metal Encyclopaedia* by Malc Macmillan.

Videos

A Year And A Half In The Life Of Metallica, Pantera: Vulgar Video, Paradise Lost: The Child Murders At Robin Hood Hills, Paradise Lost 2: Revelations, Some Kind of Monster, Live Shit: Binge & Purge, Cliff 'Em All, Cunning Stunts, Metallica – S&M.